TO WIN THE INDIAN HEART

First Peoples: New Directions in Indigenous Studies

To Win the Indian Heart
MUSIC AT CHEMAWA INDIAN SCHOOL

Melissa Parkhurst

FIRST PEOPLES
New Directions in Indigenous Studies

Oregon State University Press   Corvallis

The paper in this book meets the guidelines for permanence and durability of the Committee on Production Guidelines for Book Longevity of the Council on Library Resources and the minimum requirements of the American National Standard for Permanence of Paper for Printed Library Materials Z39.48-1984.

Library of Congress Cataloging-in-Publication Data

Parkhurst, Melissa.
   To win the Indian heart : music at Chemawa indian school / Melissa Parkhurst.
      pages cm
   Includes bibliographical references and index.
   ISBN 978-0-87071-738-3 (alk. paper) — ISBN 978-0-87071-739-0 (e-book)
   1. Chemawa Indian School—History. 2. Off-reservation boarding schools—Oregon—Salem—History. 3. Indians of North America—Education—Oregon—Salem—History. 4. Indians of North America—Oregon—Salem—Songs and music. 5. Music--Instruction and study—Oregon—Salem. I. Title.
   E97.6.C3P37 2014
   371.829'97079537--dc23

2013040032

Oregon State University Press
121 The Valley Library
Corvallis OR 97331-4501
541-737-3166 • fax 541-737-3170
www.osupress.oregonstate.edu

Contents

Acknowledgments

This book could not have been completed without the generous assistance of many people. I am deeply indebted to Chief Cliff Snider, my father's high school gym teacher, for bringing Chemawa to my attention in a conversation about his mother, a Chemawa alumna. Historians SuAnn Reddick and Cary C. Collins were supportive of my initial inquiries and graciously helped fill gaps in my understanding of Chemawa's history. Professors Andy Sutton, Lois Anderson, Jim Leary, Susan Cook, and Ned Blackhawk were wonderful teachers and dissertation readers at the University of Wisconsin-Madison. Stephen Dow Beckham at Lewis & Clark College gave me the initial encouragement that these stories should be published in book form.

My deepest gratitude and respect go to this book's consultants, the Chemawa alumni, faculty, and staff who opened their heart and homes to me, sharing their experiences and tirelessly answering my questions: Warner Austin, Linda Begay, Chet Clark, William DePoe Jr., Em Dickey, Karen Graham, Kathryn Harrison, Max Lestenkof, Ted Mack, Chance May, Rosemary McGlashen, Ted McGlashen, Millie Metcalf, Don Moccasin, Arlie Neskahi, Betty Pearson, Dee Pigsley, Bob Tom, Ted Young, the late Ed Bartlett, the late Hal Beyers, and the late Charles Holmes. Their openness and generosity propelled the work forward, and I hope the book meets some of their expectations.

The staff at OSU Press was instrumental in helping transform my manuscript from that of a novice to a more cogent, integrated work. Their support was constant and creative in every step of the process. My hearty thanks go to Mary Elizabeth Braun, Jo Alexander, Micki Reaman, and Tom Booth. Anonymous reviewers offered insightful feedback that gave the book more clarity and vigor. Steve Connell at Verse Chorus Press graciously improved the quality of the photographs and accommodated all requests for last-minute adjustments to the text and layout. Mary Harper of Access Points Indexing skillfully created an index that is functional and effective. Also, I am indebted to the First Peoples Publishing Initiative, for supporting the writing process, enabling me to attend a NAISA conference, and bringing new authors together for study and support.

Cliff Trafzer was a generous mentor, graciously reading through chapters and offering wisdom on matters both detailed and over-arching. His counsel helped the work feel less solitary and, when a dead end presented itself, helped me find a way forward.

Fellowships and professional societies provided material support and testing grounds for new ideas. A Vilas Travel Grant from the University of Wisconsin-Madison allowed me to venture to Anchorage, Alaska, to meet with Chemawa alumni and attend a reunion. Conferences of the Society of Ethnomusicology and the Public Memory Conference at Lewis & Clark College provided encouraging and dynamic forums for portions of the book.

For assistance with the archival portions of this research, I am grateful to the Multnomah County Library, the National Archives at Seattle, the Grand Ronde Cultural Resources Division, and the Tamástslikt Cultural Institute. The Friends of Historic Forest Grove, particularly Mary Jo Morelli, graciously helped refine my understanding of Chemawa's early history. And at the Pacific University archives, Santha Zaik and Eva Gugemos answered my questions tirelessly and connected me with precious letters, articles, and photographs.

Our community of relations in Portland, Oregon, helped in many ways. My friend and neighbor, Margaret Davis at Ma Nao Books, provided skillful editing at various phases of the manuscript's development. Philomena and John McGill offered stretches of uninterrupted writing time at their quiet second home on Washington's Long Beach Peninsula. And countless hours of caring for our son, Oliver, were gifted from our loving friends—especially Audrey Sackett, Elise Robbins, and Alison Lentz.

My family has sustained me both before and during my years of research and writing. I wish to thank my parents for developing my inquisitiveness from an early age, as well as my curiosity about Pacific Northwest history. They raised me and my sister to know that the present is infused with the past. My sister, Valerie, has been my most unwavering source of cheer and encouragement throughout the challenges of writing. My husband, David, has been my patient companion and sounding board; his material support and steadfast love made the book possible. And our toddler son, Oliver—as he grows, he may not remember the crafting of the book, but it is through him that I came to more fully understand the Chemawa parents' desires for their children to have a more expansive future, one where their gifts would be honored.

Introduction

In 1879, the fate of the Indian people in the West was yet undetermined. Many Indian groups had been recently forced onto distant, unusable lands and, facing imminent starvation, they attempted to flee. In late January, a group of Cheyenne refugees led by Chief Dull Knife broke away from their containment at Fort Robinson, Nebraska. Mounted troops followed the band of refugees into the snow, shooting at the 150 starving men, women, and children. Nearly all the escapees were quickly killed or captured.

Within a week, newspapers from San Francisco to Boston covered the Fort Robinson massacre, and the public responded passionately. An editor for the *Atlanta Constitution* proclaimed, "The affair was a brutal and inhuman massacre, a dastardly outrage upon humanity and a lasting disgrace to our boasted civilization."[1] But the Cheyenne escape proved to be only the first in a yearlong series of disastrous encounters between the government and American Indians. In late January, a small band of Poncas, led by Chief Standing Bear, escaped home to Nebraska from Oklahoma, only to be arrested and jailed.[2] Soon afterward, more than five hundred Northern Paiutes were forcibly moved 350 miles north, during the middle of winter, to the Yakima Reservation, with dozens of babies, young children, and elderly dying en route. In the Southwest, Warm Springs Apaches fled from their disease-ridden San Carlos Reservation, and in southern Idaho, soldiers and settlers took arms against the Bannocks, who faced starvation after their food supplies were disrupted by white settlers.

The forced, often violent transfer of frontier lands to white control continued unabated as settlers flowed steadily westward. But public opinion on the treatment of the remaining Indian groups grew increasingly circumspect as awareness of governmental abuses mounted. Given the recent series of bloody skirmishes, talk of a military solution now seemed inhumane to all but the most violently obdurate Indian hater. Even General George Crook, known for his numerous campaigns against Indians in the trans-Mississippi West, declared, "Our treatment of the Indian is an outrage."[3]

As the public came to identify the government's treatment of its Indian wards as unnecessarily cruel, discussions of the "Indian problem" were marked by the reappearance of an old theme: Indians not only needed to be saved from the white man, they needed to be saved from themselves. As historian David Wallace Adams explains, "In the beginning, it was remembered, Indians had been promised the gift of civilization in exchange for their land. Indian land, for the most part, was now white land. Indians, on the other hand, were still largely savages. It was time to redeem an old promise."[4]

Amid a reform frenzy sweeping through America's upper middle class in the 1870s, a variety of political organizations concerned with the treatment of Indians emerged, including the Board of Indian Commissioners, the Boston Indian Citizenship Association, the Women's National Indian Association, and the influential Indian Rights Association. While these early reform groups did not count Indians among their members, they did share a common vision of reforming Indian policy.

The reformers were all from the upper echelons of eastern society and were almost universally guided by the tenets of evangelical Protestantism. Uplift of Indians was the fulfillment of one's Christian obligation to extend the blessings of Christianity to all the world's peoples. To this end, the reformers' efforts were animated by what historian Carl F. Kaestle has termed "the Protestant-Republican ideology." Core elements of this belief system included the sanctity of the republican polity (with its concomitant ideals of individualism, liberty, and virtue), personal industry, social mobility made possible through individual character, a respected but carefully circumscribed domestic role for women, the social virtues of property ownership, the grandeur of America's destiny, and the necessity of a concerted public effort (i.e., education) by which to unify America's polyglot population.[5]

Philanthropists alighted on the idea of "civilization" as a shorthand method for referring to these numerous values. Because Indian ways differed from those of whites, Indians were deemed to be the less civilized. So that Indians might reap the benefits of civilization, the Indian organizations lobbied for several distinct but related reforms. Reservations were a gross impediment to assimilation and had to be dismantled; this ongoing process was codified through the 1887 Dawes Act, which constructed a system for dispersing tribal lands to individual Indians, thus divesting the tribes of their land holdings. Tribal legal systems were deemed insufficient, savage, and backward; to extend the protection of the nation's legal system to Indians, Congress created an Indian police force in 1878 and in 1883 Indian courts wherein minor crimes such as "participation in heathenish dances" might be addressed. But of greatest importance to the reformers' agenda, for its presumed power to reach into the psyches of Indian youths and ensure the assimilation of future generations, was the need for education reform.

Arguments for Indian education rested on the premise that for lasting assimilation to take place, young Indians had to be taught the values, mores, and knowledge of Christian civilization. Older Indians were deemed incapable of becoming civilized; at best they could be "tamed," and hence finite resources should be allocated more effectively to the young. Most reformers adhered to an idea of social evolution similar to that put forth in Lewis Henry Morgan's 1877 treatise, *Ancient Society: Or Researches in the Lines of Human Progress from Savagery Through Barbarism to Civilization*, and in turn reasoned that education could exponentially quicken the process of cultural evolution. Thomas J. Morgan, Commissioner of Indian Affairs from 1889 to 1893, argued that "a good school may thus bridge over for them the dreary chasm of a thousand years of tedious evolution."[6]

Reformers also couched their arguments in terms of economic prudence. Secretary of the Interior Carl Schurz estimated that it cost nearly $1 million to kill an Indian in warfare, whereas it cost only $1,200 to put an Indian child through eight years of schooling.[7] Education could, in effect, augment the country's natural resources as well, since assimilation could be exploited to help dislodge tribal people from their vast landholdings. As a means of inducing Indians to cast off tribal ways and learn to operate within Euro-American society, education made sense on a variety of levels. For reformers, assimilation seemed to require nothing short of total identity transformation. To effect a complete transformation of Indian identities, education appeared a vital and indisputable moral imperative.

Indian people, however, likely did not share such a grand, all-encompassing vision of education; assimilation and identity were distinct ideas, a change in one not ensuring a transformation of the other. Many Indians accepted assimilation as an attainable or even desirable outcome that could be pursued without diminishing their Indian identity. They could selectively embrace parts of American society and still maintain a clear sense of themselves as Indians. Moreover, Indians often experienced attempts at education and land reform that left them segregated and isolated, and further prevented their full participation in American society. Historian Cary C. Collins has characterized the relationship between the national government and the Indian people: "The federal presence, ubiquitous and intrusive, enveloped Indian Country, seeking a victory of assimilation at any cost and wreaking enormous havoc on everyone and everything it touched, Indian and white alike. Equally debilitating to both patient and doctor, the encounter diminished each."[8]

But reformers in the late nineteenth century remained optimistic that the federal government's assumption of a parental role in the education of Indians would humanely offer them a chance for survival in the modern world. Prevailing ethnocentric appraisals of the Indian peoples' collective future were bleak, with many well-meaning Indian reformers warning that the alternative to total assimilation was total obliteration or, perhaps worse, the Indians' endless suffering in a status of inferiority and subordination relative to the non-Indian population.

To save the Indians, policy makers would need to accomplish their process of social reconditioning quickly, within one or two generations. Thanks to the far-reaching efforts of missionary-run schools dating back to colonial times,[9] a variety of models for Indian education existed. Which might promise the best chance of rapid assimilation?

The kind of complete transformation envisioned by federal policy makers required more than academic and vocational instruction, however successful these might be in preparing students for trades and domestic labor. For civilization to really take hold in Indian communities, the students' interior lives and emotional allegiances had to be remade as well. Music instruction promised to fill the vital role of replacing the "heathenish" pleasures of Indian ceremonial activities with more acceptable pastimes that would reinforce Anglo-European social customs. By breaking up the otherwise grim life of prayer, work, and study, school officials hoped musical activities would be sufficiently compelling that students might be more amenable to and complete in their conversion to civilization.

School songs were memorized in music class and sung en masse at student assemblies, and such songs often encapsulated a school's goals and teaching philosophy. The following school song, in use at Chilocco (near Ponca, Oklahoma) in 1906, embodies the intrusive parental role assumed by the school in its effort to control Indian bodies, thoughts, and spirits.

> There once did live an Indian youth
> His tribe Chey-Sioux-Chip-Pot-Jo
> His Uncle Sam said—which was the truth,
> "To school you ought to go, LO"
> So he left the reservation
> Left it far behind
> Came to seek an education
> To soothe his savage mind
> Learned to cultivate the land;
> Learned how to keep accounts correctly,
> Head applied to hand.
>
> There also lived an Indian maid
> Her tribe O-winne-paw-pa;

Her Uncle Sam said, and was obeyed,
"To School, my Minnehaha."
So she left the reservation
Left it far behind
Came to seek an education
To soothe her savage mind
Came to study at Chilocco
Learned to sew and bake good bread
Learned to keep a home in order
Hands controlled by head.[10]

In addition to repertoires of school songs that were known to entire campus communities, extracurricular activities offered various forms of music instruction to students who were interested in music or were advised by their teachers and administrators to pursue it. Marching bands, orchestras, dance clubs, drill teams, theater troupes, and glee clubs all offered forms of entertainment and self-development that were deemed acceptable by school administrators.

Extracurricular music activities fulfilled the goals of federal Indian policy by strategically using music to inculcate patriotism and a national identity. By reinforcing Anglo-European artistic sensibilities, school officials sought to erase Indian culture and history from students' memories. Students were taught "safer" forms of music than those of reservation life, and nationalistic musical pageants such as "Columbia's Roll Call" were devised to steep students in the mythologies of colonial America. Music quickly became a feature touted by school officials and maligned by critics of Indian schools, who acknowledged music's power to entice students into potentially dangerous environments. After learning of the scandalously high death rates among students in many boarding schools by the late 1890s, Indian Inspector William J. McConnell conveyed his alarm to Secretary of the Interior Ethan Hitchcock: "We are little less than murderers if we follow the course we are now following after the attention of those in charge has been called to its fatal results. Hundreds of boys and girls are sent home to die that a sickly sentiment may be patronized and that institutions where brass bands, foot and base ball are the principal advertisements may be maintained."[11]

In the early years of the boarding schools, teachers' and administrators' journals and letters reveal a pervasive fear of tribal music. Administrators deduced that running away from school, a common expression of student resistance, was provoked by the combination of "the roving disposition" and "the sound of drums reverberating against the mountains."[12] School officials thus perceived tribal sounds as insidious; they noted that even when a boarding school was walled up, guarded, and surrounded by a tall fence, music could still penetrate the compound. During a measles epidemic at the agency boarding school in Fort Defiance, Arizona, some parents succeeded in collecting their sick children for treatment at home, and the school staff listened anxiously to the "tom-tom and the barbarous howl of the medicine man at night, and the death wail from the same wickiup in the morning."[13] For many school officials, tribal music represented the unknown, the wild, the disorderly, the un-Christian, and possibly the dangerous. Even accounts given by more progressive teachers are notable for their savage depictions of tribal sounds. Flora Gregg Iliff, superintendent at Truxton Canyon, Arizona, recalled seeing Don, one of her prized older students, dancing at a late-night Walapi curing ceremony she attended:

> The muscles of his face were drawn in tight ridges, sweat rolled
> down his cheeks and dripped from his chin; his eyes were those
> of an Indian, a fanatical Indian, straining with all that was in
> him to lay hands on that magic power. He would support with
> the last breath of his life that thin, mummified zealot that sucked
> and gurgled and screamed in a wild frenzy. And I wondered,
> "Tomorrow will he stand in front of his company at school and give
> his commands to his boys? Will he sit at the head of his table in the
> dining room and help serve the younger children? Tonight he is
> steeped in Indian tradition. Can he change by the time the breakfast
> bell rings in the morning?[14]

Superintendent Iliff ultimately departed mid-ceremony, around three in the morning, panic-stricken.

A common lament among teachers was the special problem posed by tribal dances held off school grounds, which caused a buzz among the students and distracted them from their studies. The boarding schools' mission of identity transformation was compromised, and teachers believed that, after a dance, students would take days or even weeks to resume their regular work.[15] From the perspective of the teachers, tribal musics carried degenerative potential, creating unproductive students and thwarting organized education.

The students, however, were not savages, but emissaries from societies with cultures that were sophisticated and viable. Though early sources regarding students' opinions of music in school are fragmentary, we can glimpse some of their experiences through passages in autobiographies, letters, interviews, and oral histories, plus find clues in federal records, albeit mediated by non-Indian authors. Collecting anecdotes from around the boarding school system, we know that some students continued to practice their tribal musics, dances, and rituals secretly, while publicly embracing the school-sponsored programs that administrators had designed to engage the Native heart. Secret participation in such activities as stomp dances and peyote rituals was self-selective and often tribe-specific. For example, while groups of Creek and Cherokee students at Chilocco Indian School sometimes ventured to a nearby field to do stomp dances together, one Eastern Cherokee alumna confessed, "There's nothing in this world that will put me to sleep faster than a stomp dance . . . these Cherokees are so *colorless*, they have no feathers, no nothing . . . so now for our celebration every year we have the Plains Indians, now they can really get it on."[16]

Some students came to regard music classes as the saving grace of boarding school life; Fort Defiance alumna Irene Steward recalls discovering the "unexpected joys" of school life in fifth grade when she developed a talent for singing, lost some of her shyness, and enjoyed participating in the school's holiday programs.[17] Many students brought humor to bear on their newly learned music skills, as a way of coping with the disheartening day-to-day realities of boarding school; girls at one school acknowledged their inadequate food rations by composing such jingles as "Too much government gravy / Make me lazy."[18] Other students found the regimentation that was deeply engrained through daily dress parades to be stifling and downright embarrassing. Anna Moore Shaw, who attended Phoenix Indian School, resented the cadence of military marching that had become indelibly engrained in her own gait.

> At first the marching seemed so hard to learn, but once we had
> mastered the knack, we couldn't break the habit. Sometimes on our
> once-a-month visit to town, a talking machine would be blasting
> band music outside a store to attract customers. Then we girls
> would go into our act; try as hard as we could, we just couldn't
> get out of step. It was impossible! We'd try to take long strides to
> break the rhythm, but soon we would fall back into step again. How
> embarrassing it was![19]

For a few students, music instruction paved the way for professional success. Yakama vocalist and Haskell alumnus Kiutus Tecumseh became a celebrated tenor following World War I; Pima trombonist Russell Moore (known as "Big Chief" Moore) graduated from the Sherman Institute to tour with Lionel Hampton, Louis Armstrong, and his own Powwow Jazz Band; and Lakota student Gertrude Simmons Bonnin (Zitkala-sá) toured to the 1900 Paris Exposition as a violin soloist with the Carlisle Band, later parlaying her celebrity into a long career in

Indian policy reform. Responding to their boarding school music experiences in individual ways, students put the training to their own social, political, and economic uses.

For students' families, as well, music represented many things. Letters that students sent home reveal this diversity. Rip Van Winkle, a Navajo student whom agents had forcibly enrolled at the boarding school in Grand Junction, Colorado, staged a letter-writing campaign that eventually succeeded in securing his release. In a letter to his brother, his favorable reference to the school's band music stands out in stark contrast to his isolation:

> March 28, 1894
>
> Dear Brother Will Price
>
> I am going to write to you this afternoon. I stay house and three
> day. I dont feel better every day. I dont think stay here but I like
> go home this summer. I am very sorry all time and the boys march
> with the brass band and I think them play pretty good. I do not like
> to stay here because the superintendent don't like the navajo boys.
> I will ask him if I can go home summer. If he dont let me go, I will
> runaway from him. He told me. He said put me guard house and
> stay four day said that. if you will write *to me* again.
>
> from your brother
>
> Rip Van Winkle[20]

For some families, enrolling a child in boarding school was a conscious and deliberate choice, and parents often regarded music instruction as one of the schools' primary selling points. A father from South Dakota with two children at Flandreau wrote that he wanted to "see that Raymond works in the carpentry shop all winter," but he also stipulated that his daughter Phoebe learn music by having "lessons on the piano."[21] Another Flandreau parent, viewing music as an integral part of his sons' total education, wrote to request that his boys "take lessons of violin and also keep on in training as farmers."[22]

Some students wrote their own letters of application, as did George White Bull. In his request for enrollment at Flandreau, he uses his experience in a band as his opening argument for admission.

> I am going to write to you and asked you how I can come to school
> and so wish you would give me the proportion to come I play in
> band for two or three years and I'm just in fifth grade and I am
> very glad to learned little more if I can I have looked over all the

non-reservation school but I dont think I can go any wheres but to come over to your Flandreau Indian School as I thought this School will give me a little more education so that I can make an honest living when I get out. I know several Indian boys from here that had been there before and as they tell me about how the School is over there and so I thought I will get my learning from you Well Sir I wish you would kindly send me some blanks so that I can fill them up The very first time I want to do when I get over there is to join the band.[23]

Occasionally, students were descended from families with multigenerational legacies of musicians; such families often used the boarding schools as a way of ensuring that the musical training their children had begun at home would continue. Later in the boarding school era, some families were reluctant to enroll their children without some assurance that their own tribal cultures would be taught alongside the non-Native. If parents judged that tribal ways were neglected or denigrated in the schools, they often pulled their children from enrollment.

The phenomenon of "Indian Clubs" emerged on school campuses in the 1930s[24] as a way for schools to combat parental resistance by honoring students' tribal heritages. The tellingly named "Indian Clubs" were an outlet for Native dress, music, dance, and ceremony that was supervised and deemed safe by school administrators. At a time when many Indian groups had been dispersed and driven from their ancestral lands, many students welcomed a chance to research their background and tribal heritage, and it became a popular campus activity. One San Juan Pueblo student at Santa Fe Indian School reflected, "I don't think I appreciated my Indianness until I . . . became a senior in high school, when we had our Indian Club here, and I joined the Indian Club."[25]

As students learned to perform dances and songs from tribes other than their own, they took new songs and dances back to their communities, cultivating intertribal ties among boarding school students and their families. Boarding schools would prove themselves hotbeds for traditional arts, syncretism, and cultural exchange.[26] This history of sharing has been particularly pronounced at the longest-operating boarding school in the federal system, Chemawa Indian School, located four miles north of Salem, Oregon.

This book consists of nine chapters that explore the principal forms of music making that Chemawa students have engaged in from the school's establishment in 1880 through the present day. Organized by genre, the chapters overlap in the span of time each covers; together, they form a multi-layered account of music in campus life and its changing meanings for individual students, faculty and staff, school administrators, and families.

Chapter 1 opens with a Haida creation story as an invitation to consider the fundamental ways music has always been important to Indian people. This chapter then recounts the complex events that led to the establishment of Chemawa Indian School, and why Office of Indian Affairs officials deemed the practice of music—with its performance of both Indianness and whiteness—pivotal to their assimilation campaign.

Chapter 2 explores the school band—the juggernaut of the residential school's music program—as a social barometer, chronicling changes in the membership, repertoire, and functions of the band over the course of Chemawa's history. Military-style bands that were used to instill order and obedience for the entire student body gradually gave way to more diverse repertoires and the inclusion of female musicians. Alaska Natives in particular often arrived at Chemawa familiar with brass band instruments; at many Alaska villages, Native communities had already established their own brass bands.

Chapter 3 considers Chemawa's student singers and choirs, and the fundamental conflict between pedagogical approaches that emphasized music instruction for *all* students versus music instruction for the talented few. Choirs and small vocal ensembles were a key part of the school's public relations campaign, and students chosen to participate functioned as public ambassadors to the off-campus community.

Chapter 4 examines the extension of private lessons to students who were deemed talented, and the transition from the unbridled optimism of early reformers to the more qualified version of equality expounded after the turn of the century. This chapter also chronicles the colorful and complex life histories of two famous Chemawa musicians, Will DePoe and Spade Cooley.

Chapter 5 considers the role of theater and pageants in shaping campus life and student identity. Originally mounted for their perceived ability to inculcate students with the virtues of patriotism, Christianity, and civilization, the early dramatic productions eventually gave way to the performance of dances and stories from students' tribal communities. Supervised by staff and faculty members, students exchanged expressive culture, participated in each other's dances, and strengthened town-gown relations between Chemawa and the greater Salem community.

Chapter 6 charts the various forms of dance that Chemawa students have engaged in, first assessing governmental prohibitions of Indian dances and ceremonies and highlighting how these prohibitions were employed in western Oregon. The progressive reforms of Commissioner John Collier allowed for students to practice some tribal dances as well as Euro-American social dance forms, through which students learned prescribed social etiquette and gender norms.

Chapter 7 examines the historically recent phenomenon of garage bands, and how a group of Chemawa students chose to be active players in this regional trend. It identifies new ways student musicians have expressed themselves individually and collectively, and profiles The Meteors, a Chemawa garage band that met with considerable professional success.

Chapter 8 explores the unique role of powwows at residential schools, and the implications for the dynamic processes of identity formation, intertribalism, and cultural revitalization. Participation in traditional performing arts at Chemawa has become largely student-driven, and the students who choose to participate often return home to form drum groups or otherwise transmit their knowledge to youth in their tribal communities.

Chapter 9 returns the focus of the book to resiliency and the ability to bounce back from adversity—a necessary skill for all boarding school attendees. It invites consideration of Chemawa musicians' diverse life paths as proof of the ways that the students' musical involvement has supported their later successes in personal growth, work, relationships, and service to their communities.

Chemawa's founding was predicated on the erasure of all aspects of students' culture, language, traditional beliefs, spirituality, and connection to their tribal communities. Music was a critical component of this assimilation campaign, for its perceived ability to reach the hearts of Indian children and enable the total transformation sought by social reformers. One hundred and thirty years later, music is now used in the service of a new mission for Chemawa, one that recognizes "the oneness of all indigenous people, tribal self-determination, and respect for the inter-relatedness of all peoples and life."[27] The form of cultural expression that policy makers had pinned such high hopes on for its promise to reach the Indian heart became *not* a tool for mindless assimilation, but a way for Indian students to define themselves, to create social networks, and to gain the competencies that would promote their own resiliency both during their time at Chemawa and afterwards. How this remarkable change came about is the subject of this book.

Chapter 1
The Origins of Chemawa Indian School, and Why Music Mattered

Raven and the First Human Beings

Everyone knows that a long time ago, the world was covered by a gigantic flood. It covered up islands, shores and even many of the mountains. Eventually, the flood receded. Raven was flying around, happy that the floodwaters were gone. He was bored with a waterlogged world. So he was out there, flying around, flying around. Finally hungry Raven landed on a beach and began looking for good things to eat. Raven hopped and flapped along the seashore. From a distance, as Raven hopped along the beach, he spied a gigantic clamshell. Always interested in anything new or different, Raven waddled over to the shell. He heard strange sounds coming from that clamshell-little squeaks and funny noises: "Yakity, yak-yak." He had never heard such sounds coming from a clamshell before. He cocked his head and fixed his shiny black eye on the shell.

Raven was curious to find out what was inside the clam shell, but he knew that he would have to soothe its fears, whatever it was. Raven has a beautiful voice: He can croon and sound like a beautiful bell. He can sing and make pleasant and reassuring sounds, comforting sounds, sounds that bring joy to any heart. So Raven decided to sing to the clamshell. He sang a song that sounded like gurgling and happy water. After his song, he called out to the shell, "Come out, whatever you are, whoever you are. Come out. I am Raven, Creator of the World, and I will not hurt you. Please come out and play with me. The flood is over; I have given light to the world. Please come out and we will play together." Again Raven sang. Raven is not only the Maker of Things, not only the Transformer; he is also a Magician and a Healer. His singing contains magic and his voice, while sometimes annoying when he is hungry or frightening when he is angry, can also be lulling and soothing.

Finally, the clamshell opened, and a little being with long black hair, a round head, and brown, smooth skin popped out. Raven looked at his creature, with two legs like himself (but no feathers) and two arms and two hands: a very puny and scrawny being. Raven heard the murmur of other voices in the shell. Because he didn't want to scare the little thing, he continued singing, and he called the others out. Slowly, these little creatures emerged from the clamshell and onto the beach of what is today called British Columbia. These beings were the ancestral Haida.

"Come and play in my beautiful world, a world with warm, rich sunshine and sounding seas and dark nights for telling stories and sleeping. Come and play with me, and we will eat salmon and berries and all types of good things," Raven sang to the First People. At first, the People were frightened and bewildered. They were frightened of the sea-noise, the crashing of waves against rocks, and the pounding of the surf. They were frightened by the sound and movement of the wind. They were frightened by the darkness and size of Raven; they were afraid Raven might eat them. But slowly, one by one, they emerged and played with Raven and ate the delicacies he brought to share with them.[1]

Music has always been of vital importance to Indian people. For some Native groups, their very creation is predicated on it. The Hopi gods sang the world into being; the spirits that would become the Modoc people first gathered in the underground world to sing and dance; and for some tribes in the Pacific Northwest, Raven sang a song of greeting to the first people as they emerged from a clam shell. In effect, Raven used his voice to sing the first people into existence.

For children at Chemawa Indian school, the Raven story holds striking parallels and contrasts. Emerging from their tribal communities into the new world of the school, some children liked what they heard, others decidedly did not. The song of the reality of residential school life emerged regardless. Some students embraced it, and others did not. Most integrated parts of it into their identities, and discarded or left alone other parts that did not prove useful. Regarding their musical knowledge, all students arrived at Chemawa with backgrounds in music acquired through years of life experience. The students did not arrive without a song.

The goal of assimilationist reformers, then, was not to bring music to an unmusical people—though some reformers no doubt viewed their pedagogic aspirations in this manner. The reformers' real purpose was to replace the Indians' existing cultural life with a new one befitting a Christian, civilized, de-Indianized people. Indian people already had music; they just had the *wrong* music—music that was deemed uncivilized, savage, steeped in barbarism, and even prone to lead the practitioner towards Satan. Eventually, federally sponsored reformers would seek to rectify this most thoroughly by means of the curricula and campus life of off-reservation residential schools, but the first groups of reformers to attempt this task were church missionary societies.

In 1824, Indians of the Pacific Northwest first experienced a formal boarding school education at the Red River School at Fort Garry (now Winnipeg, Manitoba). Anglican Reverend David T. Jones and Governor George Simpson, of the Northern Division of the Hudson's Bay Company, agreed that the school's opening mandate was to bring thirty children from tribes across the continent to be educated at Red River. Operated by the Church of England's Church Missionary Society, the school sought to provide an education that missionaries considered similar to that of an English boarding school, with English-language instruction in European history, geography, agriculture, and "white man's ways," bracketed by morning and evening prayer. Students sang hymns and learned to read the Bible and the *Book of Common Prayer*. The first groups of students included the sons of Spokane, Flathead, and Kootenai chiefs, as well as the sons of HBC fur traders who had married Indian wives (one wife being the daughter of Chinook Chief Concomly). As the Red River School and its surrounding community grew, many of the Métis alumni and families left to make new homes in the Willamette Valley, some in clusters around French Prairie and Forest Grove. One graduate of the Red River School, Garry (the son of a Spokane chief), established an Indian-run school in Spokane in 1832, where Indian people from around the region came to learn Christianity, English, and basic agriculture.

Missionaries in the United States observed these early successes and were inspired to attempt ventures of their own. In 1835, Methodist missionary Jason Lee and his nephew built a twenty-by-thirty-foot log structure to house Oregon Country's first Methodist Episcopal Indian manual labor school. Located at French Prairie in an area known as Chemaway, the log house functioned not only as the precursor to Chemawa School but also as a church and hospital until it was washed into the Willamette River during the flood of 1841. The following year, Lee convinced the Mission Board to invest $40,000 in the construction of a new school at Chemeketa (now Salem). Rather than enrolling the "one to three hundred children" that he had promised the school would serve, however, Lee retained only twenty-three "scholars," using the bulk of the Mission Board's funding to secure valuable real estate, possibly to further colonization at a time when Oregon was still a contested territory. Reverend George Gary, whom the Mission Board sent as Lee's replacement, reported after arriving at Chemeketa that "some of them [the students] have run away and many have died. The dead have been decently buried. Runaways have been punished as criminals." Gary admitted to "blush at the information" that "the most of them have taken their stolen budget and when found have been brought back, put in chains, severely whipped . . . and guarded and kept within a high enclosure, like prisoners."[2] Gary sold the campus property and transferred the school at Chemeketa to the Oregon Institute, which operates today as Willamette University.[3]

Over the next three decades, missionary efforts continued in the form of small schools scattered throughout the Northwest. Despite Indian Commissioner T. Hartley Crawford's advocacy in 1938 of "establishing a large central school for the education of Western Indians,"[4] federal efforts at Indian education in the Northwest consisted mainly of subsidies for the various mission schools, eventually codified under the Grant Peace Plan in the 1860s.[5] Through the efforts of missionaries, reservation day schools became scattered throughout the West, with forty-eight already in existence by the era of the American Civil War.

In the Pacific Northwest, treaties negotiated with the Indians during the 1850s displaced the Willamette Valley tribes to the Coastal and Grand Ronde reservations. Pacific Northwest treaties often included promises of educational support, stipulating that vocational schools would be established with no-cost enrollment for the children of the signatory tribes. The Medicine Creek Treaty of 1854, for example, promised to Nisqually, Squaxin, Puyallup, and Steilacoom tribes that an agricultural and industrial school would be "free to the children of said tribes for a period of twenty years," with school expenses covered by the federal government and not deducted from annuities; the Treaty of Point Elliot, signed by tribes in the greater Puget Sound region in 1855, contains a similar clause, promising "to furnish them with schools, teachers, farmers and farming implements, blacksmiths, and carpenter, with shops of those trades." While the United States did not fully fulfill these articles, they did provide limited funding for day schools. Such schools were relatively inexpensive to operate, and engendered little parental resistance, but did not prove to be effective instruments of civilization. Much to the schoolteachers' consternation, the lessons, manners, and values taught in the five-hour school day were negated each evening by the realities of camp life. One Indian agent disgustedly summarized his day school's progress as of 1879: The natives seemed "content and happy; happy in their degradation and filthiness; seemingly content to remain as they are with little ambition to change for the better."[6] Had he attempted to sing Native songs with tribal leaders and women, other outcomes might have been possible. But white bias, combined with a lack of understanding of Native languages, culture, and religion, could yield no success. In such an environment, a day school was ineffectual at best.

Reservation boarding schools appeared as a promising alternative to day schools, with students only returning home during the summer vacation period, and in some instances over the Christmas holidays. In the Pacific Northwest, missionary-run schools at the Colville and Tulalip reservations eventually received federal funding as contract Indian schools, for which the government provided annual funds to maintain the buildings while the Catholic Church furnished books, clothing, housing, and medical care. Even after Congress gutted the contract Indian school program in 1896, these two schools persisted as federal facilities, offering education through the 8th-grade level. [7] The children ranged in age from six to eighteen, and they hailed from a variety of Indian communities that lived both on and off reservations.

A recurring phenomenon emerged, however, which alarmed and aggravated schoolteachers and administrators: the relapse. After going home for the summer, children tended to slough off their newly acquired habits of civilization in favor of more engrained, familial tribal ways. Indian parents also persisted in visiting their children at school. Seasonal camps were set up immediately outside the school grounds, facilitating student-family communication that subverted the efforts of the schools. One Indian agent explained, "Members of the tribe daily visit the school to its detriment in many ways, notably in retarding English speaking by the pupils, in persuading the children to run away, or to refrain from performing their allotted work, or in giving notice of the time of dances and their whereabouts to the pupils."[8] Dances were a common threat to the process of identity transformation; another agent explained, "A dance is announced a week in advance, and at once you see the young mind reveling in the thought until study and all thoughts of books are driven out and nothing but Indian remains, and weeks pass before the scholars get back to their regular work."[9]

As the day schools and reservation boarding schools, which were within visiting distance of the students' homes, developed patterns of shortcomings and complications, policy makers sought a more effective instrument of assimilation. Clearly, a higher degree of institutional hegemony was needed for a child to undergo the desired transformation. At this opportune moment an educational experimentalist emerged in the form of Captain Richard Henry Pratt, an army officer turned educator. In April 1878, he had been charged with the guardianship of seventy-two young Cheyenne, Kiowa, Comanche, Arapaho, and Caddo prisoners, Pratt had successfully transported them to Virginia and enrolled them as students at Hampton Normal and Agricultural Institute, a school for African Americans.[10] Encouraged by his experiences at Hampton, Pratt sought funding from Congress to establish a federal residential school in Carlisle, Pennsylvania, with the goal of assimilating Indian children by completely submersing them in

Table 1: Locations and Opening Dates for Off-reservation Boarding Schools (from Adams 1995:57)

Location of School	Date Opened	Fort Lewis, Colorado	1892
Carlisle, Pennsylvania	1879	Fort Shaw, Montana	1892
Chemawa, Oregon	1880	Flandreau, South Dakota	1893
Chilocco, Oklahoma	1884	Pipestone, Minnesota	1893
Genoa, Nebraska	1884	Mount Pleasant, Michigan	1893
Albuquerque, New Mexico	1884	Tomah, Wisconsin	1893
Lawrence, Kansas	1884	Wittenberg, Wisconsin	1895
Grand Junction, Colorado	1886	Greenville, California	1895
Santa Fe, New Mexico	1890	Morris, Minnesota	1897
Fort Mojave, Arizona	1890	Chamberlain, South Dakota	1898
Carson, Nevada	1890	Fort Bidwell, California	1898
Pierre, South Dakota	1891	Rapid City, South Dakota	1898
Phoenix, Arizona	1891	Riverside, California	1902

the white man's world. "In Indian civilization," Pratt contended, "I am a Baptist, because I believe in immersing the Indians in our civilization and when we get them under holding them there until they are thoroughly soaked."[11] Congress approved, and within two decades, an extensive off-reservation boarding school system was established, with twenty-five schools scattered across the country, mostly concentrated in the recently settled western states.

Earlier boarding schools had been located within visiting distances of the students' villages, but the more ambitious, modern government school system transported many students to school from halfway across the continent. Memoirs of Indian writers from the assimilation era (defined by historian Frederick E. Hoxie as 1880 to 1920) contain vivid descriptions of the enrollment process. Luther Standing Bear recalls being rounded up and loaded onto a train with no explanation, with even the older boys so frightened that they began to sing the death songs of Sioux warriors approaching battle.[12] Once students arrived at their schools, they were given new names. As Omaha writer Francis La Flesche recalls in his boarding school memoir, "The aboriginal names were considered by the missionaries heathenish . . . in the place of Tae-noo-ga-wa-zhe came Philip Sheridan; in that of Wa-pah-dae . . . Jonathon."[13] Music programs were a prominent feature at all the schools, and new students quickly encountered choirs, bands, dress parades, and football games.

A peculiar set of regimented experiences became common to students throughout the boarding school system. Newly enrolled students all received haircuts upon arrival, boys' hair clipped close to the skull. School administrators forbade the speaking of native languages, often under the threat of physical punishment. A typical daily routine followed a strict schedule of classes, work periods, study hall, prayer times, housekeeping, and recesses. Most schools had extensive working farms and vocational units, and the costs of keeping these up—as well as the costs of the kitchen, laundry, and campus infrastructure—were defrayed by the use of student labor. Some students went to boarding school expressly to learn trades, including music, both for their future livelihoods and personal enjoyment.

As their time in school lengthened from weeks to years, students exhibited markedly varied reactions to the new regimes. Some flourished and grew into compelling Indian activists who credited their success to their education. Some found the harsh treatment and separation from home untenable and ran away as soon as possible, only to be apprehended and returned to the school to await the next chance for escape. Others learned prodigiously yet returned home upon graduation to find that there was no place for them in their communities of origin, where prejudice against those perceived as having forsaken their Indian identities could sometimes lead to subtle taunting or outright ostracizing.

Despite their youth and the intensity of the boarding school indoctrination process, most Indian students were loath to give up their tribal ways. Songs, languages, and rituals continued clandestinely as students struggled to remember home and find security in a strange new world. Paradoxically, the remote locations of boarding schools, meant to speed indoctrination, also resulted in the mixing together of students from a variety of Indian groups. The students quickly realized that, contrasting cultures notwithstanding, they shared many common interests and experiences simply by virtue of being Indians.

Students learned songs and music from each other, and the intertribal bonds that would later facilitate many Indian groups' struggles for justice, federal recognition, and restoration were forged through these processes of acculturation. While *assimilation* implies conformity and the one-way transmittal of knowledge, *acculturation* allows for selective adoption, multidirectional sharing, and polyvalent meanings of cultural phenomena. Broadly defined by American dictionaries as "the adoption of the traits or patterns of another group," the idea of acculturation engenders a more accurate appraisal of how elements of culture were creatively shared, accepted, or rejected by players in the boarding school system—students, faculty, and staff alike—with all parties transformed in the process. Policy makers never anticipated that Indian students would actively participate in the acculturation drama, but faculty and staff working in the schools saw that student responses proved far less predictable than had been assumed. Understanding the complex, multidirectional cultural work that has taken place at boarding schools requires a sharper notion of acculturation, one where "acculturation comprehends those phenomena which result when groups of individuals having different cultures come into continuous first-hand contact, with subsequent changes in the original culture patterns of either or both groups." [14] Moreover, when people from different cultures interact, the process of acculturation is inescapable and necessarily involves all parties, all the time. No one can remain unchanged by an interaction, be it as fleeting as an algebra lecture or as momentous as the weeks of campus preparation for an Indian Day pageant. Despite the profoundly deleterious effects of assimilationist education policies and the undeniable cultural losses wreaked by the boarding schools, staff memoirs reveal periodic changes in their understandings of the acculturation process,[15] and students drew unanticipated strength from the bonds they formed with each other.

As Lieutenant Richard Henry Pratt was establishing his school at Carlisle, Pennsylvania, in 1879, Interior Secretary Carl Schurz also allotted funds for the establishment of a parallel boarding school to be located on the West Coast. Army Captain Melville Cary Wilkinson, inspired by the efforts of fellow Congregationalist General Oliver Otis Howard in establishing the Freedmen's Bureau and offering education to former slaves, was new to the Indian service, and was an ardent assimilationist with a passion for Indian education. Wilkinson was already living in Oregon, serving under General Howard's command at the Department of Columbia. Federal law prohibited army officers from holding civilian positions, however, except for certain loopholes, such as being appointed a military instructor at an established college. Wilkinson received just such an appointment, as professor of military science and tactics at Pacific University in Forest Grove, Oregon. Multiple factors rendered Forest Grove an ideal site for the Indian school: Sydney Harper Marsh, the president of Pacific University, was a great-grandson of Eleazor Wheelock, who had founded Dartmouth University as an early trial of Indian boarding school training. Missionaries Elkanah and Mary Richardson Walker, who had established the Tsimakain Mission for the Spokane in 1839, now lived in Forest Grove and were active in the life of Pacific University. Also, Forest Grove was a dry town, helping create a moral climate that federal officials believed would support their attempted transformation of Indian lifeways. In February 1880, Wilkinson recruited eighteen Indian boys from the Puyallup Reservation in Washington Territory to establish a new school at Forest Grove.

Using $5,000 of appropriations, Wilkinson oversaw the construction of Forest Grove Indian Industrial and Training School by the hands of the students themselves on four acres of land loaned by Pacific University. The school would operate as an instrument for assimilation, with Western music—in the form of Christian hymns and marching band music—as an integral part of its curriculum. Once the dormitories were completed, Wilkinson began recruiting female students as well, and by October 1881 he reported having the school "filled to one more than the maximum allowed: seventy-six students from Puyallup, Warm Springs, Wasco, Piute, Pitt River, Spokane, Chehalis, Nesqually, and Oyster Bay Agencies."[16]

Photographs of the students, taken both before and after their enrollment, were used as part of a public relations campaign to create a lasting, tangible sense of the transformation that the school might produce. Figure 1 shows Spokane students who had just arrived at Forest Grove in 1881, and the same students seven months later. Five of this group were dead by February 1888.

These images highlight the school's overtly stated purpose of assimilation. In reality, the students acculturated instead, taking *some* aspects of the new education into their lives. They remained Indian people, adding new elements like the knowledge of Western music; in doing so, they embraced acculturation rather than assimilation.

While instructors at Forest Grove focused their school curriculum on vocational instruction, with students learning farming and other forms of manual labor, part of the day was devoted to traditional academics, taught from a stridently Euro-American perspective. Wilkinson considered Forest Grove's geographic isolation from tribal communities a "bonus," and believed that education could proceed effectively only if the students were made to shed their Native identity. He reported on his progress and strategies, summing up: "Pushing general Indian Education rapidly and to successful issue." Affirming his deep personal commitment to the process, he explained that effective transformation "can not be done at the end of a pair of tongs nor by those who have an idea that their Creator must have made a mistake in creating this race." He sought to divest students of their Indianness by attacking the most fundamental aspects of identity, mandating that "the final rule here, after cleanliness and obedience, is no Indian talk. The delegations, from different tribes, are divided and subdivided, until all tribal associations are broken up or lost."[17] "No Indian talk" included a ban on the singing of traditional Indian songs.

While the United States government strove to provide formal education for Indians, it simultaneously waged wars against the last groups of resistant Indians. Wilkinson returned to his regiment in July of 1882, and Ojibwe Indians eventually killed him in a skirmish between U.S. soldiers and the Bear Island band of Ojibwe at Leech Lake, Minnesota in 1898.[18]

The school at Forest Grove continued to expand despite its scant farmland and building space. With no prospects of further expansion at Pacific University, a fire that destroyed the girls' dormitory in 1885 allowed the school to relocate.

Figure 1. Spokane Indians, as new boarding school students and again seven months later. Though not individually identified in the photos, they included James George, Florence Hayes, Garfield Hayes, Louis Isaacs, Eunice Madge James, Julia Jopps, Martha Lot, Frank Rice, Ben Secup, Susette Susan Secup, and Alice L. Williams. Photos by I. G. Davidson. Courtesy of Pacific University Archives, Forest Grove, Oregon.

Two additional circumstances coincided to make the move possible: the U.S. government offered $20,000 for the construction of school buildings if another party would donate land for the school, and a group of citizens from Salem eager to attract federal money to jump-start the local economy donated 171 acres of land just north of town, the site of present-day Chemawa.

The school opened its doors on October 1, 1885, as the Salem Indian Industrial School. It assumed a series of names—Harrison Institute; Salem Indian School; United States Indian Training School; Indian Industrial School; again in 1909, Salem Indian School; and finally, Chemawa Indian School. While the source of the name "Chemawa" remains a topic of debate, the name existed in reference to a location and possibly a band of people long before any school was built there. Evidence suggests that Chemawa was once a campsite for a band of Kalapuya Indians, a group who thrived in the Willamette Valley for centuries only to lose 92 percent of their population to European diseases between 1838 and 1841. In 1930, Chemawa Indian School's annual, *The Teepee*, offered the following summation of theories on the name's meaning:

> It is said that the word "Chemawa" is from the Calapooia language
> meaning "a place where no one lives." And again it is claimed
> that the name is from the Chemeketa tribe of Indians and means
> "Happy Home." There has also been advanced the theory that the
> name was taken from the Chinook language and that originally the
> name was "Chewawa," the "che" meaning new and "wawa" talk
> or language—in other words, "new education." In the course of
> time it is suggested that somebody blundered and the first "w"
> in "Chewawa" got changed to an "m," thus making the name
> "Chemawa," as at present known to all.[19]

A more recent consideration of the native language sheds further light: in the Santiam Central Kalapuya dialect, Chemawa means "place of low-lying, frequently overflowed ground." Such places were often good sources of camas, a critical root crop for local peoples. Kalapuyans applied the term Chemawa to at least three different locations in the Willamette Valley: a prairie north of Salem (near Lake Labish and what would become Chemawa Indian School); a place near Forest Grove; and a place near the town of Independence, just southwest of Salem.[20] Recently, Chemawa students themselves embraced the Kalapuya etymological concept of "happy home" in their production of the "Happy Home" video, designed to complicate the idea of "home" and showcase how they feel about attending Chemawa today.[21]

A common theme in the official rhetoric surrounding the inception of the Indian boarding school system was that of economy. To maintain itself, Chemawa needed a land base large enough to produce the requisite food to sustain its student body. Rather than returning home during the summer months, students were hired out to work in local hop fields. After a season of picking hops, they received half of the wages paid to them by landowners, the other half being used to secure additional acreage for the school. School administrators justified the use of student labor to purchase school real estate by touting the practice as a means of inculcating a Protestant work ethic in the students.[22]

The campus expanded to more than three hundred acres by the turn of the century, and the student body increased accordingly. By 1920, the school enrolled nine hundred students from ninety western tribes, with nearly a third of the students hailing from Alaska. At this time, the physical plant consisted of sixty-six buildings and more than four hundred acres of agricultural land that contained a variety of crops, orchards, and gardens. Rich soil, ample moisture, and the good drainage of the Willamette Valley provided exceptional resources for the vocational component of the school's "half-and-half" (academic and vocational) curriculum,[23] and Chemawa attracted students from throughout the West.

To be admitted, students needed to be at least one-quarter Indian (a blood quantum law), pass a physical examination, and have their parents' consent. The regions from which students came fluctuated over time as the Bureau of Indian Affairs adjusted its educational policies and strategies. From 1925 to 1960, Alaskan Natives were not allowed to enroll, barring a few emergency situations. From 1957 to 1960, the Navajo Project mandated that Chemawa provide education for Navajo students, who were without schools in the Southwest, rendering Chemawa a Navajo-only school for several years. Between 1960 and 1967, Chemawa admitted only Alaskans and Navajos. In 1967, the Indian Bureau ended the Navajo Project.[24] Students from the Pacific Northwest began attending Chemawa the following year, and today Chemawa educates more than four hundred students from seventy tribes in fifteen states.

Academic instruction at Chemawa underwent several structural changes during the school's initial development, but music remained a constant, with many forms of musical expression always present on campus. The first graduates received the equivalent of a fifth-grade education. In 1888, an eighth-grade curriculum was instituted, and in 1917, this was expanded to a ten-grade progression. In 1926, Chemawa finally expanded to include a full four-year high school, with total enrollment approaching a thousand students. The primary grades were phased out by 1933, though in 1936 younger children were again allowed to attend Chemawa while receiving treatment for conjunctivitis.[25]

As we have seen, at the time of Chemawa's inception the school's goals were overwhelmingly assimilationist. The residential schools were charged with integrating the Indian population into the general society through education, in effect swallowing up the students into the Euro-American social order. As students from disparate homelands encountered each other, however, they were prone to engage in cultural mixing, sharing the stories, songs, and foodways of their home communities and forging new intertribal relationships. Not only did these new alliances help give birth to the modern Pan-Indian movement, but they also posed serious impediments to the schools' indoctrination processes. Students who developed a sense of shared identity as Indians could sustain a coexistence of Indian and white beliefs and practices within themselves, fend off undesired indoctrination attempts, rely on each other for emotional support, and reinforce Indian values. School administrators quickly realized this and that, while Christianity, vocational training, and academic classes might reach an Indian's head and hand, a deeper, more lasting assimilation could take place only if a way was found to reach the Indian heart.

Music promised to provide just that intimate access. School officials knew that music had always been important to Indian people, figuring prominently in feasts, rituals, and day-to-day life. They hoped to replace tribal music forms with "proper" forms of music, in the process instilling ideas of order, work ethics, gendered behavior, religion, and patriotism. Through music making—the right sort of music making—students could be thoroughly transformed from the inside out, and could then share evidence of that transformation with the greater community through concerts and recitals. On occasion, the music making prescribed by school officials would highlight paradoxes of federal Indian policy by romanticizing the very behaviors and Indian-ness the schools sought to eradicate. Students were enjoined to perform such popular tunes as "Red Wing: An Indian Fable" and "By the Waters of the Minnetonka: An Indian Love Song." Shy Indian maids kept campfires burning patiently, bold warriors "fell bravely in the fray," and primitive love calls issued forth to tunes that were "founded upon a Tribal Melody."[26]

Despite these romantic images of Indian life that Chemawa musicians were made to bring alive, student choristers and band members learned, in no uncertain terms, the behaviors that Euro-American society deemed acceptable for the confines of their particular gender, race, and class. Students marched in neat formation, sought companionship at carefully scripted social dances, and received lessons on wind and brass instruments (boys) and piano (girls)—until Superintendent Reel deemed such lessons wasteful because "in all likelihood" these were "expensive instruments the students would . . . never own."

Somehow, although the music was foisted upon them, many students liked the music they performed at the school, took it in, modified it, and made it their own, using it to their benefit both during school and afterwards. For some, it provided a means of getting away for performances and breaking up the routine of daily campus life. For others, it gave them the training they would rely on after graduation to pursue music performance professionally or as an unpaid vocation. Still others went on to teach music in other Indian Office schools.

Even though they both operated under the same institutional umbrella and with ostensibly the same mission, Chemawa differed somewhat from Carlisle in that it more closely reflected Grant's Peace Policy rather than the U.S. Army's "force policy." Many of Chemawa's students had been voluntarily enrolled by their families and tribal communities, who sought to give their children knowledge of spoken and written English as a means to protect and advance themselves. The different schools used different means to further their agendas, as a result of individual administrative leadership, the participating tribal communities, and the degree of each school's geographic engagement with or isolation from the central offices in Washington, D.C. Carlisle's physical plant was patterned on that of the prisons and workhouses General Pratt had overseen before designing his method of Indian education, including a prominent elevated bandstand, which served as a symbol of surveillance, and a six-foot fence that completely surrounded the campus. Since Chemawa, however, was first established by Wilkinson, who had served only briefly in the Indian service, the "rude wooden structures" of its physical plant more closely resembled those of a working farm, as was befitting the local community in Forest Grove, Oregon. Following the school's 1885 relocation to Keizer, Oregon, its twelve new large brick buildings and many wooden structures more closely resembled a small college campus with dormitories and extensive agricultural/vocational units. Though Chemawa certainly sought to control Indian bodies and behavior, it had no equivalent to Carlisle's "man on the bandstand,"[27] who claimed an omnipresent status to inspect, judge, and control student deportment. In the early decades of the boarding school system, rules regarding displays of expressive culture would differ wildly from school to school, as would the performative deployment of Indian-ness, even as the top Indian Affairs officials attempted to assert bureau-wide policies on acceptable music making.[28]

The Chemawa campus would prove home to a diverse array of musical forms and activities, from glee clubs and pageants to powwows and garage bands. That said, Chemawa's early years were marked by Christian hymn-singing and military-style marches, with students lining up in formation and marching in a dress-parade style. The genre of music that featured most prominently in early campus life, accordingly, was the school band.

Chapter 2
"Chemawa Always Had a Huge Band":
The School Band as Social Barometer

> "Chemawa always had a huge band. It was one of the real highlights of
> the school. At the reunions, the older guys would sit down and try to
> play. They had all been in the band. The music was extremely important.
> It seemed to spark a lot of pride in the school."
>
> —Dee Pigsley (Siletz), recalling growing up on or
> around the Chemawa campus from 1945 to 1971

Because early Indian boarding schools took their organizational cues from Richard
Henry Pratt's military structure at Carlisle, the first cohesive school music programs consisted of marching bands that could accompany the student body in
marches, drills, and parades.[1] The administrators' initial goal was to bring order
and discipline to the seemingly chaotic, undisciplined lives of their young charges. This differed from the slightly later use of school bands in non-Indian schools;
bands in Indian schools, established by an army general as a means of instilling
order, were specifically targeted to wipe out and replace Native musical practices.
Comparable forms of cultural imperialism have long been one of the hallmark
strategies of colonialism, as the organizers of society—politicians, theologians,
academics, and families—institute cultural practices to impose and ensure order,
the shape and requirements of which can change over time. Music and language
are popular tools for these hegemonic processes, and parallel examples abound,
including the beating of Hawaiian children for speaking in their native language
in school during the early territory period,[2] the forced use of French—through
la vergonha (shaming, particularly in school)—as the language of Occitania, and
the imposition of Japanese language and music upon schoolchildren in Korea,
Okinawa, and Indonesia.

While the use of marching bands in Indian schools began as an intentional,
wide-sweeping hegemonic device, the practice never achieved anything close to a
wholesale replacement of tribal music forms, which were remarkably malleable in
terms of how different tribal communities appropriated and used the new music.
The instruction was not solely externally imposed; there was input and direction

from individual students and their families. After the initial imposition of order that school administrators achieved with the bands, the student musicians quickly excelled at their instruments and became creative and enthusiastic band members whose dedication and love of the music helped the school band program to persist for several generations. Some students—Alaska Natives in particular—had even arrived at Chemawa with competence in their instruments; these students would become the backbone of the band ensemble for years to come. The enduring presence of the school bands is underscored today by Siletz elder Dee Pigsley who, when reflecting back on Chemawa's music program, recalls that "Chemawa School always had a huge band. It was one of the real highlights of the school."[3]

The historical longevity of Indian school bands is all the more impressive when one considers that the boarding school bands existed long before their public school counterparts. Bands and orchestras did not appear in public high schools until after the founding of the Music Educators National Conference in 1907, and did not become a common institution until the 1920s. Indian school bands, however, appeared in the late nineteenth century, shortly after the schools were first established. The musicianship, uniforms, and modes of behavior characteristic of military-style wind orchestras relied upon a system of discipline and control that appealed to early school administrators, as they sought an antidote to tribal musics they perceived as chaotic or threatening. Wind orchestras, particularly marching bands, offered an effective way to establish military discipline and regimentation for the musicians themselves as well as for the student body as a whole, who could be taught to march in formation for drills and dress parades. Under Pratt's leadership, Carlisle Indian School formed its first band in 1880, during the first year of the school's existence. The band soon became renowned nationwide for its polish and talent, and accounts of the band's early history attribute its beginnings to a charitable contribution from Mrs. Walter Baker of the Baker Chocolate Factory. Here the story is told from the perspective of Carlisle's administrators:

> During the first year's existence of the school, the two great musical instruments to be heard were the "tom tom" and Indian flute, which were as annoying and unmusical as they were constant in their use. From early morn until obligated to retire at night, the only musical sounds coming from the boys' quarters were the tom tom, tom tom, tom tom or other like melody.

The annual appropriation was not calculated to cover the luxury of musical instruments which prevented the replacing of the Indian drum and flute with clarinets, cornets, and pianos which were very much desired. The question, therefore, was one of finance.

Finally, however, Mrs. Walter Baker, of Boston, came to the rescue. During a visit she had been making, she was very much delighted with the prospect of the school and its Indians, and as she was about to leave said to Captain Pratt, the superintendent:

> "Captain, what can I do to help the school which would be distinct and by itself, and not be part of some general contribution?"
>
> The Captain replied: "Since you have been here you have heard the 'tom tom' and Indian singing down in those quarters?"
>
> "Yes."
>
> "Well, I want to stop that, but feel it wouldn't be fair to do unless I can give them something else as good, or better, on the same line. If you will give me a set of brass band instruments I will give them to the 'tom tom' boys and they can toot on them and this will stop the 'tom tom.'"
>
> And so Mrs. Baker sent the boys a set of Boston instruments and the girls were provided with pianos. Strange to say, the order to stop the singing of Indian songs was never issued, but as the first band became more musical, the Indian songster in proportion became musicless.[4]

The tropes in this recollection—the savage beating of the "tom tom"; a bifurcation of Western instruments into appropriate types for girls and boys; and the notion that music exists in a realm closer to the heart than other human pursuits—occur throughout early boarding school records. Also pervasive was the idea that Western music had a natural superiority over Native music, and that once exposed to both, Indian youths would inevitably choose the former, in tacit acknowledgment of its beauty, refinement, and complexity. Marching bands in particular were a symbol of civilization, intelligence, culture, and refinement. In administrative discourse, music thus became a stand-in for the more generalized concepts of culture and lifeways, and assertions of the inherent appeal of Western music always implied something larger that was at stake: competing social systems, in which the Indian would presumably disintegrate in the face of the Western.

Whether because of its smaller student body or for lack of a similar benefactor, Chemawa's band was not founded until 1892. Reports to the Commissioner of Indian Affairs suggest that instrumental music education existed at Chemawa even before that, as Silas Whitman, the brass band teacher in 1892 at the Fort

Figure 2. Earliest known band photo, from 1892, when the school was briefly named Harrison Institute. The band was later known as the Chemawa Indian School Band. Members unidentified. Robert Thomas papers. Courtesy of SuAnn Reddick.

Lapwai, Idaho, school, was himself a graduate of Chemawa and likely learned his trade there.[5] Documentation of this period in Chemawa's history is scant, and little is known about the band's early days. Its repertoire may have paralleled that of the Carlisle Indian School Band; if so, it would have included such overtures as *William Tell*, *Tannhäuser*, and Auber's *Fra Diavolo*, as well as classical music by Grieg, Schubert, Weber, and Mozart. School records from the mid-twentieth century make reference to Chemawa's "grade school band" folding in 1915, and so it is probable that Chemawa's first bands included ensembles for students of various age brackets. A few existing campus photos reveal military-style band uniforms (figures 2 and 4), a special gazebo from which the band would play (figure 3), and a large quad area where the entire student body would stand in formation, but little is known definitively of the band's practice habits, repertoire, or membership requirements.

Stories of an early practice of "serenading" persist, in part because the practice has been revived at later points in Chemawa's history. On days of special significance, such as the band's anniversary each March, the band members would rise before dawn, assemble outside, and play beneath each of the campus dormitories and staff housing areas, waking up the Chemawa community with the strains of their music. High school student Lucetta Hahn, who attended Chemawa in the mid-1950s, described the earlier practice by explaining, "Many years ago, on the band's birthday the members used to get up early and go out to serenade on campus. First they would go to the superintendent's house, and then around to the other buildings." Hahn further describes the disappearance and revival of the practice:

Figure 3. Chemawa's bandstand, adjacent to the tall evergreens that rendered its campus grounds distinct from those of other Indian schools. Behind the bandstand is Cramton Hall, the dining hall. Photo circa 1913, from Robert Thomas Collection.

Figure 4. The Chemawa Indian School Band, circa 1930, in front of the Academic Building at Chemawa. Courtesy of Grand Ronde Archives.

"The band has not done this since about 1920. But on March 18, 1955, on their sixty-fifth birthday, the band went out during their practice period and played two marches in front of the high school building, the administration office, and the home economics building. The marches were 'Honor Band' and 'Military Escort.'"[6]

As we have seen, the band had ceased its serenading practice in or near 1920, and the grade school band had folded entirely in 1915. These breaks in the timeline of Chemawa's band program stand out for their contrast with the burgeoning public school band phenomenon of the time. The patriotism and martial spirit of World War I had held wide appeal for much of American society, and bands— more than orchestras—were a natural marriage with the war effort, for their mobility, volume, sonority, uniforms, and repertoire.[7] Why did this intense increase in the popularity of school bands not translate to Indian schools, or at least not to Chemawa? One factor may be the lack of donated instruments available from instrument manufacturers during the years of World War I. Another may be the growing wealth and social mobility that World War I brought to America—the rush of vertical mobility experienced after the war helped families to secure the purchase of musical instruments for their children, and helped communities to afford instruments for their schools. But for the most part, Native American populations did not benefit proportionately, and thus did not have the income at their disposal to purchase or promote this type of instrumental music instruction.

Perhaps because Chemawa could not afford to maintain a large band program during the war years, a group of select students formed the Indian String Quartet (see figure 5), a small ensemble that made few fiscal demands on the school.[8] Assembled by music teacher Ruthyn Turney, the group included students who had arrived at Chemawa as early as 1908, all of whom had come to Chemawa with the express purpose of studying music. The Indian String Quartet eventually left Chemawa (without Turney) to tour extensively in the years from 1915 to 1917, garnering rave reviews from Lyceum audiences and fellow musicians alike as they played their first (classical) act wearing suits, and their second (featuring Turney's Indianist compositions) wearing Native regalia. Interestingly, the Quapaw and Haida members of the quartet would forgo their traditional clothing (basket hats and porcupine roaches, respectively) in favor of the long Plains-style war bonnets that white audiences instantly perceived as Indian; Inuit violinist Alex Melovidov may have played up his Arctic origins by performing in fur clothing and sealskin *kamiks* (boots). When the Redpath Bureau, their Chautauqua employer, froze their salaries during the war, first violinist Fred Cardin enlisted in the Army and the group disbanded.[9]

In 1928, as Congress received the scathing report by Lewis Meriam, "The Problem of Indian Administration" (commonly known as the Meriam Report) and

Figure 5. The Indian String Quartet, ca. 1916. Left to right: Fred Cardin (Quapaw), violin; William Palin (Flathead), viola; William Reddie (Haida), cello; Alex Melovidov (Inuit), violin. Photograph from the records of the Redpath Chautauqua Collection, Special Collections Department, University of Iowa, Iowa City, Iowa.

implemented its demands that more resources be allocated to the Indian schools, Chemawa set about rejuvenating its band program.[10] New music was purchased, and special attention was given to the space in which the band could perform for the campus community and for visitors. An anonymous (likely staff-written) article in the school paper announced, "Mr. Robert DePoe, our bandmaster, has just received quite a consignment of new music for the band, marches and standard overtures, etc., and the organization is now well supplied with good music." The author was particularly excited by improvements to the safety and acoustics of the performance space: "The task of moving our bandstand is under way. It is to be located on the campus just in front of Cramton Hall. The old location was too close to the road and S.P. tracks. The children crowded onto the road and R.R. tracks, to the endangering of their lives, and passing trains and autos made too much noise, hence the change." Hot autumn afternoons would be rendered more comfortable, as "Supt. Lipps expects to put in a number of seats under the trees and in reality to make a little park for band concerts."[11] Clearly, Superintendent Oscar Hiram Lipps regarded the band performances as central to campus life.

As support increased, the band went through a series of directors who often did not stay at Chemawa for more than two years, a puzzling development if not for the fact that most of them proceeded from Chemawa to assignments at other Indian schools that were also enthusiastic supporters of their own band programs. In the period of 1928 to 1932, Chemawa was assigned in succession the band directors Robert R. DePoe (father of Chuck and Will), Hermann A. Kunkel, Amos Vosburgh, and Charles ("Chuck") DePoe. Biographical blurbs printed in *The Chemawa American* and *The Salem Statesman* reveal the band directors to be college-trained, active, professional musicians. While both DePoes were graduates of Indian schools (and Siletz bandleader Will DePoe is profiled in Chapter 4, "Private Lessons"), biographical sketches of Kunkel and Vosburgh (who hailed from Connecticut and New York, respectively) make no reference to Indian schools or tribal affiliations, suggesting that they were likely non-Native.[12]

Besides playing for school football games, the school band appeared in a variety of contexts, both on and off campus. Under the direction of Robert DePoe, the band continued the Indian school tradition of holding dress parades on campus. On Sunday afternoons, students marched in formation in time with the band music, clad in wool uniforms even in late summer temperatures that could exceed 90°F. Following the dress parade exercises, the band often performed an outdoor concert, with visitors witnessing both the dress parade sequences and the band offerings. One Turtle Mountain Chippewa alumnus who attended Chemawa from 1927 to 1933, from age fourteen until graduation, recalls the discipline and decorum particularly required of the students on Sundays: "That's the way it was . . . we'd dress in uniform every Sunday. In fact we had to be in uniform practically all day Sunday because we had to go to chapel in the evening and dress parades, just like West Point." Even in the 1930s, the codes of dress and behavior Chemawa required of its students were still akin to those of a military academy. Students responded in various ways to this high level of structure. Some enjoyed the excitement of performances and competition; this particular alum was one who lauded it, explaining, "All these Indian schools followed the military . . . To me, we had discipline [and] I think that was the best thing Chemawa ever had around there. They had competition for different companies. It was a lot of activity."[13]

The evening displays were particularly well attended by the public in the springtime—the most temperate time in the Willamette Valley—and served a critical public-relations role for the school. Students and faculty alike were keenly aware of being on display, as a staff member described in the school paper: "It is now the season of the year when auto loads of people begin to show interest in us by motoring to the school about the time for flag salute on Sunday evenings to hear the band play and watch the maneuvering of our various student companies."[14]

Chemawa also brought the band out to the Salem area, to represent Indian education at community events. Under H. A. Kunkel's direction, the band appeared in countless area parades, including the parade of the Modern Woodmen of the

World, the Armistice Day parade, and the Spring Opening parade. The band often performed in non-marching concert settings as well, with recitals for the State Tubercular Hospital, the state convention of the Christian Endeavor Association, and the annual community concert held in the Salem Armory. Accounts of these performances, written by Chemawa staff members, focus not on the music per se nor on the students' experiences of the events, but rather on the quality with which the band represented Chemawa. Post-concert summaries are replete with variations of the phrases, "It was another case of Chemawa to the fore," "the band proved themselves a credit to the school," and "our band acquitted itself most creditably and added to Chemawa's fame as the home of better things."[15] Occasionally, school officials asserted the civilizing effects of the music overtly, such as in this 1929 encomium from Supt. Lipps: "It is quite clear . . . that they [students and band members] are an indication of Indian possibilities in civilization."[16]

Some students arrived on campus already proficient on band instruments. This was particularly common among the students from Alaska, whose villages often had traditions of community brass bands that had been brought by the Russians in the early twentieth century. Whether in the larger cities of Juneau and Sitka or in smaller villages like Klukwan, band music had been eagerly taken up by Alaska Native men, and most villages boasted at least one marching band or dance band (see figure 6).[17]

Judson Brown—whose father James Wheeler Brown is pictured in the center of the back row—commented, "Some of these men could read music, but couldn't read or write!"[18] The sons of these musicians would arrive at Chemawa in the 1920s and 1930s with similarly surprising skill sets.

During the period just before the Great Depression, Oregon public schools were also implementing orchestral training. While orchestras had come to flourish in many of the nation's schools by the 1920s,[19] Oregon's geographic position on the western frontier and its accompanying culture of individualism had discouraged its investment in musical ensembles, as well as in public schools in general; when Chemawa was founded in 1880, Portlanders were still debating whether public high schools should even exist.[20] In 1925, however, the Portland Junior Symphony Orchestra gave its first concert at Lincoln High School, and a survey conducted in 1931 by the Oregon Music Teachers' Association identified "between 60 and 70 of these organizations in the counties [i.e., rural or semirural areas] and between 30 and 40 in the first class [i.e., urban or more densely populated] districts."[21] Clearly, the resurgence of the instrumental music program at Chemawa now coincided with a regional trend.

The nation also was in the midst of a sharp upswing in the manufacturing of musical instruments. The sudden ubiquity of wind bands during and following

Figure 6. Haines Native Band, ca. 1910-1920. Photo courtesy of Judson Brown.

World War I had demonstrated the possibilities of expanded sales for many types of instruments, and within a decade instrument production increased exponentially. Related businesses, such as uniform makers and music publishers, increased their production accordingly. Uniform companies began a conscious effort to produce more appealing and versatile band uniforms, and music publishers responded to the demands of band teachers by standardizing arrangements for particular groupings of instruments, and publishing ever-increasing amounts of music from a wider number of genres.[22]

Band genres evolved rapidly in the 1920s, yet the band repertoire at Chemawa still remained firmly in the classical realm, as school administrators regarded jazz with suspicion or outright contempt. An unsigned two-page manifesto against jazz appeared on the front page of *The Chemawa American* in March 1930, beginning with the opening salvo, "We believe that 'Jazz,' so-called, represents a state of mind. If such is true, what an indictment of the American people!" The author continues, linking jazz to the listener's personal character: "Jazz is not only represented in music, as the result of a state of mind, but we venture the opinion that whoever is wild over musical jazz will be found of not over-serious mind in regard to other features of the life they live." Stereotypes of race and savagery are both implicit and explicit, as the author deduces that, "It appears logical to assume that as our minds are supposed to govern all of our acts that where one revels in barbaric music (deficient in all the laws of harmony and musical form) some vital cell in the brain must fail to function. Jazz is strictly the product of 'Yankee Land' and came from the African jungles with the importation of slaves to the United States." The remainder of the article contrasts young people who live for "genuine and legitimate pleasures that are born of noble aspirations" with those who live "for sensations and experiences that tend to wreck mind and body and leave them as . . . human derelicts."[23] The parallel constructions of primitivism affixed to African-American youths and American-Indian youths are striking; while these are not identical, they do include similar tropes: the dangers of pleasures that appeal to the body (presumably at the expense of the mind), the need to take a stand against jazz before it inflicts its evils on white populations as well, and the insidious power of tribal musics to lure heretofore promising youths down a path of delinquency and wasted potential.

Interestingly, isolated voices in academia were just beginning to challenge the tenets of social Darwinism, and while their studies were sometimes spurred by an interest in racial distinctions, the findings increasingly pointed to a lack of different aptitudes between ethnic groups. In a 1929 study that appeared in the *Music Supervisors Journal*, Thomas R. Garth (chair of the Department of Education at Columbia University) and Sarah Rachel Isbell (mathematics teacher with an M.A. from the University of Denver) sought to employ scientific methods to answer the question, "What musical ability does the American Indian possess in comparison with the white man? Does he excel in the latter or is he less gifted?" To this end, they surveyed 769 students of the Indian schools in Chilocco, Oklahoma; Rapid City, South Dakota; and Santa Fe and Albuquerque, New Mexico, administering a detailed questionnaire that assessed abilities of pitch discrimination, intensity, time, consonance, musical memory, and rhythm. The results came back the same for all groups—mixed blood or full blood, males or females, or grade in school (5th through 9th); moreover, "no racial differences are indicated here" between the musical talent of Indians and the musical talent of whites. The article appeared as a follow-up to an October 1928 study by Guy B. Johnson, published in the same journal, treating the area of "Musical Talent and the Negro." Garth and Isbell's write-up was billed as a "companion discussion" and "the result of a long and difficult study."[24] The progressive nature of their study and its results becomes clear when one considers that, only a decade earlier, esteemed music critic Charles Wakefield Cadman expressed widely held public opinions in his essay "The 'Idealization' of Indian Music," an exploration of the potential for using Indian-based themes as building material for American classical music: "It is really true that no [primitive] race is more music-loving than the American Indian. If you talk with those at the head of any Indian school or those in authority on the many reservations scattered over the West and Southwest, you will find evidence for a firm conviction that Uncle Sam's little wards are in the main quite musical . . . The girl students show a singular aptness in the study of the piano and singing, and without a bit of urging on the part of their teachers."[25]

While Indian school music programs of the 1920s and '30s were still grounded in the notion that Indian students had a unique potential to be transformed by exposure to Western music, scholars were mounting the first challenges to the stereotypes of Indian people as innately more rhythmically oriented (and more harmonically challenged) than non-Natives. For the time being, however, school administrators seem to have been unswayed by findings such as those of Garth and Isbell. Convinced that rhythmic jazz music posed a particularly virulent threat to Native students, they deemed that the civilizing effects of the school band could only be achieved by a hearty diet of Western music. Chemawa's music students received a heavy dose of classical training, often leading to the development of technical skills they could later use to pursue other genres (for example, see the profile of western swing band leader Spade Cooley in Chapter 4, "Private Lessons"). Despite increased interest on the part of the student body in the popular dance music of the time, as evidenced by spoken and written accounts of students pooling their money to buy phonograph records to dance to in the dorms, the school band's repertoire stayed in the realm of the classical. Not until the 1950s would Chemawa see more vernacular music programming.[26]

Eventual changes in repertoire notwithstanding, there were several aspects of the ensemble's functioning that remained constant over the history of the band's existence: students arrived with prior training that ranged from nominal to extensive, they had to audition to become band members, and practices were held during school hours on week days, with the band assigned to a designated elective period. Often, the band room would also be kept open in the evenings for those who wished to rehearse during their free hours. Each new school year was guaranteed a rocky start as students arrived at various times over the course of two months, and it was never certain which of the previous year's players would be returning. But once a critical mass of students had arrived (typically by late September or early October), band practice resumed in earnest.[27] Sometimes, the decisive factor in determining when band rehearsals could resume in the fall was not the arrival of the students, but of the band director; a turnover of the position sometimes led to a gap in leadership, and students awaited their band work with anticipation. Written accounts of the waiting musicians attest to this form of student agency. Student agency is most broadly defined as the students' ability to take action, but in this context, it also implies genuine enjoyment of their time in the band. Band culture included member-generated initiation rites, the students' favorable descriptions of band parties and out-of-town gigs, and instances of the students planning surprises for their band directors, such as the gift of a new baton.[28] Engaging with school band music had become a new way for students to express themselves, and to experience a common, shared history with fellow students.

Students' satisfaction with their band experiences seems to correlate largely with the amount of support the school superintendent gave the band at various times, and the upswing both in support and in student gratification is particularly evident for the period of the late 1920s through the early 1950s. While public schools at this time enjoyed support from commercial interests such as instrument manufacturers and music publishers, Chemawa saw far fewer of such benefits, as the public expected the Office of Indian Affairs to supply the lion's share of resources for the band program. Despite perpetually having to operate a complex institution with limited resources, however, Chemawa strove to maintain a strong music program in the 1920s to 1950s, and its support of the band included a bandstand, fresh sheet music, newly constructed bleachers, a renovated practice space, and new uniforms.[29] Though alumni recall that "the band sometimes marched, but not in the rain," the band maintained special white raincoats in the 1950s to cover their bright red V-neck sweaters when rain was forecast for parade days.[30] A show of the school's support of the band can also be gleaned from its willingness to provide the band with their uniforms outright, while other campus organizations (such as the pep squad cheerleaders) had to pick nuts or hops to earn money for their uniforms.

Over the course of Chemawa's history, the school offered its students membership in several types of musical ensembles, but the presence of the band remained constant even while other ensembles were formed and dismantled. A school orchestra sometimes existed, but always with numbers much smaller than the band; the band consisted of wind and percussion instruments while the orchestra included strings as well. In public schools, the orchestra initially had a more central role, and the band was much slower in gaining academic recognition. For Indian schools, however, it was the band that was given the more central role in campus life, and in addition to playing for football games and parades, bands were expected to fill many of the functions that orchestras assumed in the public schools: performing as a concert unit, playing for dances and soirees, and providing music for various school functions.

The 1950s also saw the addition of several majorettes, who would march with the band while twirling batons; they were just as often complimented on their "cute new outfits" as on their twirling. The Girls Athletic Association (G.A.A.) also formed a drill team, which functioned as an auxiliary group to the marching band; with twenty-four members, they had a strong visual impact at school sporting events, and their adviser, Mrs. Mary Bartolome, was able to secure for them red-sweater uniforms similar to those worn by the band. In addition to performing with the band at sports meets and parades, the G.A.A. drill team sponsored school dances and played basketball against Chemawa's regular intra-murals team, sometimes winning.[31]

The band often marched, and while early formations were based on the clean grid lines of military regiments, later formations grew increasingly whimsical, with the band assembling in the shape of a trombone, or a "C" for Chemawa.[32] Changes in the styles of band marching came with changes in repertoire. The three pieces the band played for the Class C band meet held at Salem High School on April 22, 1950, exemplify the older tradition of concert pieces that could be performed by band or orchestra: the "Golden Glow" overture, "Passing of the Red Man," and the "Normal" march.[33] For the band's fifty-seventh birthday celebration, held on March 15, 1952, the band played a grand march, jitterbugs, and waltzes, and a panel of faculty judges awarded several students awards for being the best dancers.[34] For the Winter Band Concert, an annual event, the 1952 program under the direction of Vincent J. Matt included a mixed program typical of public schools at the time: "marches, popular numbers, novelties, and an overture."[35] An even greater proportion of vernacular pieces comprised the repertoire of Chemawa's newly formed pep band, which appeared on Salem radio station KOCO in the spring of 1954 with the pieces "Military Escort March," "Sugar Blues," "You," and "March of the Trojans."[36] Later that winter, the annual band concert consisted largely of vernacular, dance-oriented numbers: Sousa's "Washington Post March," Bennette's "Ambition," Yoder's "Tiger Rag," Weber-Aronson's "Loveliest Night of the Year," Huffine's "Them Basses," Zamacnik's "Fortuna," and, lastly, Sousa's "Stars and Stripes Forever."[37]

Ad hoc bands occasionally sprang up on campus, with students employing the common areas of their dormitories as practice spaces. The unsigned (and thus likely staff-authored[38]) article "All-Girl Band" gives the instrumentation for one of these student-generated campus dance bands, proclaiming, "When a certain group of girls get together in the living room at Winona Hall they make real band music. Myna Kennedy plays the piano, Myrtle Racine and Florence Hall strum guitars, Rebecca Andy plays the snare drum, and Dorothy Harris plays the bass drum and cymbals. We hope to hear them play at a dance sometime soon."[39] The author intended to be laudatory and encouraging, but in the process revealed a bit of surprise at the girls' ability to make "real band music." This surprise may be attributed to the girls' ability to achieve a tight ensemble outside of normal class hours, rather than surprise that the girls could successfully harness their instruments. Since the early 1940s, the school band had admitted an increas-ing number of girls into its ranks, transforming the band in the decade between 1941 and 1951 from a male-dominated group to one in which a majority of the members were female. After women nationwide had filled the vacuum created by professional jazzmen who were drafted during World War II,[40] female musicians likewise became commonplace in public schools and Indian schools, and they weren't displaced after the war ended. For Chemawa, the shift to increased female membership proved a definite boon for athletic meets—whereas the 1941 band had five of its twelve members on the football team and was thus reduced to a skeleton crew at football games, the 1951 band had only twelve males out of fifty-four members, allowing it to play easily for interscholastic sporting events, which were still male dominated in the 1950s.[41]

When the band reached fifty-four members, the band program's resurgence became official, as staff and faculty who had long been affiliated with the campus declared, "We believe this is the largest school band Chemawa has ever had."[42] The band's heyday in the early 1950s can be attributed to numerous factors, including: Chemawa's increased enrollment, as the school embarked on its Navajo program while still accepting Northwestern students and Alaska Natives; the admission of female students into the band, thus doubling the pool of potential auditioning musicians; a growing general budget in the years between World War II and the tribal termination era[43]; a general public acceptance of school bands' playing of vernacular music (including jazz, which had been considered degenerate just twenty years earlier); and the able leadership of Vincent J. Matt, Sr., a longtime beloved band director at Chemawa (see figure 7). At its peak, the band program included the large Chemawa Band, a twelve-member pep band, a dance orchestra made up of five students and three employees, and a grade school orchestra of forty-eight students, reinstated in 1950 after being defunct for thirty-five years.

Navajo student Betty Pearson, who had transferred to Chemawa from Flandreau, South Dakota, remembers playing in the band with her sister Margaret in the mid-1950s. "Margaret played the trombone," Betty explained, "and I played the sax—I think it was the alto sax. And we'd march downtown in the parade. We had a band director, Mr. Matt." Betty laughed, saying, "I think that [the sax] was the only instrument left. It had a good sound. I really wanted to play the clarinet, something small. But I played the sax, and it was big, and had a big sound." Teachers worked with groups of musicians, rather than with private students: "We learned in a big class. Sometimes, he'd divide us up into sections, and we'd work with just the horns, or just the clarinets." Betty recalls the band performing publicly and, during her time in the band, the students wearing street clothes for performances: "We'd march in town, on Columbus Day and other holidays. We didn't have uniforms—we wore our own clothes." [44]

Betty had very little family—only her sister Margaret and a brother she would not know until later—and her involvement in music was one factor that

Figure 7. Chemawa Indian School band, late 1950s. Courtesy of Grand Ronde Cultural Resources, Charles Holmes papers.

contributed to her resiliency, and one of the main reasons she chose to attend Chemawa. Betty explained, "I was born without parents. So, I spent the winters in school, and the summers in foster homes. I went to a lot of different schools! When you don't have parents, you get bounced around a lot from place to place. I was at Chemawa from 3rd grade to 8th grade. This was in the mid-1950s [as part of the Navajo 5-Year Program]." Like many residential school students, Betty attended other Indian schools in addition to Chemawa, allowing her to make comparisons between the schools. "Then [after Chemawa], I went to the school in Flandreau, South Dakota. It was cold! Otherwise, there was no difference [between Flandreau and Chemawa]. There was no music there [at Flandreau], just the basics. They only had about three hundred students, while Chemawa was closer to a thousand."[45]

Soon after Betty Pearson's time at Chemawa, band members received new caps and uniforms and the latest recording technology to assist their practice regimen as the band tried to "rub out the rough spots . . . with the aid of a tape recorder and phonograph records."[46] The band kept an active performance schedule at this time, with regular off-campus appearances in parades and civic gatherings; to create a sharp image, the school administration sought to support the band's musical development and showmanship, viewing the band members as unique ambassadors who would shape many people's first encounters with Chemawa.

Siletz student Dee Pigsley grew up at Chemawa; her mother worked there as a matron, and her father as the night watchman. She lived there from age two (in 1945) till her family moved to a house in town in the late 1950s. One of eight children, four of whom played musical instruments, Dee recalls the band's vibrant uniforms, and their role in starting school dances: "They did march, and they wore red sweaters, with a 'C' in front, in black letters. They all looked really good. The band always started the dances with a march, like a Sousa march. That's what got the kids mixed up, so the boys didn't all sit on one side of the room."[47]

In the late 1950s, the band began to gradually decline in numbers. The initial drop-off resulted from fluctuations in Chemawa's total enrollment, but the continuing decline in the 1960s coincided with a more general phenomenon that took place in public schools throughout the country. Education reformers maligned marching bands for their presumed emphasis on showmanship over musicality. A panelist for a discussion at the New Jersey Education Association meeting in 1962 encapsulated the conflict with the challenge, "I defy any French horn players to produce sounds related to musical endeavor while prancing around the grass at 160 gyrations to the minute, bobbing up and down like yo-yos and standing with one foot facing east and the other foot facing west." The author of this critique attributes this degraded state of affairs to music teachers who, increasingly faced with students untrained in music, tried to maintain their positions "by showmanship rather than musicianship," and who thus fooled themselves into believing that "teaching discipline, sportsmanship, and physical control"[48] were the reasons for the existence of music in the public schools. Educators voiced similar opinions through the 1960s, decrying an overemphasis on pageantry and other nonmusical experiences of marching bands. William Thomson, then chairman of the Theory Department at Indiana University's School of Music, expressed a common critique of bands as a force working against universal music education when he argued, "The music educator who regards ensemble performance as the sole means of training literate musicians in the public schools is deluding himself and prostituting his students . . . the crucial test of the validity of a school's music program must be what the individual student knows about music when he leaves that program, not how well his band played when he was in it."[49]

As such arguments denigrating bands became more prevalent nationally, many school music programs shifted their resources away from school bands and into music appreciation classes. Chemawa took a middle path, still maintaining its band yet offering a music appreciation class as a fine arts elective. When the new campus, with a design taken from a community college in the Dakotas, was built in the 1970s, there was no dedicated space for a band, and the lack of infrastructure further marginalized the music program.[50] The band survived into the 1980s, taking a less central role in campus life and public relations but still playing for sports meets, through the efforts of a small group of dedicated students as a succession of band directors came and went. Siletz tribal leader Dee Pigsley attributes the decline to multiple forces, including changes in campus space, personnel, and the school's focus and priorities: "V. J. Matt was the director for years. He died a while back, though, and the [music] program never really got going again after he was gone." The new physical space, though it had a modern gymnasium, was not designed with a large school band in mind, either: "The old school had a huge gym where the band played. I don't think they ever did that anymore after the new school came. My neighbor across the street taught music there for a while at the new campus, and she said there just wasn't much interest. It seemed like it wasn't a high priority." [51] Ultimately, Chemawa donated its musical instruments to the Siletz charter school, gifting them a grand piano, a grouping of brass instruments, and assorted other instruments.

Back in the early 1970s, when a Colville delegation had visited Chemawa, they reported that only $3,000 was budgeted for student recreation, of which the band was considered a part. They also noted that there was "little in the way of cultural activity." Subsequent Chemawa superintendents Al Ouchi and Ed Lonefight instilled more structure, disallowed tours by visitors' groups (Ouchi explained, "We're a functional unit . . . we're not some place where people can come look at us because they want to see an Indian"), and restored funding for a number of clubs and activities. [52] The extracurricular activities that emerged in the 1980s, however, were mostly student generated, and while there was a ski club, a kayaking club, a drama club, and money for ice skating or going to the beach, student interest was not sufficient to consistently maintain a band.

The last music teacher to direct a band at Chemawa was Hal Beyers, who worked there for nine years and retired in 1997. While the primary focus of Chemawa's music program at that time was its music appreciation classes, Beyers sometimes organized a small band for students who wanted to play. There were no formal lesson times allowed for in the school curriculum, yet Beyers offered private lessons on several band instruments, and arranged for interested students to meet with him outside of class, while enrolling in his music appreciation courses in order to get credit for their work. In this way, Beyers attempted to accommodate the students' diverse interests and talents.[53]

Ted Mack, recent vice principal of Chemawa, explains the current—and fundamentally different—music coursework, along with the challenges it entails: "Now, what [music] the kids get is through a course that the BIA requires: the 'culture cluster.' It's difficult [teaching tribal traditions] here, for two reasons: not all faculty are Native, and there's not one tribe in the majority."[54] The "culture cluster" is a single course that is part of the graduation requirement for Chemawa students. It fits into the curriculum as follows:

Graduation Requirements[55]

Language Arts	4	units
Mathematics	3	units
Culture Cluster	1	unit
Social Studies	3	units
Science	3	units
Health	1	unit
Physical Education	1	unit
Keyboarding	0.5	unit
Fine Arts	1	unit
Practical Art	1	unit
Electives	6.5	units
Total	25	units

With the culture cluster course being a general survey of cultural traditions from around Native America, with some emphasis on the cultures currently represented at Chemawa, any teaching of music is perfunctory at best; the course cannot sufficiently draw on all the students' tribal backgrounds, nor can it offer the ongoing campus presence effected by the marching band, which impacted the whole Chemawa community.

To meet the fine arts requirement, Chemawa offers an exceptionally strong visual arts program, and a large portion of the students choose to study drawing or painting. With educators of American Indian and Alaskan Native students increasingly concerned about the growing number of students who do not find school a meaningful place,[56] the fact that high numbers of students flock to Chemawa's visual arts program suggests that it may be a more effective vehicle than marching bands for helping students learn technical creative skills while allowing for authentic self-expression. And the art that now bedecks the walls of Chemawa visually represents the diversity of the student body in a more conspicuous, undeniable, and potent way than marching band music ever could.

Certainly, the more options that students have, the greater the likelihood of their achieving academic and social success. Were a band to be reinstated at Chemawa, there would likely be some percentage of students who would connect with it in a meaningful way. But for a student body that now numbers less than four hundred, current levels of school funding simply cannot support the large palette of activities from which earlier students could choose. That a band-centered music program has gradually transformed into the culture cluster course, focusing on traditional forms of cultural expression, is sometimes lamented by alumni, who remember the band as a symbol of thriving campus life. But current students find relevance in other types of music, including powwow drums, guitar rock, and hip-hop. While bands remain relevant at many public schools today, the general social climate of the past thirty years has rendered other concerns—issues of tribal sovereignty, access to health care, cultural recovery, and the rebuilding of families and communities fractured by generations of systematic disenfranchisement—more pressing for today's Indian students. Students took hold of the hegemonic device of the school band for a time, squeezed what usefulness they could from it, and allowed it to fall away when it no longer served their purposes.

Chapter 3
A Hegemonic Tool Redeemed?
Chemawa's Voices and Choirs

"How to love and how to sing, are the same lessons. It begins inside with the breath and courage accumulated in one vibration, from the solar plexus."
—Elizabeth Woody (Warm Springs), granddaughter of Chemawa alumni, remembering the gifts of singing passed down from her grandparents.[1]

When the first boarding schools were established on the heels of the Indian Wars, students often arrived with extensive skills in their tribal languages, songs, and musical instruments. Familiarity with the English language and with Western classical instruments, however, was less predictable. Vocal instruction therefore emerged early on as a seemingly effective means of harnessing Indian bodies, minds, and hearts. All students, irrespective of their various language fluencies, were presumed to be capable of singing. School officials reasoned that patriotic, Christian, or otherwise pedagogic song lyrics were edifying even for those who did not yet understand English, and early accounts of Sunday chapel services testify to the teaching of songs to all students, even the newest charges. The vocal arts became the area in which the early boarding school policy of "music for all" was most heartily adopted. The emphasis on singing underscores the early social reformers' enthusiasm for the complete identity transformations that they believed boarding schools were capable of carrying out.

Singing lessons helped the youngest students learn to pronounce standard American English vowel sounds and consonant clusters that did not necessarily occur in their tribal languages. For example, third-graders at Carlisle Indian School were taught to sing "Little Brown Sparrow," complete with hand gestures (figure 8).

Songs about animals often resonated with children, Native as well as non-Native, and most children's songbooks contained many of them.[2] To effect the complete transformation sought by school administrators, it was deemed best not to present the human relationship with animals from a tribal perspective. In song lyrics, humans learned moral lessons through animals (e.g., the value of

Figure 8. Singing class at Carlisle Indian School, ca. 1890. Photo by Frances Benjamin Johnson. Courtesy of Cumberland County Historical Society.

hard work in a squirrel's storing nuts for the winter), yet maintained dominion over them.

All boarding school students engaged in some form of vocal music making, and it was often built into a school's daily schedule. This was common in federal boarding schools and even more prevalent in church-run schools. The Cherokee Female Seminary's daily schedule included "Afternoon Music," and teachers were expected to participate regardless of their expertise: "The board . . . required seminary teachers to instruct students in vocal music."[3] This injunction took root with American Christianity's emphasis in the late nineteenth century on congregational singing as a form of communion with the divine (an oft-quoted patron was St. Augustine of Hippo: "He who sings prays twice"). Chemawa maintained Catholic and Protestant church choirs in addition to the regular campus choirs. Students sang in their classroom hours and in their free time, in their required courses and as an extracurricular activity. While there is little documentation of how students felt about the extensive singing they did in the early boarding school days, we do know that all students who were enrolled in the boarding school system were made to learn a large repertoire of vocal music—a powerful hegemonic tactic. In time, the focus of this compulsory singing would change in response to new philosophies guiding federal Indian policy.

As the first two decades of America's Indian boarding school endeavor passed, former students did not disappear or blend seamlessly into non-Native society, and social reformers qualified their earlier optimism. Changes in federal Indian policy reflected the new goal of fostering Indian youth who would not be the equals of their white counterparts but would more likely work in service positions. In 1895, Superintendent Hailmann declared that "the stress of work on the part of the schools should be placed upon industrial and manual training rather than upon literary advancement." Literature could be studied, he allowed, but this should be "in the service of the respectively fundamental aim of securing industrial fervor and efficiency on the part of the children."[4] A decade later, his successor, Estelle Reel, would go so far as to disallow non-industrial instruction altogether, mandating that girls "become proficient in cooking, sewing, and laundry work" and that boys study such topics as "the anatomy of the horse's foot" rather than "the chemical and physical properties of matter, a knowledge which will be of little practical value to Indian children."[5] Intellectual pursuits were positioned in opposition to the practical, and the practical always trumped the intellectual. The system-wide curriculum was rapidly overhauled to emphasize the acquisition of skills deemed practical for the students' eventual employment, which was presumed to be agricultural or, in the case of female students, domestic.

This meant instruction in vocal music could only be offered to a small number of students, those who evinced unusual talent. With half of the school day devoted to vocational activities, the remaining classroom hours were scarce, and students could not be allowed to squander time on tasks that did not contribute directly to future work prospects. It didn't matter that Indians in the rural Northwest enjoyed classical music, with the Pendleton Drug Company reporting in 1920 that it had sold many phonographs and a "surprising . . . number of grand opera selections" to local Indian community members.[6] Universal music instruction fell prey to vocation-centric pragmatism. By the late 1920s, Chemawa openly acknowledged the policy in its promotional materials: "Music, both instrumental and vocal, is given to a selected few who show aptitude and talent for the work."[7]

The vocal ensembles that were active at Chemawa in the 1920s met outside of regular classroom hours. The new music policy favored small ensembles agile enough to rehearse outside of class, in the students' limited free time. These included a girls' octet, a boys' octet, Catholic and Protestant church choirs, and an occasional ad hoc trio or quartet. Their off-campus performances continued to fill a vital public relations role for the school, and students were taken to area churches, high schools, and civic events to accompany Chemawa officials as they touted the school's good work. The students' singing was central to the success of one lunchtime speaking engagement before local business leaders, as "Supt. Lipps took with him to the Chamber of Commerce a quartet of girls, Martha Packineau, Melba Arnoux, Katherine Soldier and Serena Twiggs, who contributed musical numbers at intervals and were splendidly received . . . We are truly proud of the event in every way."[8]

Small ensembles of a few talented vocalists could cultivate skills that students already possessed upon arrival at school, and could strategically represent Chemawa to the non-Native public. Even if the complete assimilation of all Native children as equals to non-Natives was no longer deemed possible, students with specialized vocal training became examples of the school's transformative potential, and helped earn support from the local community. At this time, Chemawa's "Outing" system of vocational and domestic apprenticeships was in its early stages of development, and finding homes for students who were ready for placements likely grew easier as local farmers and tradespeople witnessed the students' ability to sing Western art songs. The students' performances rendered them seemingly more "civilized" and less Native, assuaging any fears about their ability to assimilate into local households.

Students who represented Chemawa by singing at off-campus events hailed from a wide range of areas and tribal communities. Despite their diverse musical backgrounds, all were trained at Chemawa in the singing of popular "Indianist" compositions of the time. As America emerged from the late nineteenth century and its Victorian sentimentality, the prevailing culture and marketplace remained preoccupied with music that depicted sanitized and stereotyped Indian-themed songs, usually written by non-Indian composers. Sometimes incorporating bits of melodies from Native music,[9] the songs were replete with romantic frontier images of primitivism, innocence, and noble savagery—the very qualities boarding schools were supposed to minimize in their young charges. This irony seems to have been lost on school officials, whose accounts of students' performances never commented on the discrepancy between the values espoused in the songs' texts and music and the assimilationist values touted by the federal boarding school system.

"Indianist" compositions used various techniques to evoke the sounds and images that the popular imagination associated with Indian culture. Musicologists Michael Pisani and Tara Browner have used Charles Pierce's semiotic relationships between "sign" and "object" to group musical works based on Native American subjects into three categories: symbolic (merely Native inspired), indexical (attempting to approximate Native sounds), and iconic (using materials from Native music).[10] Pieces derived from these three approaches made it into the popular repertoire of the early twentieth century, and became regular fixtures at Chemawa despite the Native values they crudely displayed—values that were, from a school administrator's perspective, antiquated at best, and dangerous at worst.

Vocal works that were performed regularly throughout the 1920s and '30s include the operettas *Pocahontas* and *The Captain of Plymouth*, Glick and Logan's "Pale Moon," Lieurance's "By the Waters of Minnetonka," Roos and Zamecnik's "Indian Dawn," and, later, Rudolf Friml and Oscar Hammerstein's "Indian Love Call." Of these works, the two that were performed by far the most frequently over the years were "Pale Moon" and "By the Waters of Minnetonka."

First published in 1920, "Pale Moon" featured lyrics by Jesse G. M. Glick (1874-1938) and music by Frederic Knight Logan (1871-1928).[11] Logan was better known for "The Missouri Waltz" and did not usually write Indian-themed pieces.[12] "Pale Moon" was a surprise hit that was published in numerous arrangements during the 1920s and '30s. To depict the deep and "natural" pain of forsaken love, Glick's lyrics employ a variety of stereotypes that anchor Indian people firmly in a timeless, primordial way of life:

> Out of my lodge at even-tide,
> 'Mong the sobbing pine,
> Footsteps echo by my side,
> A spirit face, a sign.
>
> Twilight skies all a-light,
> Across the deep lagoon,
> A face is breaking through the night,
> My Indian [maid/brave], Pale Moon.
>
> Speak to thy love forsaken,
> Thy spirit mantle throw,
> Ere thou the great white dawn awaken,
> And to the sea thou swingest low.
> — "Pale Moon, An Indian Love Song"[13]

Various indexical features common to "Indianist" music of the time—grace notes, pentatonicism, "tom-tom" fifths, octave leaps, downward melodies, and short-long rhythms—appear in the piano accompaniment, though only sparingly; Logan was not as heavy-handed in his use of "Indian" signifiers as were other composers of the day.

Such musical references appear more conspicuously in Thurlow Lieurance's "By the Waters of Minnetonka."[14] Written circa 1912, "Minnetonka" takes its melody from a flute piece Lieurance transcribed after one October night in 1911 when he sat around a campfire with several members of the Crow, Cheyenne, and Sioux tribes, his Edison phonograph at the ready to record any songs the men were willing to sing for it. Sitting Eagle (Sioux) first sang and then played a love song on his cedar flute, and Lieurance found it haunting for its pentatonicism, its sharp iambic rhythms, and the accompanying legend relayed by Sitting Eagle in which "Moon Deer" and "Sun Deer" escape tribal animosities by fleeing to the Minnetonka, where they choose to drown themselves rather than be captured by the enemy Cheyennes on the opposite side of the lake.[15] Here is Lieurance's rendering of the legend:

> Two lovers of the Sun and Moon clans of the Sioux Indians, loving against tribal law, fled to escape torture, and let themselves sink together into the waters of the lonely Northern Lake. The silver ripples, it is told, mourn above them, and the winds bear the cry afar. But in the song they will arise from the depths of the lake for you; you will hear the steady and regular beat of their paddles and see the diamond spray drip off in the moonlight as they pass, once again, in their ghost-canoe.
>
> A violin typifying the wind, if you choose, echoes the soft harmonies of the accompaniment which rocks to and fro on harp chords, between the major key and its relative minor, in and out of that singular domain musicians know as the "added sixth" chord and its derivatives.[16]

"Minnetonka" proved an enduring hit. Operatic singers such as Nelson Eddy and Mohawk baritone Oskenonton popularized it; it became an important jazz standard during the big-band era, and it would eventually be used humorously by Lucille Ball in the May 4, 1953, episode of *I Love Lucy*, "The Indian Show." Obviously, the sounds and words of "Minnetonka" and the meanings they evoked resonated in non-Native America, as they confirmed non-Indian ideas about Indian culture.

Determining the young Chemawa soloists' thoughts and feelings as they sung these "Indianist" pieces is difficult, if not impossible, as most of them have since passed on and did not, to my knowledge thus far, share these specific remembrances with their survivors. We do know that students at Chemawa were aware of the romanticized legend associated with "By the Waters of Minnetonka," and one student's storytelling skills were even elicited by Chemawa administrators when they desired a retelling of the legend for the school paper.[17] Students seem to have been aware of the popular lore surrounding the Indianist compositions, and still many came to embrace the repertoire as something they could perform and enjoy. As historian John Troutman asserts, the singers of Indianist compositions didn't necessarily have problems reconciling the songs' fraught histories with their own performative identities as Native people. The students constantly expanded their repertoires of expressive culture "in ways that both reflected their experiences and transformed their circumstances."[18]

Early evidence of students' claiming Western vocal traditions as their own lies in the accounts of what they did after attending Chemawa. The students who represented Chemawa as vocal soloists often distinguished themselves as alumni as well, actively pursuing professional involvement in music. This phenomenon was not lost on the school administrators who authored Chemawa's promotional materials. School correspondence and newspaper articles show that many of the star soloists sought opportunities in music after they graduated from Chemawa, whether in radio, university choirs, or teaching music. One student whose successes were periodically chronicled in school publications was Raymond Haldane (Tsimshian, class of 1928). The February 20, 1929, issue of *The Chemawa American* noted that Haldane "is employed in Ketchikan, Alaska, and is getting along nicely in every way . . . Raymond was popular while here as a singer of unusual ability and also as an actor above the ordinary."[19] Following a visit by Haldane to Chemawa the following spring, the paper reported, "Our orchestra was the attraction at the weekly 'open house' event of the Salem Y.M.C.A. last Friday night. A 'capacity house' greeted our musicians on their arrival and the orchestra played unusually well and proved splendid entertainers in a fine program, many prominent people voicing most complimentary views on the work of the organization." Specific praise was reserved for Haldane, who "accompanied the party as a vocalist and he, too, proved a 'hit,' being recalled on both of his solos. He was in splendid voice and did credit to himself and our school. In every way the concert was of high order."[20]

Another student whose progress was charted was Reno Booth (Tsimshian, class of 1928). After graduating, he was invited to return to Chemawa for chapel exercises, where he appeared following Dr. Sisco's speech on the health of the Indian people of the Northwest. The post-chapel article recounts, "Lack of scientific knowledge with which to combat the ravages of disease was what rendered the Indian forefathers helpless . . . The blood is really the greatest factor in health, good or bad . . . [Also] Reno Booth (alumnus) gave a vocal solo, after which there was a recitation, choir, and orchestra."[21] Updates on Booth's work became more detailed and laudatory in tone as he secured more professional engagements: "Reno Booth, a member of our graduating class of last year, is now singing over the radio from Portland regularly. He sings over KOIN and KXL. His regular night is on Tuesday, between 11 and 12 o'clock. This is known as the 'Varsity Hour.' On Thursday nights he is on from 10:30 to 12 with the Portland Tomcats." School officials further sought to promote Booth's work by helping build up an active listening audience and by tracking down regalia for him to wear for performances: "He is anxious to have request numbers sent in for that makes business for him. It should be mentioned that he expects to do some stage work pretty soon and is anxious to secure a genuine Indian costume for the work. If any one of our readers have something in that line to loan or sell they will favor Reno by addressing him at Portland, Oregon, general delivery."[22]

Sports also remained a selling point for the few off-reservation boarding schools that remained open in the 1930s, and the Chemawa school paper cited alumnus Alpheus Norwest (Rogue River) for his work in both basketball and music teaching. "A recent subscriber to the *American* was Alpheus Norwest, class of '24, who is teaching music and coaching athletic teams at the St. Labres Mission, Ashland, Montana. He has 16 in his band, 12 members in his orchestra and 42 music students in his classes." Norwest's coaching met with similar successes, as "his basketball team is enjoying a good season having just trimmed a rival Montana school and contemplating the downfall of still more opponents."[23]

Faculty newspaper editors presented different coverage of female alumnae, who were less often singled out with detailed information but were often grouped in a single write-up. According to one, "It is possible for those really interested in music to advance themselves more than they realize. For instance: two former members of our club, Lena Louie [Coeur d'Alene, class of 1933] and Marceline Seltice [Coeur d'Alene, class of 1934], who are now attending the University of Idaho at Moscow, are reported to be members of the University singing organization." The newspaper's editor mined local successes, as well, for their potential to inspire current students: "And this isn't all, for returning to our home-ground we find Mary Iyall [Yakama, class of 1934] singing in an organization of Salem High. This should awaken some serious thought on the part of all our members and encourage them to make the best of present day opportunities to step outside and [build on the] works of our club."[24] The paternalistic, didactic tone of the article was typical of boarding school publications through the 1930s, and was especially pronounced when directed at female students. Not unlike their non-Native counterparts, female students' aspirations in music were assumed to be primarily in the realm of unpaid community-based activities, while male students were lauded mostly for their forays into the professional realm. For male and female vocalists alike, graduation from Chemawa often brought opportunities in music that may have included, but were no longer limited to, the "Indianist" compositions with which they had received their early training. And the number of them who returned to their home communities while still engaging in non-Native music forms reflects their choice to live in both worlds, in the process breaking down the Native/non-Native dichotomy even further.

In the years that followed the release of the Meriam Report in 1928, public outrage led the Office of Indian Affairs to drastically change the operation of its boarding schools, closing down many and mandating that those still operating adopt a healthier, more holistic approach that would not be geared solely toward vocational training. One result was that, by the late 1930s, a veritable uproar of nonstop musical activity took hold at Chemawa. Students engaged in singing through small vocal ensembles, Glee Club, Catholic and Protestant choirs, dormitory sing-alongs, talent shows, impromptu sing-alongs during power outages, singing for guests, off-campus performances, segments on local radio stations, special gigs for soloists, Christmas pageants and caroling, singing at dances, school songs and pep rallies, patriotic assemblies, the National Day of Prayer, National Music Week,[25] cantatas and operettas, senior students bequeathing favorite songs to underclassmen in their class wills, music clubs, witty songs for literary societies, class song leaders (an elected office), Sunday chapel, and singing along with the radio, with movies, and with visiting choirs. The dizzying amount and variety of vocal music making engaged all the students at Chemawa and permeated campus life.

The school's policy of "music for a select few" had, over a few short years, reverted back to "music for all," only this time not with the express intent of eradicating Native ways. An article from the school paper in 1933 reflects the initial changes—opening music classes to all students, and allowing students to form extracurricular music organizations: "Classes in public school music have started, the choir practices daily and helps with chapel exercises, the orchestra has been rehearsing and performs in chapel, the band has been working hard and has appeared on the bandstand on Sunday a couple of times." The overall campus exuberance was hard to stifle: "Various unofficial music groups have sprung up—and, to make a long story short, at most any hour of the day 'there's music in the air.' "[26]

By 1950, all high school students at Chemawa were required to be enrolled in some form of music class. A dispatch from "Melody Lane" describes the three choices available to students: "For their training in music, all Chemawa high school students belong to one of the three groups: choir, chorus, or class. The choir is working on music to be sung in a cappella style. The chorus sings a variety of songs." Students who did not wish to perform could elect to join the music class: "The class sings, but for the most part is a listening group. The choir and chorus will appear on programs during the remainder of the school year."[27]While having prior vocal training was useful for students' participation in these classes (especially choir), other qualities were deemed important by the music faculty. "Mrs. Johannaber adds that for membership in such organizations, a good voice is an asset, but that interest, dependability, and a spirit of cooperation are qualities of great importance."[28] The focus on the development of particular aspects of personal temperament and character was nothing new for a BIA school, but it was a focus that had fallen away in the years immediately following the Meriam Report, in favor of approaches that honored students' inherent dignity. Because public school choirs were one realm in which such traits were often stressed for non-Native students as well, however, choir remained one endeavor at Chemawa where character still could be emphasized.

The high school choir served different roles at different boarding schools, in part depending on whether participation was mandatory. At schools where choir was mandatory, it was often endured with resentment. Basil Johnston (Ojibwe, class of 1950) recalled his time in choir practices at the Rainy Mountain school in Spanish, Ontario, as "interminably long and much too frequent." The choir director, Sister Leutsch, was "a very severe woman" who taught "armed with a pointer that served as a baton," and she cracked the knuckles of boys "if they happened to play fortissimo instead of pianissimo during practice . . . She would not tolerate mistakes, and would make us sing passages again and again until she was satisfied that no note was abused."[29] At Chemawa, however—a BIA-administered school in the U.S., rather than a church-run school in Canada—choir was an elective, and alumni remember it positively. Millie Metcalf, from Hooper Bay, Alaska, recalls with a smile, "The teacher, he was always kind, and we loved singing those songs . . . I have lots of good memories of choir,"[30] even in the midst of deep homesickness during her time at Chemawa.

Choir at Chemawa had become a popular elective in the years following the Meriam Report, and would serve as the backbone of Chemawa's vocal music program for the next four decades. The choir performed frequently, both on and off campus, and it served as the feeder group for smaller, more agile vocal ensembles. The school yearbook of 1932 included a retrospective of Chemawa's choir from the 1931-1932 academic year: "A group of students with good voices and strong wills to practice diligently compose the Chemawa choir of 1932. Practices are conducted daily and the result is the fine leadership of the singing at Sunday night chapels." While all the choristers were expected to exhibit perseverance and diligence, some students stood out as exceptional and were chosen for smaller ensembles and the solo work in pageants and operettas: "From the choir are selected the sextet, male quartet and operetta leads. The Christmas pageant, a beautiful old custom here, is given a week before Christmas by the choir, and this year's group staged a very effective presentation. Vocal music is appreciated more and more at Chemawa as the years go by."[31]

Not long after the Meriam Report, Mrs. Gertrude A. Turney (wife of faculty member and composer Ruthyn Turney) assumed direction of the choir and its popularity and participation in campus events would remain steady under her leadership and beyond her retirement in 1941.[32] Notes from Sunday chapel services reveal that many of the choir selections were four-part arrangements. The 1937 yearbook describes the choir as a reliable, stalwart presence: "A fine, respectable group is the choir of the Salem Indian School which has been an active organization for many years. The choir has never failed to render special musical numbers for Sunday night chapel services and has faithfully and gladly rendered its services to any occasion for which choral voices were demanded." The writer alludes to the variety of vocal styles that students brought to the endeavor, explaining, "Membership in the choir is open to any student, either boy or girl, interested in music and voice. From this group of selected students one finds a surprising assortment of voices." The choir director was lauded for her high standards and for the music's edifying properties: "Mrs. Gertrude A. Turney sponsored this group and the members, she is to be complimented on their high ideals, on their seemingly untiring devotion to rehearsals, and last to their splendid achievement in offering an opportunity and opening a road to better music."[33] The accompanying photo shows thirty-five singers, with an equal distribution of male and female students. The article's characterization of the choir as having been "an active organization for many years" is true in the sense that a choir existed pre-Meriam Report, though with fewer voices and a reduced role in campus events.

How students felt about their time in choir can be gleaned through the remembrances of alumni and through published references to telling incidents that speak to the students' agency in choir activities. One such incident was written up by Martha Brown, a student reporter for the school paper in 1956; she described a special choir performance off-campus, and noted how the choir members surprised their director, Mrs. Johannaber, by wearing coordinating dress clothes, not school clothes, to the program.[34] Motivated either by a desire to look smart or to please Mrs. Johannaber, this small action reveals a measure of self-motivation on the part of the students, as well as a sense of ownership of their performing ensemble.

Students did not have total free agency in their choir participation. As with a typical public high school choir of the time, students didn't choose their repertoire or their performance contexts. However, the evidence suggests that many found choir a bright spot of their stay at Chemawa—a time for enjoying camaraderie, building skills, exhibiting leadership in school events, and representing Chemawa to the greater community. The vocal music training that had originally begun as a compulsory hegemonic device was now—with voluntary participation, an increased role in campus events, and a concomitant increase in student motivation—beginning to redeem itself, and some students took a particular interest in maximizing their opportunities to perform.

From among the ranks of the Chemawa choir were chosen a handful of singers who could work on more challenging repertoire in smaller ensembles. The two primary ensembles were organized by gender, and served separate functions accordingly. Kathryn Harrison (née Jones; Grand Ronde, class of 1941) remembers her time in the female ensemble fondly: "I was in the Girls' Septette.[35] My sister [Dorothy Jones[36]] was in it when it was the Girls' Quintette.[37] Each girl would step forward and tell what tribe they were from, and about the tribe. They did dances, too." The students were selected for participation by the choir director, and they performed for various campus events. "We sang for each class, and in the dorms. You were asked to be in the group. She [Mrs. Turney] picked us." Repertoire consisted partially of Indian-themed popular songs. Harrison recalls, "We sang oh, like 'Pale Moon,' 'Waters of the Minnetonka,' songs that were culturally related. Whatever she picked for us." The small ensembles were not backed by any instruments, and the vocal arrangements were not easy! "It was all a cappella—that was hard! She had an ear as sharp as a tack, and she knew who made a mistake."

Harrison recalls some students being singled out for their talents, and being groomed for future music endeavors and to represent Chemawa to the outside community. "One boy, he was really talented; the matron took him under her wing. He even sang in the opera *Carmen*. And that was Henry SiJohn [Coeur d'Alene]—he could sing, and he represented us all over." SiJohn would go on to become a music teacher himself, as well as a tribal leader and a World War II veteran. Even during Chemawa's egalitarian "music for all" era, exceptionally talented vocal soloists who could represent the school off-campus also were chosen to serve in leadership positions in the small vocal ensembles. Harrison remembers the boys' group contemporary to the Girls' Septette: "There was the Serenaders, the boys' group. They'd come out, and sing under the girls' windows at night. It was a surprise. They'd sing, and you'd say, 'Oh, there's the Serenaders!' They'd sing any kind of song that was popular in the day. It kept them out of trouble, you know. It was one of their pastimes." Membership was select. "That was a hand-picked group, led by Mabel R. Cornick [the boys' dormitory matron]. And there was a student leader, Henry SiJohn. She [Cornick] was sponsoring him for voice lessons." [38] The 1937 Chemawa yearbook shows SiJohn in a white suit, with the other members wearing black suits.

The 1937 yearbook characterized the Serenaders as an "independent musical organization" made up of a "group of talented McNary Hall boys" whose appeal soon grew beyond the Chemawa campus: "At first the organization confined its activity to local serenading. Gradually their unusual ability and close harmony caught the fancy of music lovers and their fame became wide-spread." It was not possible for Mrs. Cornick and the boys to fulfill all requests for performances, as the invitations came from all parts of Oregon and from community organizations in Washington as well. Some of the group's success was attributed to the boys' receptive attitudes and eagerness to collaborate: "Membership was restricted to twelve boys of good moral standing, and who were willing to react to suggestion." Regular periods of time for practice were observed and, as touted in the yearbook, "the reputation and popularity of this organization speaks for itself."[39]

The tradition of serenading was an effective means of enforcing Euro-American gender norms, and it was a long-standing practice at other Indian boarding schools as well. In her description of campus life, Devon Mihesuah alludes to the careful etiquette prescribed for night-time serenades at the Cherokee Female Seminary: "Male seminarians often serenaded the girls at night, and all the girls were allowed to listen at their windows, providing they did not converse with the singers." Surveillance was paramount. "On those nights that the boys serenaded the girls, Wilson [the dormitory matron] often walked quietly past the girls' rooms in her stocking feet and lay down on a hall table and listened to their conversations."[40]

In this earlier era (circa 1900), Victorian standards of womanhood were taught through musical behavior and response, and response was closely monitored, out of concern that it could become sexual. By the 1930s at Chemawa, the practice of serenading still entailed the acting out of romanticized gender roles, yet in a looser environment with fewer strictures on conversation. Small vocal ensembles now had a decidedly different and expanded role than the early ensembles of 1900 to 1920, with more opportunities for the students to sing for each other as part of the campus community, rather than solely representing Chemawa to the greater public. Gender norms notwithstanding, the small vocal ensembles offered students greater freedoms and community engagement than they had previously experienced in Chemawa's vocal music program.

Sanctioned singing organizations took place against the backdrop of spontaneous forms of singing as well. Groups of students often arrived at Chemawa with knowledge of, and competency in, various ceremonies from their respective tribes. This was particularly true for older students, whose years at home had made possible the retention of tribal ceremonies and songs, whether from elders, other family members, or a spiritual leader such as a medicine man. Students often guarded this knowledge when they came to school, and used it to help them manage difficult times, such as their initial arrival at boarding school.

Toward the end of my first conversation with Bob Tom (Siletz), who grew up on the Chemawa campus in the 1950s, I asked if he wished to add anything that hadn't been covered in his responses to my questions. He first reflected that "Chemawa produced a lot of Indian leaders for the Northwest, and a lot of good marriages." Then, his tone shifted as he told one last story about the start of school in the fall: "The other thing—it's really sad but it's engraved in my mind—is the Navajos. The school was grades one through twelve then, with no vacations during the school year." Students had free time in the evenings for homework or extracurricular activities. "Those kids would come up, around sunset, in the football field. This was in August, when the weather in Oregon is real nice. They'd go out there, make a circle, and sing. The older ones and the little ones. These were ceremonial songs, *not* powwow songs. It was the most beautiful music.

"Then the dorm attendants would come out, and they'd chase 'em off, run 'em off, make 'em quit. They chased 'em off with sticks. This would go on for a week or two, with the kids going out on the field every day at sunset, and getting chased off, until they just didn't come out anymore."[41] Tom's family lived in staff apartments adjacent to the football field, allowing him to hear the music clearly and witness the forced dispersal of the students. He recalls these incidents clearly even now, fifty years later.

This remembrance speaks to the tenacity of Chemawa's Navajo students in the 1950s as they forged ways to manage the transition to boarding school life. When asked why the dorm attendants had run the students off so insistently, Tom explained, "It was a control thing." He further elaborated that many good people who went to work for the BIA were changed by the culture of the institution, and that he didn't want to judge them. In nipping an unauthorized gathering time in the bud, the school staff apparently believed they were acting in the best interests of the students. Indian education in the 1950s—and the Navajo Special Education Program was just one example—was geared towards helping students assimilate into city life, rather than preparing them to return to the reservation. This philosophical shift fit with the realities of the termination era that ensued in the postwar years.[42]

The dormitory staff was intent on establishing control of the students early in the school year, and in boarding school culture this meant complete authority over the students' bodies, minds, and souls. Music proved to be an area in which these elements of personal identity converged, where students and dorm staff fought the battle of what it meant to be an Indian and an American. In the 1950s, students' spontaneous practice of tribal traditions—rather than under the auspices of the Indian Club or some other supervised activity—was still perceived by school officials as threatening. Allowing the students to perform tribal music at will could sow the seed for future discipline problems, and this was deemed contrary to the goals of civilization. In the Navajo students' repeated attempts to sing together, the dorm attendants' desire for control met with the students' capacity for resistance. The desire of the older students to pass on tribal traditions to the younger students, even when the traditions conflicted with the mission of the school, was paramount for the new arrivals at Chemawa as they sought to maintain connections to home. The music they sang on the football field was not intertribal, but ceremonial, music that left Bob Tom with lasting impressions of its power, beauty, and importance for cultural persistence. Summing up the significance of the Navajo students' singing, Tom noted, "Anytime there's a congregation of Indian people, there's songs. If Indian people hadn't protested-protected—hadn't kept the beat of their drum, they wouldn't have survived."

Forms of music making that persisted with the greatest continuity tended, not surprisingly, to be those that were officially sanctioned by the school. Chemawa's music clubs, designed as an extracurricular activity, first appeared in the 1931-1932 academic year. Split along gender lines, the clubs exhibited different emphases from their inception. The girls' club, Treble Clef, met on alternating Mondays under the faculty sponsorship of Mrs. Turney. It was organized "for the purpose of giving girls who are musically inclined an opportunity to give pleasure to music lovers, and a chance to practice their talents on an appreciative group."[43] The designated colors were pink and green, and the first officers were: Helen Welch, president; Lena Louie, vice president; Verna Starr, secretary and treasurer; and Laura B. Boye, reporter. In short, it was an inclusive group designed for girls who wanted to pursue music for the love of music itself, not out of professional aspirations. The Boys' Music Club, on the other hand, had a membership that was "composed of only those boys who know how to play a musical instrument." The officers were: Lonnie Weeks, president; LeRoy Pepion, vice president; Robert Thomas, secretary and treasurer. Mr. VosBurgh, bandmaster, was the sponsor and director. Even in its first year of existence, the boys' music club furnished music at all the school dances.[44] Compared with the girls' club, the boys' club took a more public role, performing both on and off campus, while the girls focused on music as performed in domestic settings, such as small social gatherings in the home. Social interactions were an important component of the girls' club, and sorority-type rituals[45] and sanctioned etiquette practices figured prominently. A blurb in an October issue of the school paper read, "Initiations are the order of the day. The Girls' music club staged one Monday night, putting it's [sic] neophytes through their paces in grand style. Refreshments were served."[46] The girls' meetings were structured like salons, typically consisting of short programs of pieces rendered by several members or, alternately, lecture-recitals by Chemawa's music faculty on topics such as "The Life of Schubert." The boys' meetings were more geared toward ensuring their readiness as a public performing group. One such meeting was recounted as follows: "The main question brought up was how we were to know the boys that joined had musical ability. It shall be determined at the next meeting for all the new members are to do their try-outs. A committee of four has been chosen by the president to pass judgment on the new members. A constitution has been drawn up and it shall be read at the next meeting."[47]

The boys' group also appears to have been more member directed than the girls' group, wherein Mrs. Turney figures prominently. The invisibility of the boys' club's sponsor may be due to a conscious effort to teach the boys the skills of establishing group guidelines through the creation of a written constitution, running meetings by something akin to Robert's Rules, and recruiting or excluding members. For girls at Chemawa in the 1930s, such business-oriented skills were not deemed quite as relevant.

The clubs' heydays were in the 1930s, and the boys' club in particular motored to surrounding towns and performed at Grange halls and other community events. During the 1940s, student interest in the music clubs remained, but the focus shifted to ensemble singing. By 1948, the clubs had reorganized into a single co-ed organization known simply as the Music Club. The emphasis was on learning vocal music, and most of the club's meeting time was dedicated to four-part singing. Faculty sponsors limited the enrollment to eight students per part, so as to achieve a balanced, focused sound.[48] By the 1950s, the Music Club seems to have disappeared, likely because of the popularity of other campus music groups and the myriad music activities that had sprung up at Chemawa.

Some modes of musical performance offered many students a level of excitement and occasional off-campus travel opportunities, namely, the special engagements of radio shows and traveling operetta performances. Various subsections of Chemawa's student body participated in such engagements. Students were not usually paid, but they received public recognition of their talents, as well as opportunities to visit places they might not otherwise experience, providing breaks from everyday campus routine for young musical adventurers.

From the 1920s through the 1950s, radio played a big role in daily life at Chemawa, as students gathered around dormitory radios in the evenings to listen and dance. Donations of radios were often solicited from the Salem community, and when they broke, students took collections from among themselves to pay for new tubes and repair services. Chemawa students received opportunities to perform on area radio stations, particularly in the 1940s and 1950s. The appearances included an interview with Chemawa Superintendent Kelly on KOCO (formerly an Oregon radio station; now the call letters are used in Oklahoma City) in February of 1949; a vocal group traveling to Portland for a spot on KPOJ in February 1952; the eighth-grade class visiting the KOAC studio in Corvallis in May 1954; and a mixed group of Chemawa students featured on Portland's KEX station in December 1955 for the Westinghouse Project, a public service effort that sought to help students recognize their talents. The topic for the Westinghouse discussion was "Problems of Teenagers," and compared with past radio appearances Chemawa students had engaged in, the appearance included less singing, showed less of a public-relations bent, and featured more honest reflections on the experience of being a teenager while living away from home at an Indian boarding school.

Other Indian schools, too, took part in radio shows near their campuses, thus suggesting that the students' activities were of interest to the non-Native community. Music students from the Sherman Institute in Riverside, California, appeared on the KNX radio station on December 9, 1932; even though the broadcast came from Hollywood, the AM signal traveled as far north as Chemawa.[49] In 1942, boys from South Dakota's Flandreau Indian School went to Omaha, Nebraska, to perform on a Mutual Broadcasting radio show for which they sang two songs in Meskwaki, a dance song and a deer-hunting song. Several of the students who had previously felt alienated and depressed at school later reported that they were adjusting better to Flandreau following the positive attention they had received from the radio appearance.[50] Again, this reveals the redemptive potential of an originally hegemonic tool (vocal music in boarding schools), and suggests that group singing was particularly helpful when the repertoire included songs from students' tribal communities.

Operettas were another special engagement for which boarding school students received public attention, and one instance in particular speaks to the high degree of exposure of these events. In July 1926, a group of forty Chemawa students (comprising the cast and the orchestra) traveled to Spokane, Washington, to perform their production of the operetta *Paul Revere*.[51] Accounts in the days leading up to the performance list the ranchers and local businessmen who purchased the first tickets and box seats, and note that revenues from the production would help defray the expenses of Spokane's upcoming annual Indian congress. Six thousand tickets went on sale, with Camp Fire Girls constructing a special "picturesque" ticket booth in the Union Pacific downtown ticket office. Part of the buildup to *Paul Revere* was the dramatic lighting of the street before the Thursday and Friday evening performances. The *Spokane Chronicle* excitedly previewed, "Red fire will glare up and down Post Street from Riverside to Trent on both Thursday and Friday evenings, the nights of the performances. A teepee, smoke curling out from the top, will be pitched at the entrance to the theater. Boy Scouts have charge of these two features."[52] As with the Camp Fire Girls, the Boy Scouts who were providing support for the show were likely not Indian youths themselves, though Chemawa had only five years previously become the first Native American community to organize Boy Scout troops.[53]

In addition to the involvement of local scout troops, Spokane business leaders helped to build awareness of the operetta, albeit in a way that played on common and damaging stereotypes of the day: "Scalps of those attending the Chamber of Commerce Luncheon tomorrow noon will be in danger when the Pocahontas tribe of the Redmen's lodge swoops around the corner of Riverside onto Washington just on the stroke of 12. The ticket drive will be given a big send-off at the luncheon."[54]

This Spokane production stands as a good example of large-scale off-campus musical performances, before the Meriam Report. Many students lived at Chemawa during the summers, and while the usual rules and structure of the academic year were relaxed somewhat, students still had to participate in planned activities and follow the dictates of the school. This occasionally entailed opportunities for adventure, when work in the farm fields or on the school's physical plant was interrupted by interactions with the local community or by trips to represent Chemawa elsewhere in the greater Northwest. The actual parameters of the musical productions that were mounted, though, were not decided by the students, but rather by a combination of school administrators, faculty advisers, and liaisons in the host communities where the students would be performing. Patriotic themes supported the mandate of the federally run schools to produce assimilated Indians, and the productions allowed students to experience travel and the limelight in ways they might never have anticipated.

Music making at Chemawa went beyond the special productions for which interested students auditioned or were otherwise selected. There was a distinct body of songs that all students experienced just by virtue of having attended Chemawa. The songs that everybody sings together are critical for the creation and maintenance of group identity, and to the body of common knowledge that, for a time, all students at Chemawa acquired.

Beginning in the 1920s, state songs were sometimes sung at school assemblies and often at the conclusion of Sunday chapel services. "Oregon, My Oregon"— written for a song contest in 1920, and officially adopted as the state song in 1927 by a joint resolution of the Oregon State Legislature—champions two main themes: honoring the early settlers and pioneers of Oregon, and praise for the natural beauty of the state.

> Land of the Empire Builders,
> Land of the Golden West;
> Conquered and held by free men,
> Fairest and the best.
> Onward and upward ever,
> Forward and on, and on;
> Hail to thee, Land of Heroes,
> My Oregon.
>
> Land of the rose and sunshine,
> Land of the summer's breeze.
> Laden with health and vigor,
> Fresh from the Western seas.
> Blest by the blood of martyrs,
> Land of the setting sun;
> Hail to thee, Land of Promise,
> My Oregon.[55]

For reasons not explained by the school administration, "Oregon, My Oregon" was gradually abandoned in favor of another Oregon-themed song, "Oregon, Dear Oregon" (also known as "Oregon Song"). The lyrics center on Oregon's natural grandeur, and make fewer references to the state's non-Native "conquerors," though the second stanza still refers to Oregon as "The land our fathers won."

> Oregon, oh Oregon, out where the tall trees grow,
> Oregon, oh Oregon, the state you ought to know,
> Oregon, oh Oregon, majestic ranges high.
> Fishing streams and mountain lakes, where snowcaps touch the sky.
>
> Oregon, oh Oregon, With valley broad and fair,
> Romance rides on ev'ry breeze, And roses scent the air.

> Oregon, oh Oregon, The land our fathers won;
> Oh come and live in Paradise; In dear old Oregon.
>
> Oregon, oh Oregon, Your highways are most grand,
> Beaches fair beyond compare, Beside the sunset strand,
> Oregon, oh Oregon, Your rivers deep and wide,
> Latent wealth of energy, Within their depths they hide.

The origins of "Oregon, Dear Oregon" are less well known than those of "Oregon, My Oregon." Still, it was adopted by Chemawa's administration, and for the 1930s through the 1950s, the student body sang it far more often than they sang Oregon's official state song.

Class yells were another type of music making in which all Chemawa high school students engaged. Performed with a declamation halfway between singing and speaking, the yells were segregated by class, with particular ones allotted to the freshmen, sophomores, juniors, and seniors. Just as in public high schools of the time, class yells were a way of establishing group allegiance, and a way to motivate students to perform certain collective activities for the good of their peers. Three yells typical of Chemawa are those used by the senior class of 1929:

> Who's got the pep?
> Who's got the rep?
> S-E-N-I-O-R-S!
> S-E-N-I-O-R-S!
> S-E-N-I-O-R-S!
> Seniors! Who? Seniors! Alee Gazel, Ala Gaza
> We're on today
> We're on today
> C-H-E-M-A-W-A
> C-H-E-M-A-W-A
> Rah, rah, rah!
> SENIORS!
> Winniemucka, Washkie,
> Massoit, Yahola,
> Chiliquin, Pontiac,
> Motezuma, Zula,
> Red Cloud, Crazy Snake,
> Boss-Ribs, Multnomah!

These are the Chiefs
Of the Indian race—
Yes, we'll add ol' Rain-in-the-face.
Listen to us holler,
Listen to us yell!
Yes we'll holler
Till we raise—CHEMAWA!

Of these three senior yells, the first two could have been sung at any public school, and the third was penned expressly for Chemawa, though the last four lines were likely interpolated from a popular public school yell. Coinciding with the release of the Meriam Report, these particular yells came at a time when boarding school culture still required that Indian identities be regarded with sentimentality at best, or ridiculed at worst.

School songs were another perennial means of establishing school pride. Though the earliest school songs were racially based (see Chilocco Indian School's song in the Introduction), racial references at Chemawa soon disappeared in favor of more subtly stereotyped representations of the beauty of nature, patriotism, and the quest for knowledge. One such song, named for Chemawa's symbolically freighted school colors, was "The Red and the White":

Sheltered by the state fir trees,
With its flowers so bright,
Stands our noble Alma Mater,
Colors red and white.
Just at the break of dawning,
When the bugle sounds,
As Old Glory waves to heaven,
Looks she proudly down.

[Chorus]
Raise the chorus, Shout it onward,
Chemawa Hi we'll hail.
Firmer may her sons tread onward
Onward, never fail.

Thru the many years of school life,
'Midst the scenes we know so well,
And the mystic charms of knowledge,

We vainly seek to spell.
Or we win athletic victories,
On the football field we fight.
Still we work for old Chemawa,
And the Red and the White.[56]

The lyrics enforce a sense of American identity, through the symbol of the flag, "Old Glory"; more subtly, knowledge is represented as perpetually out of grasp for Chemawa's Indian students: "And the mystic charms of knowledge / We vainly seek to spell."

More typical for Chemawa were school songs that, for the vast majority of Chemawa's history, have resembled those of countless other public high schools and colleges. Many students of the 1960s remember singing "On, Chemawa" (a typical high school anthem, sung to the same tune as "On, Wisconsin"), and students of the 1940s and '50s invariably recall "Chemawa, We'll Love Thee Forever":

Chemawa, we'll love thee forever,
Thy maples and walnuts so fair,—
The sunlight that falls on the fir trees,
Thy walks and thy flowers so rare;
And over the western mountains,
Our banner is floating above—
And dear to our hearts will be ever,
Chemawa, the school that we love,—

[Chorus]
Oh, here's to our dear red and white
For you all our lives we will fight,
Our homage we bring,—
The welkin shall ring.
All hail to our dear red and white.

Thy sons and daughters so loyal;
Proud to own the dear name that we bear,
For the truth and the knowledge thou teachest
We are ready to fight and to dare;
For our friendship so valued we thank thee,
Our grateful tribute we bring—

All hail to our Alma Mater,
Chemawa, to thee we sing——.[57]

Though its tune may have been composed for Chemawa, the lyrics bear striking resemblance to other school songs of the time, albeit with an abundance of agriculture and nature references appropriate for the Willamette Valley.

One form of group music making that bears special mention is that of farewell songs, songs the students sung together at the end of the school year. One that elicits strong feelings from alumni even now is "God Be With You Till We Meet Again," a Christian hymn based on the etymology of "good-bye" (i.e., "God be with you").[58] Grand Ronde elder Kathryn Harrison recalls, "We all went to church—Catholic or Protestant. The Catholic Mass, that was in Latin, and it was interesting. So sometimes we'd go to that instead. We had to borrow a hat and gloves." The students sometimes found the music deeply meaningful, especially when it connected directly with events and current circumstances in their lives. "When we sang 'God Be With You Till We Meet Again,'" Harrison explains, "it was at the Protestant service. It was right at the end of the school year, and we had our bags packed already. We really didn't know if we'd see each other again—some kids would die in the summer, and some kids wouldn't come back to school . . . I could never make it through that song."[59]

When being interviewed for her memoir, Kathryn Harrison also took care to mention how she felt when singing the hymn. "We would sing 'God Be With You Till We Meet Again.' We held hands. We knew it was going to be hard, but it was our tradition. We never got through it. It was always too hard. Then school ended." In this case, students were leaving for their respective homes, and in the 1940s, many were not to be connected by telephones or easy methods of communication. "Some of the students were leaving on the bus that brought them. You always knew when to be ready. They would post it—Flathead bus is leaving on such and such a day. Some would go by train. The rest were left behind, and there were quite a few. The train whistle became the loneliest sound of all when you knew they were taking your friends away."[60]

Harrison's remembrance of the farewell hymn speaks to the power of communal singing at difficult moments. It was a way for the students to recognize and to physically mark the trauma of a situation, all the while knowing that they were experiencing its harshness together. A Christian hymn could have deep personal meaning for students from various locations and tribal communities, whether they identified with Christian faith traditions,[61] or syncretic practicing of Christianity and indigenous religion, or were not Christian themselves, but found resonance in the sentiments expressed by the song and by their classmates.

Figure 9. Chemawa Choir performance, circa 1970. Photo courtesy of Jesse Matt.

Over the past thirty years, the use of non-Native vocal music at Chemawa has gradually fallen away. The large-scale societal forces of the Civil Rights movement, war opposition, and anti-establishment sentiment took hold of the national consciousness in the 1960s, and Chemawa operated within, not outside of, these phenomena. Organized choral ensembles continued in the 1970s (figures 9 and 10), but grew less popular after the new campus was built, at a time when students sometimes perceived energetic professions of school allegiance as hokey and insignificant in the face of the Vietnam War and the struggles waged by the American Indian Movement. Organized non-Native vocal music finally disappeared in 1991, with the departure of Chemawa's last music teacher, Hal Beyers. Chemawa did not replace Beyers after he left.

The lack of a choral program is a loss for students who are inclined toward the choral singing tradition. The school's identity as a whole, however, has grown to include students' pride in their tribal singing traditions, and resource allocation has shifted to reflect this emphasis. While school officials initially instituted vocal music at Chemawa as a deliberate hegemonic tool, students gradually claimed the music, made it their own through voluntary participation and graduates' subsequent singing endeavors, and eventually allowed the program to fall away once it no longer retained its usefulness. Just as Indian peoples have selectively adopted colonial religions, so too have Chemawa's students been selective in

Figure 10. Chemawa Choir, circa 1970. Photo courtesy of Jesse Matt.

their favoring of different vocal music forms at different historical moments; by the 1970s, Chemawa's revised mission of education "by Indians, for Indians" allowed students to explore and perform musical genres that bore relevance to them, and to let go of genres that did not. The current choral music void at Chemawa has made room for types of music making that were novelties there just two generations ago, types in which the students have found renewed meaning: singing in powwow drums, learning traditional songs from local elders, and making new songs to share at school events. The forms of expression may be markedly different, but the impetus to sing together continues.

Chapter 4
Private Lessons: For All, or the Talented Few?

"Please see that my boys take lessons of violin, and also keep on in training as farmers."
—David Dorian, letter to Flandreau School, 1913[1]

"Music, both instrumental and vocal, is given to a selected few who show special aptitude and talent for the work."
~ *The Chemawa American*, March 28, 1928[2]

During Chemawa's earliest days as Forest Grove Indian School (1880-1885), the primary focus of school superintendents Melville C. Wilkinson and Henry J. Minthorn was the establishment of the school itself, both physically and in terms of curriculum. Students constructed the buildings, began learning trades such as blacksmithing, and were used to elicit visits from tribal leaders in hopes of increasing enrollment. To prove its worth to BIA leaders back in Washington, D.C., Chemawa needed to become productive quickly, and there was little time for music at first.

Soon after Chemawa's 1885 move to its present location near Salem, however, the school's more robust numbers and more generous federal funding allowed the ideals of racial equality touted by social reformers to be expressed in the curricula and campus life. Chemawa (then known as Salem Indian Industrial School) soon developed a band, and boys and girls alike were granted musical training both through classroom instruction and private lessons. Regardless of whether students had come to Chemawa with prior knowledge of Western art music, social reformers' basic assumption that education could quicken the process of cultural evolution led schools to purchase instruments and hire music teachers in order to rapidly render the Indian "a refined, cultured, educated being" who would "assume the title of an American citizen, with all the rights, privileges, and aspirations of that favored individual."[3] To produce these cultured citizens, the imposition of an alien music system emerged as a comprehensive and deeply transformative tool, but one that required intense private study if students were to learn the complexities of European instruments. In an intentional hegemonic strategy, students were not expected to master their instruments solely outside of school but were given private lessons on campus. Thus, a modest student body size and reformers' early optimism propelled the personalized mechanizations of cultural imperialism in the boarding schools.

After twenty years of off-reservation residential schooling, when a generation of Indian people had been subjected to rigorous education in boarding schools but still had not vanished into Euro-American society, reformers' early optimism was gradually replaced with darker judgments. Articles in the popular press increasingly referred to the "shortcomings" and "crudeness" of the "Red Man," and asserted that the Indian was hampered by a "strong streak of childishness."[4] Even those who had so recently sympathized with such reformers as Helen Hunt Jackson and Alice Fletcher now expressed disenchantment with Indian progress. Journalist and social critic Ray Stannard Baker, who had only recently decried stereotypes and segregation in *Following the Color Line*, now reported for *Century* magazine that even after receiving education and land allotments, tribal members continued living "exactly as before, looking on imperturbably, eating, sleeping, idling, with no more thought of the future than a white man's child."[5]

Not surprisingly, the music lessons that had once been deemed so integral to the process of civilization began to be questioned for their efficacy, and their usefulness became suspect to Indian Affairs administrators. A decline in access to private music instruction was particularly evident with regard to female students. Early reformers had viewed women's education as particularly vital to the civilization process, popularizing such revolutionary aphorisms as "Educate a man, you educate an individual; educate a woman, you educate a race."[6] Instruction in advanced needlework and piano playing had been plentiful, in an attempt to make these realms as accessible as they were for the students' middle-class non-Native contemporaries. Instruction in the refined arts was abruptly curtailed, however, when Estelle Reel became Superintendent of BIA Schools in 1898. Reel toured the country inspecting off-reservation boarding schools, and relentlessly urged the implementation of the idea that schools should emphasize the practical over the intellectual. Following a visit to Chemawa in 1904, she reported to the Commissioner of Indian Affairs that too many girls were "practicing on the piano" when they should be mastering the "household arts." From that point on, Reel demanded that superintendents ensure that their "large Indian girls become proficient in cooking, sewing and laundry work before allowing them to spend hours in useless practice upon an expensive instrument which in all probability they will never own."[7] Just as piano production was reaching its peak in the United States in the first decade of the century, the instrument that had become a fixture in white middle class homes was being withheld from their Indian counterparts. Girls who wanted piano lessons would have to seek them outside the confines of the campus, and evidence from the Carlisle, Flandreau, and Bismarck schools suggests there were families who found ways to support their daughters in this endeavor.[8]

Thus Chemawa entered an era of musical training that, in some respects, exists there even in the present day: that of lessons for the talented few. Students who arrived at Chemawa already demonstrating knowledge of and talent on a particular instrument might be granted lessons during their time at the school, but instruction for beginners would not be offered. Resources were finite and admissions were often competitive. Even though Chemawa's hierarchical policies regarding private lessons sprang from the notion that musical skills were impractical for Indian students, a select group of student musicians found their talents affirmed as they were able to aid Chemawa's public relations by standing as exemplars of the school's civilizing influence. Those youths who could demonstrate their musical expertise were often granted priority in admission. One male alumnus (Turtle Mountain Chippewa), who attended Chemawa 1927-1933, recalls, "We had to make application in those days, way ahead of time. Everybody was trying to get in. Then if you had a background in music or [if you were] a good athlete, that's what they'd do in the old days."[9]

Those who attended Chemawa in subsequent decades report similar practices. One Umatilla elder—a female alumna who also chose to remain anonymous—affirms that when she attended Chemawa in the early 1940s, "Instruments were rare, because of budget restrictions, but they did have some. Students who showed promise were the ones who utilized them the most." Interestingly, she contrasted the prevalence of music instruction at Chemawa with that of the Catholic schools her peers attended, where "they were more strict about music and everyone took choir or band."[10]

One trend that emerged as a less-costly alternative to private lessons was that of learning musical instruments through clubs dedicated to the performance of particular instruments. During the era of Superintendent Harwood Hall (1910-1926), Chemawa had a Mandolin and Guitar Club in which an unidentified male staff member led high school-aged girls in playing a dozen mandolins, several guitars, and a double bass (figure 11).[11] Later, during the 1950s, Navajo students could partake in the weekly instructional meetings of the Harmonica Club. Today at Chemawa, several students meet during free hours in the evenings to develop their guitar skills, using a small collection of electric guitars that have been donated to the school by the Native rock band Red Thunder.[12] In all of these instances, the clubs were not initiated by the school administration but rather arose when the availability of instruments coincided with the specific expertise of a faculty or staff member.

Figure 11: Mandolin Club. Photo courtesy of Confederated Tribes of Grand Ronde.

To be sure, Chemawa's approach to individual instrument training has been largely haphazard, even through to the present day. The vast majority of students arrived at Chemawa with no previous instruction on Western instruments and thus could only avail themselves of training by way of classroom electives such as band or choir (both of which were ultimately discontinued in the 1990s). Chemawa's selective approach, however, has allowed for the development of a few stand-out musicians. These students have complicated the hegemonic process by taking whatever musical training they could get at Chemawa and using it to their own devices, whether for the good of their tribal communities or for themselves as individuals. Two of these men in particular are notable for their regional and national fame: one for his impact on Northwestern Indian tribal relations, and the other for his role in shaping an emerging American music genre.

Chemawa has produced many tribal leaders for the Northwest, and occasionally, a student outstanding in his or her craft has parlayed this success into a means of helping Native people attain social justice. Such was the case with Chief William Charles DePoe (Siletz and Cheyenne), grandson of Siletz Chief William DePoe ("Old Charley") for whom Depoe Bay, Oregon, was named in 1836. "Witty" DePoe was born William Hauser DePoe in Logsden, Oregon (a small town in Lincoln County), on Christmas Day of 1912. His parents had recently moved to Oregon from Kansas, bringing them closer to the husband's tribal community. Music making was part of the everyday life of their household. William DePoe's son, William H. DePoe, Jr., explains, "His mother was a music teacher, a piano player. She went to Carlisle College and met my grandfather there. Then they moved out to Siletz and taught school there. She was Cheyenne, descended from Chief White Antelope, and my grandfather was Tututni, from the Rogue River."[13]

The first of four brothers, William was nicknamed "Witty" for his keen sense of humor. All the boys played musical instruments, and together they formed a band. DePoe, Jr., explains, "It was pretty well-known. The youngest was a drummer, then there was clarinet and saxophone, and my dad played piano." In addition to his early training on the piano, DePoe grew up playing basketball, and he continued developing both his musical and his athletic passions when he arrived at Chemawa Indian School in the mid-1920s. A strong athlete, he played for the school football, basketball, and track teams. All the while he was an active performer in the school band, and in a smaller ensemble that played for the high school dances. It was DePoe's musicianship that ultimately drew the attention of young Marie LaFrance, the Chippewa student who would eventually become his wife. Their son William recalls the story of how his parents met in school: "Dad was in a band, and he played for the high school dances. Mom would see him playing there, and what attracted Mom to him was his music. Mom was a singer, herself."

William was joined at Chemawa by his brothers Chuck and Peter, and the DePoe brothers often teamed up to provide music for special events; their combo was a standing favorite among students and faculty alike. The Nonpareil and Excelsior literary societies chose the DePoe brothers to provide music for their joint annual meetings, and the superintendent periodically incorporated their band into school-wide assemblies.[14]

DePoe's training at Chemawa differed qualitatively from his schoolmates' training in farming or construction work; he had been singled out as worthy of pursuing a path not available to most of his peers. Consequently, he received more personal attention from faculty members than did other students, and this early affirmation of his talent may partially account for the strong sense of self-worth that DePoe brought to his public appearances after he left Chemawa. DePoe parlayed the piano performance skills honed at Chemawa into a successful career as a pianist and composer. He played with Lawrence Welk's traveling band from 1938 to 1941, earning a reputation that would lead to numerous collaborations with leading entertainers such as Will Rogers, Bob Hope, Tommy Dorsey, and Lionel Hampton.

At the onset of World War II, DePoe enlisted in the Navy, later explaining his preference in terms of his tribal community: "Our people, the Siletz, had always lived on the sea." He was assigned to the Wickes-class destroyer USS *Waters* (DD-115), stationed at San Diego Naval Station. Later, he was decorated for his service on LSM-59, a medium landing ship hit by a kamikaze while steaming off the coast of Okinawa on June 21, 1945. Only thirty-eight of the five hundred crew members were found alive; DePoe was one of these few, plucked from the water by rescuers on the minesweeper USS *Steady*, after floating for five days in the Pacific Ocean.

Immediately following the war, DePoe worked briefly for Boeing, having already relocated his young family to the Seattle area. But buoyed by postwar economic prosperity and the public's desire for recreation, DePoe quickly found venues that were hungry for good musicians. His son William recalls his father's livelihood with pride and enthusiasm: "Then, he made a living playing music. Dad played music all around Seattle—in cocktail lounges and places like that. Wherever there was a piano, he had it made." Successful enough to support a family, DePoe and his wife proceeded to raise five children—three boys and two girls—on a musician's income. He would continue as a full-time musician for the rest of his working life.

Though he was in demand as a soloist, much of DePoe's work took the form of collaborations. He played with several of the leading big bands of the 1940s and 1950s, including the Dorsey Brothers. Circumstances allowed him to perform for Queen Elizabeth, and he later appeared in four films, including Elvis Presley's twelfth movie, *It Happened at the World's Fair*, set in Seattle in 1963. Chief DePoe acknowledged his Native identity publicly (figure 12), and the musicians with whom he played always knew that he was an Indian. Audiences likely viewed DePoe as an Indian as well, not for any special dress or regalia but for his openness about his identity and his interest in arranging for Western instruments the Indian music he had heard while growing up in Oregon. To this end, he utilized his familiarity with a variety of instruments, many of which he had learned while working with the band at Chemawa—DePoe could play the piano, organ, saxophone, clarinet, accordion, banjo, and mandolin, not just passably but well.[15] His early Indian-based compositions foreshadowed the cultural bridge work he would later claim as his duty in life, leading him to visit with Native and non-Native groups to improve intercultural awareness and competency.

As we have seen, DePoe had distinguished himself in his days at Chemawa not only as a musician but also as an athlete, and he continued playing basketball in his adult life. He joined the Boston Braves, a semi-pro team active in the 1940s and '50s, and later coached several youth teams. He was esteemed in the adult basketball community, and even in middle age he regularly worked out with members of the Harlem Globetrotters.

During his career as a professional musician, DePoe returned several times to Chemawa, sharing his life experiences in an expression of gratitude for the

Figure 12. Original portrait of Chief DePoe by Carol Hamersley. Courtesy of artist.

formative role the school had played in his early musical development. DePoe played for Chemawa assemblies and classroom groups, entertaining the students with his stories and piano playing. He spoke both of his time in the entertainment industry and of the teachings he had received from his family, and how those had served him well in life.

Besides DePoe's public advocacy of musical studies, his transmission of musical knowledge also flowed through the more intimate routes of family relationships. His sons were exposed to a variety of instruments, and son William, Jr., played the clarinet and the tenor sax ("just for a hobby—not for a living"). It was Pete, the youngest of his sons, who would claim a career path in music. A drummer, he excelled in lessons as a teenager, and played in such Pacific Northwest bands as Mr. Clean & the Cleaners (A.K.A. Mr. Lee and the Exotics, based in Seattle, Washington, 1964-1966) and Witness (based in Kirkland, Washington, 1971-1972). He later went on to become the original drummer for the band Redbone. An American rock group that was most active in the 1970s, Redbone takes its name from a joking reference to a Cajun term for a mixed-race person, as the band members themselves were of mixed-blood ancestry. Pete is credited with pioneering the "King Kong" style of drumming, which features sharply accented polyrhythms involving the bass guitar and the snare drums. After making several albums and touring with Redbone, Pete left the group to live with his aging parents. Now he gives lessons to young people, and has a conscious desire to pass on his musical knowledge. Though his chosen genre of music is very different from that of his father, Pete DePoe shares his father's awareness of the importance of intergenerational transmission. According to his brother William, Jr., Pete also acknowledges the spiritual aspect of music making as something inseparable from the music itself—a belief that had informed his father's music as well.

As he grew older, the elder William DePoe's role in the public sphere shifted from that of musician to that of chief and spiritual leader. He considered his primary mission as a chief to be the preservation of his tribe's heritage, and to that end he held programs about Siletz lifeways in Depoe Bay and Lincoln City, presided over tribal ceremonies, and carefully passed on stories to his children and grandchildren. Many profound changes had recently taken place in the collective life of the Siletz Indians, a confederation of twenty-seven bands whose homelands originally ranged from northern California to southern Washington. In Chief DePoe's lifetime, he had seen termination (federal non-recognition) imposed on the Siletz in 1955, the restoration of recognition in 1977, the achievement of self-governance in 1992, and the gradual reclamation of 3,666 acres of land in Lincoln County, where the Confederated Tribes of Siletz now manage timber, fish, and water resources.

Even when he wasn't serving on the Siletz Tribal Council, Chief DePoe was often called upon to travel to Washington, D.C., on tribal business because of his collaborative work approach and his good rapport with federal officials. This collaborative spirit was also manifested locally in DePoe's efforts to improve interethnic communications, and in May 1991 he was honored by the Oregon Multicultural Education Association for his contributions to the public understanding of Native American peoples. Even while in his eighties, DePoe was willing to use all available technologies to further cultural preservation and interethnic understanding, and he lent his support to the Trophies of Honor program, a project to chronicle indigenous art by presenting works on the Internet in exhibition form, without interpretation. He helped inaugurate the program with this blessing:

> Klahyum, which is to say greetings. I am Chief Depoe. I am Siletz
> and Cheyenne. My heart is with those who have gone before me,
> and with those who have come after me. I pray to the Creator for all

those which share their native culture. May the Great Spirit bless them all. I wish you all a happy day, and good luck to all. I pray for everybody in the world. Amen.[16]

DePoe enjoyed a long marriage with Matilda (Mohawk, from New York; she was also known as Princess White Lily), who would don regalia with DePoe and visit Oregon grade schools, telling children stories about their people's lifeways. After Matilda's death, the chief's health declined rapidly, and in January of 1997, after a week-long battle with pneumonia, Chief DePoe died at age eighty-four. Over the previous five years or so, he had been passing on his family and tribal history to his son William DePoe, Jr., who resides in Seattle, Washington. The elder DePoe made his wishes clear, explaining to his son, "I don't want to just let my heritage fade away. If I stop, it will be the end of it."[17] Following his father's death, the younger William DePoe assumed the role of chief, which in the Siletz tribe is traditionally passed down through successive generations.

The life and work of the elder William DePoe presents a strong example of how a Chemawa graduate who was groomed for a career in music could capitalize on his early training. The instruction DePoe received at Chemawa led him to carve out a professional niche in music, integrate his Native identity with his work, and use his public performance skills to work for the improvement of intertribal and Native/non-Native relations throughout the Northwest. Whenever speaking publicly to adults or to children in the schools, Chief DePoe stressed the importance of treating each person as a unique individual; with this foundation, he cultivated understanding, acceptance, and effective communications between people of different backgrounds. This critical tenet in DePoe's life stands in stark contrast to the hegemonic enterprise of assimilationism still entrenched at Chemawa during his initial enrollment in the late 1920s, but the personalized musical training he received there likely circumvented the hegemonic strictures with its implicit acknowledgment of the dignity of the individual. For those who could qualify for private lessons, the extent to which cultural imperialism was exercised through the privileging of Western musical instruments and repertoire was countered by the sense of personal worth, competence, and gratitude to one's tribe that students exhibited in their post-secondary careers.

Not all successful student musicians would return home to assume leadership positions in their tribal communities. Another path was charted by Clyde Donnell Cooley, arguably the most famous Chemawa alumnus. Clyde is better known today as "Spade" Cooley, a name earned after an evening of poker when he won three straight flush hands, all in spades. In many respects, Cooley's musical journey exemplifies the trajectory of the professionally successful Chemawa musician: arriving at Chemawa with a family background of musicianship and an interest in music; gaining necessary skills through private lessons and performance opportunities while at Chemawa; and eventually, traveling away from Salem to seek different and more varied prospects for performing and recording. Cooley was unique, however, for his impact on an emerging genre of music, his level of fame and national recognition, and his eventual tragic and public downfall.

Born in a storm cellar near Pack Saddle Creek, Oklahoma, in 1910, Cooley was the son of migrant white/Native American workers whose poverty prompted the family to move westward when Clyde was only four. Eventually settling in eastern Oregon, the Cooleys worked as ranch hands, playing music for barn dances when their work was done. Clyde was the son and grandson of country fiddlers, and his father wanted him to continue the family tradition of playing stringed instruments.[18]

Clyde attended local Indian schools, and eventually enrolled in Chemawa in his late teens. Articles from the *Chemawa American* reveal that Cooley's talent was quickly recognized by the school, and that he was offered lessons in classical cello. By the fall of 1928, he was giving chamber concerts with Chemawa's music faculty (see figure 13). The performances were salon-style events in an intimate setting: "Our local trio, composed of Mr. Turney, violin, Clyde Cooley, cello, and Mrs. Turney, piano, played a short chamber music program in the music studio on Monday evening. The concert was in line with the wishes of Supt. Lipps and

Figure 13. Chemawa String Quartet, featured in 1929 Chemawa yearbook. Hermann A. Kunkel, 1st violin; Clyde Cooley, cello; Ruthyn Turney, viola; and John Dexter, 2nd violin. Courtesy of Grand Ronde Archives.

Asst. Supt. Carroll who desired that it be made a sort of cultural and educational affair." Repertoire was strictly classical, and a typical program would open with a full-length piece such as a Haydn trio, continue with a couple of short numbers, and then close with a trio by Mr. Turney. The recitals were designed as edifying special-status events for upper classmen to attend as a mark of their maturity: "The senior class members were the guests of the evening, with the addition of a number of our faculty friends also present."[19] The concert series continued through the school year, garnering glowing reviews and frequent appraisals that "the numbers were all artistically rendered." Cooley also played for the Chapel Exercises, motivational speeches that were given each Sunday afternoon in the campus chapel; typically, Superintendent Lipps would give a "frank and able talk," followed by music supplied by various campus ensembles or soloists. Gaining approval from these campus performances, Cooley soon began performing off-campus, entertaining local ladies' groups at the First Methodist Episcopal Church in Salem and the Congregational Church in Silverton. The faculty touted him as a stellar representative of the school's transformative effect, and the *Chemawa American* proclaimed after each recital that "All in all, the program was a credit to our school."[20]

The school Honor Roll that fall listed Clyde Cooley in its highest tier, that of students "whose grades average at least 90 percent, with no grade below 80 percent." Cooley's teachers looked favorably upon his academic and musical progress, and sought to provide him with special cultural experiences that might broaden his aspirations. These included frequent trips to the city to be exposed to traveling ensembles: "Miss Gunn motored to Portland last Thursday evening and had as her companion on this occasion Clyde Cooley our young cellist. Clyde was taken down to hear the Philharmonic Orchestra of Los Angeles. It was in every way a treat for Clyde and a nice courtesy on the part of Miss Gunn." Each trip was held up publicly as an example of Chemawa's cultivation of student talent and as incentive for other students. "Mr. Kunkel, our bandmaster, accompanied by Clyde Cooley and Alex Gouley, made the trip to Portland last Saturday to attend one of the concerts given by the world-famous Belgian Band which is now touring this country. All were delighted and profited in hearing this great musical organization."[21]

The following school year began in much the same way, with Cooley joining the adult musicians for chamber music events: "The string quartet rehearsals are again on with vim and vigor. The personnel is the same as last year. Hermann A. Kunkel, 1st violin; John Dexter, 2nd violin; Ruthyn Turney, viola, and Clyde Cooley, cello." Diligent practice was a must, as the series of chamber music concerts would begin early in October.[22] Some accounts identify Cooley's cello instructor as Dr. R. W. Hans Seitz, and the two would venture off-campus for performances early in the school year: "Clyde Cooley, our able young cellist, is to appear in Salem this morning in a number of cello solos. Dr. R. W. Hans Seitz will be his support at the piano.[23]

Early in February 1930, however, all references to Clyde Cooley halt abruptly with the following notice: "Last Sunday evening a telegram arrived here for Clyde Cooley, our cellist, bearing the sad information that his brother, Clarence, had been killed in a railroad accident near the parental home at Alpaugh, Calif. On Monday, Clyde and his sister, Mrs. Gladys Towns of Silverton, Oregon, departed by train for home to attend the last sad rites for their brother."[24]

While Clyde had been attending Chemawa, his family had moved south, to the area of Modesto, California. Following his brother's death, Clyde returned to Chemawa only briefly. Internal school records reveal an episode never mentioned in any Chemawa publication: on a Monday afternoon, April 7, 1930, Clyde Cooley and fellow student Anna Jackson ran away from Chemawa. Principal Sharon R. Mote explained in a letter to Superintendent Lipps, "It has come out that Clyde has not been checked up on Saturdays and he has been meeting Anna downtown on Saturday afternoons most of the year, and it finally culminated in . . . that they felt it necessary to run away and get married." Principal Mote cited the failure of "some employee" for not verifying Cooley's whereabouts on girls' town day, and posits that they received help from a staff member in their getaway, as it involved leaving campus with suitcases in broad daylight and purchasing bus tickets to Portland at the local general store.

The police departments in Salem, Portland, and Seattle were all informed of the escaped students. Searches were mounted and family members were interviewed, yet the pair was never apprehended. The *Oregon Statesman* revealed that a marriage license had, "for the first time in the memory of anyone now connected with the county clerk's office," been issued to a minor with no legal guardian. Evidently, when Clyde, age nineteen, and Anna, age seventeen, had applied for the license, local resident Mrs. P. F. Thomas (possibly a relative of Clyde Cooley) filed an affidavit stating that Clyde had lived with her since he was nine years old and that Anna had been a resident of Marion County for over ten years. The clerk's office ruled that this complied with the terms of the statute, and the marriage license was issued.

Despite being on the lam, Clyde and Anna still made appearances at Chemawa. On April 22, the principal informed school employees that Clyde and Anna had visited the campus, spent time in the dormitories, and visited freely with the students on more than one occasion since their recent departure. "The two ex-students," wrote Principal Mote, "are and should be considered in disgrace. By reason of their guilty actions they have made it necessary to consider them as suspended or expelled students, and their presence on campus is highly undesirable."[25]

School records make no further mention of Cooley, and it is likely that he and Anna lived briefly with other members of his family in the Northwest before moving to southern California, seeking work at the onset of the Great Depression. Clyde joined his family in ranch work, and increasingly drew extra income by playing the fiddle for dances. A folio of his music, published in 1945, tells of an incident that may have cemented his future career as a musician: "Later, his family moved to a ranch near Modesto, California, where Spade was an all-around top-hand. One day he made the mistake of trying to argue with the rear-end of a mule, and came out second best." This episode, whether real or imagined, is used to explain Spade's electing to be a musician rather than a cowhand: "The unfortunate incident, while leaving Spade with facial features not quite as handsome as before, was a lucky break for the rest of us; for it made him decide upon a safe career—in music, his first love. So it was ranching's loss and the public's gain."[26]

Subsequent photos of Cooley show no conspicuous scars or asymmetries. Whether his motivation was truly the desire for a safe career, or his love of music and the opportunities it afforded him for fame and wealth, Cooley made a conscious decision to pursue music wholeheartedly. In 1934, he managed an introduction to Roy Rogers, and convinced Rogers to help him get work in the movies. Short in stature, Cooley bore a striking resemblance to Rogers (see figure 14), and he served as Rogers' stand-in with parts in several films for Republic Studios.[27] He toured with Rogers as a fiddler, often contributing back-up vocals in such country groups as the Riders of the Purple Sage, the Rhythm Rangers, and the Sons of the Pioneers.

In 1937, he and Anna were still married and with a young son to support. Fortunately, the increasing demand for his playing, arranging, and band-leading skills brought him a steady flow of work in the Los Angeles area. In 1942 Foreman Phillips hired him away from the Jimmy Wakely Trio to head a band at Venice Pier, where he was joined later that year by singer and bass player "Tex" Williams.[28] Thousands of war workers migrated from Texas and Oklahoma to work in southern California's factories and munitions plants, and these workers provided a ready audience for western swing music. Prosperity after World War II only brought more success for Cooley, as country music achieved national recognition and Americans now sought the amusements and material abundance they had foregone during the war. Cross-over acts such as Bing Crosby's "Sioux City Sioux" abounded, and Spade Cooley's "Shame On You" became his signature tune and was played on jukeboxes across the nation.[29]

As Cooley's popularity soared, he returned to Salem, Oregon, for a concert, bringing along his entire band. In a January 1947 article titled "Thrills," the *Chemawa American* describes a memorable evening of cowboy music at the

Salem Armory, with the band headed by Spade Cooley, famous former Chemawa student.[30] Cooley may have agreed to this performance as a special favor to his friends and associates at Chemawa—by this point in his career, he had achieved national recognition and was playing larger venues; traveling a thousand miles with a full band to play in a small-town armory would have been inexplicable if not for Cooley's ties to Chemawa. Perhaps he wanted to show the young students the success that a Chemawa alumnus could achieve. Presumably, enough time had passed since his premature departure from high school that school officials were no longer concerned that he would serve as a bad example.

His band had risen to headliner status at the prestigious Santa Monica Ballroom, and later in 1947 Spade Cooley got his own television show on KTLA. "The Hoffman Hayride," it was named for its primary sponsor, a TV manufacturer. During the late 1940s and early 1950s, the show was wildly popular, often attracting 75 percent of the viewing audience. A variety show similar to "The Ed Sullivan Show," "The Hoffman Hayride" soon came to be called "The Spade Cooley Show," and featured highly popular guests like Frank Sinatra, Bob Wills, Jerry Lewis, and Sarah Vaughan. Hank Penny, hired by the show as a comedian, recalled, "During that era, I could walk around Hollywood and man, I was a *star!*"[31]

What set Spade Cooley's band apart from others lay partially in his instrumentation; the full brass and reed sections were augmented with fiddles, steel guitar, and occasionally a harp. His incorporation of various genres—rhumbas, boogie woogie, and the blues—produced catchy dance music, and his jazz-style arrangement techniques left space for hotshot solos, showcasing his musicians' virtuosity. While the employment of such tactics by big bands may seem commonplace in retrospect, Spade Cooley was the first to add non-country musical forms to a basic western swing sound, earning him the title "The King of Western Swing."

His keen sense of showmanship no doubt also contributed to his success. His glittery clothing featured sequins, appliquéd fiddles, and spade designs in profusion; comedic musician Hank Penny declared, "There was *nobody* dressed as sharp as him—not even Roy Rogers or Gene Autry. Cooley outdressed 'em all." Steel guitar player Speedy West describes Cooley's high-energy stage presence as riveting yet graceful: "He was outstanding, I believe as good a showman as I ever saw hit a stage as a bandleader. He was not comical or anything. He had spirit, he had poise." Cooley's physical energy was particularly memorable: "He had lots of enthusiasm, a big smile on his face and he jumped from one side of that stage to the other, constantly wavin' that fiddle bow and then pointin' it at the audience and wavin' it at the band as a baton." Having dipped into amateur boxing as a youth might have also helped his sense of movement before the public, for Merle Travis recalls that on stage, "He had the footwork of Muhammad Ali."[32]

Figure 14. Spade Cooley, ca. 1945. Photo from *Spade Cooley's Western Swing Song Folio.* Courtesy of Multnomah County Library.

Interestingly, despite Spade Cooley's being raised within Indian communities and the 25 percent Cherokee blood that gained him admittance into Chemawa, most of his fans thought of him as white, and his stage, film, and television appearances did not address his Indian identity. There was no space for non-whites in the visually oriented, Hollywood-based genre of western swing music. Students who attended Chemawa during the 1950s, at the height of Cooley's popularity, make casual assertions like, "Well, sure, everyone knew he was an Indian."[33] But while this may have been true for the Chemawa community, which had incubated Cooley as a budding musician, it is doubtful that the public at large was aware of Cooley's Indian identity.

During the height of his professional success, Cooley's marriage was disintegrating. His wife obtained both a divorce and custody of their son, John. While his divorce was taking place, Cooley hired a new back-up vocalist for his band: Ella Mae Evans, who would soon become his second wife. A series of disappointments followed, some of which Cooley bounced back from and some of which proved devastating: Tex Williams, demanding more compensation than Spade could afford, left to form the band Western Caravan, and took more than half of Spade's band along with him. A series of minor heart attacks compromised Cooley's health, a plight likely compounded by stress and his ever-increasing alcoholism. By 1956, his television ratings began to slip when, in the search for something different, he dropped his house band in favor of an all-girl band; to make matters worse, this coincided with the growing success of Lawrence Welk on KTLA. While he was still popular with the public, Cooley's gimmicks were costing him the respect of his colleagues in the entertainment industry, and at age forty-eight he entered into semi-retirement, building a huge ranch house at Willow Springs, California, for Ella Mae and their two children. Living on the edge of the Mojave Desert, Cooley turned his flashy sensibility towards a business venture: Water Wonderland, a massive undertaking that included three artificial lakes, a grand ballroom, and an amusement park.

In both financial matters and his personal relationships, Spade Cooley was known for his boundless generosity and compassion but also for his anger. This anger tragically manifested on the afternoon of April 3, 1961, when Cooley returned home from a business meeting with his Water Wonderland business partners, a meeting where he had been drinking heavily and arguing with one of his associates. He proceeded to fight with his wife; the sequence of their dispute and its escalation remains unknown, but Spade suspected Ella Mae of having an affair with Roy Rogers. Some time after 6 o'clock that evening, their fourteen-year-old daughter, Melody, arrived home to find her mother unconscious. Cooley then proceeded to stomp Ella Mae to death. Melody would later give the most damning testimony at Spade Cooley's highly publicized murder trial, resulting in a guilty verdict. In fragile health emotionally and physically, Spade Cooley was assigned to the California Medical Facility at Vacaville.[34]

In prison, Cooley made a conscious attempt to reorient his life. He spent his time making violins, teaching music, and leading an all-inmate band. He was popular with both the inmates and the staff, and at his parole hearing in August 1969 the California Adult Authority unanimously recommended that he be paroled, setting February 22, 1970, as his release date. Granted a one-day pass to perform at a sheriffs' benefit in November, Cooley was interviewed in his dressing room beforehand, and he expressed optimism for the future and his desire to return to show business after his release, saying, "I think it's gonna work out for me; I have a feeling that today is the first day of the rest of my life." After completing a successful performance before a crowd of three thousand, however, Spade Cooley returned to his dressing room, suffered another heart attack, and died.[35] Thus ended the life of Chemawa's best-known alumnus.

The past decade has seen a resurgence of interest in early western swing music, and a concomitant acknowledgment of the work of Spade Cooley. *Fortune* magazine recently included a Spade Cooley compilation in its "Transoceanic In-Flight Playlist," a short list of recommendations that included only "Five CDs worth listening to."[36] Dozens of Cooley tracks have been digitally re-mastered and re-released by record companies; a shopper on Amazon.com can choose from fourteen separate recordings of Cooley's music and spoken radio segments, in addition to dozens of compilation CDs that include tracks of Cooley's work. Cooley has a star on the Hollywood Walk of Fame at the corner of Hollywood Boulevard and North Highland Avenue, and he serves as a subject for contemporary authors James Ellroy and John Gilmore, as well as guitarist and songwriter Ry Cooder (who has a dog named Spayed Kooley). Actor Dennis Quaid has purchased the rights to the stories of Cooley's three children and has written a film that he plans to direct and star in as Spade. Whether most western swing listeners know that Spade Cooley was a product of the Indian boarding school system is unlikely, but for Chemawa staff and alumni, Cooley's career stands as both a source of pride and unease, his murder of his wife being akin to the family traumas that now lead many of today's Indian students to enroll at Chemawa.

A variety of factors likely contributed to Cooley's tragic ending, and one may have been the internal dissonance that resulted from keeping his Indian identity hidden from the public. To land the movie roles and performance gigs he wanted, Cooley followed Hollywood standards and assumed a cowboy identity, rendering himself eligible for roles of greater power and complexity. Cooley had departed Chemawa in February of 1929, only slightly before Will DePoe's graduation in May of 1933; these particular few years demonstrate a marked change in the school's increased valuing of students' tribal backgrounds that was instituted after the Meriam Report, under Indian Affairs Commissioner John Collier. While the racism endemic to Hollywood necessitated Cooley's calculated cloaking of his Indian identity, the groundwork for this deliberate denial was laid during his school days at Chemawa, at a time when the mandate of the school depended upon the eradication of Native culture.

Thankfully, Cooley's ultimate outcome was not typical of Chemawa's other student musicians. The norm over most of Chemawa's history has been to offer lessons only to an exceptionally talented few. However, a handful of motivated students have found alternative means of acquiring instruction on their instruments. During the 1960s and '70s, students in garage bands—such as the publicly successful Meteors (see Chapter 7)—sought training and technical advice from their peers. Alaska students in particular arrived at Chemawa and joined a network of older siblings, friends, and relatives. Garage band alumni recall learning from watching the older students play. Once a band was established on campus and persisted from year to year, the graduations or other departures of the older members created openings for the younger musicians to fill. From watching older students play, to patiently developing skills, to playing alongside the older musicians, students gradually carved out a trajectory of unofficial apprenticeship.

Chemawa staff members have often functioned as mentors and tutors for individual students, transmitting particular skills that coincide with the students' needs and interests. Such relationships have been particularly fruitful and vital in the area of music, where students often have no other access to instruction. Retired music instructor Hal Beyers, who taught at Chemawa throughout the 1990s, recalls circumventing the school's curriculum in order to offer private lessons to interested students: "There wasn't funding then for lessons—just band, choir, and music appreciation. Those were electives. But we'd find ways, if a student wanted to learn piano, or guitar, or some other instrument . . . we'd sign them up for music appreciation, and then I'd teach them." Beyers clearly enjoyed working with the students on a more personal level than his regular classroom work allowed, and he recalls the students responding favorably as well. "The students, they expressed a lot of gratitude. They really responded to compliments and encouragement. And they respected me. They respected their elders—that's part of their culture."[37]

Clearly, students who seek out lessons on their own already possess resiliency, going outside the established curriculum and extracurricular options to see that their own individual needs are met. But do the lessons themselves aid in further developing resilience? Hal Beyers asserts that they do, especially for students operating on the margins of campus life: "A lot of the kids, that's the only reason they stayed—for the music, or for sports." This supports one of the central findings of recent resiliency studies: that the single most predictive factor of resiliency is the presence of one attentive adult—parent or otherwise—who genuinely cares about the young person's wellbeing.[38] For students at Chemawa, an emphasis on mentoring, which is often facilitated by extracurricular activities such as sports or music, can engender these critical relationships.

Today, there is little demand for private lessons. Academic Counselor Karen Graham explains that music lessons simply haven't been a part of most students' upbringing: "Kids from reservations and small cities don't show up with instruments. Even if they've played instruments, they don't own them, and they don't have the money to buy them."[39] The overwhelming majority of students arrive at Chemawa never having been exposed to Western classical instruments in any ongoing, consistent way, and thus have never had the chance to develop a desire to play one. But a few self-motivated students with an interest in rock and popular music (most notably the guitar) continue to use a small collection of instruments that have been donated to the school, and to meet as a sixth-period elective and during evening free hours to study guitar together and help each other along. The private lessons that started out under the hegemonic auspices of assimilationism have evolved into the less rigorous but often more self-affirming practice of students wresting whatever musical training they can from Chemawa and then using it for their own purposes. Chemawa's tradition of lessons for the talented few continues, still with limited resources, but with an important caveat—rather than the teachers deciding just who has talent, the students are deciding among themselves which talents they wish to develop.

Chapter 5
Staging the Past, Preparing for the Future: Theater and Pageantry

"We talked about differences in tribal regalia, dance, and language, and learned about each other's tribal cultures. We listened to a set of phonograph records of Indian music collected from all over the United States and Canada, and we got lonesome for home. We felt comfortable together because of our shared history and heritage, and we talked about pets and siblings and life . . . I tried to make Wahpeton a home away from home for these students."

—Esther Horne (Shoshone), recalling her experiences directing pageants in the 1930s[1]

In the late nineteenth century, when the "Indian Wars" had only recently ended and public schools had not been established near many Indian populations, students who enrolled in the boarding schools arrived with vastly different religious backgrounds, different linguistic competencies in English and in their tribal languages, and radically different attitudes towards other Indian groups and individuals. Some students had already been converted to Christianity, while most came from cultures where it would have been incomprehensible to isolate religion as a separate sphere of human existence. Some were fluent in English, and some had never encountered it before; most knew only a few words and phrases. Some students came from communities that had long-standing rivalries with neighboring Indian groups, and others came from half-white families that dissuaded their children from associating with full-blood Indians. School administrators sought an efficient method of transforming these disparate identities through an experience that would be accessible to all students regardless of background. Pageants soon were incorporated throughout the residential school system as a means by which students' individual identities might be subsumed under the all-encompassing idea of being "Americans."

Weekly church services—mandatory for the first decades of the boarding schools' existence—were one form of theater by which students were bidden to act out their new identities as civilized Christians. If they were fortunate, students could choose between attending a Protestant or Catholic service. Observing the Eucharist, a weekly re-enactment of Jesus' last supper, students became participants in the Christian drama through a series of prescribed gestures and physical stances. Sitting quietly in the pews, observing hushed silences, kneeling to pray, listening receptively to sermons, singing a repertoire of hymns and liturgical music, taking communion bread and wine, genuflecting, and crossing one's self were all elements of the complex choreography of the Christian identity, publicly affirmed. These weekly services were augmented at key moments in the liturgical year by various pageants.

The term "pageant" in this context typically refers to scripted dramatic events held to commemorate a holiday or special season in the non-Native calendar. This very connection to the calendar—to the white man's way of marking time—was a way of replacing Indian people's ceremonial occasions and instilling the values of civilization that accompany sanctioned American holidays. Some boarding school pageants were religious-themed; others commemorated secular occasions. The first holiday celebrated during the school year was Columbus Day (at the direction of the Indian Office beginning in 1892), followed by Thanksgiving, Christmas, Indian Citizenship Day, Washington's Birthday, Arbor Day, Decoration Day (later known as Memorial Day), and (at a time when most students resided at the schools year-round) Independence Day.

Particularly noteworthy for its deliberate fulfillment of federal assimilationist goals is Indian Citizenship Day, also known as Franchise Day. Created expressly for Indian schools, it was a day set aside for commemorating the passage of the Dawes Act on February 8, 1887. The two main prongs of the Dawes Act were the codification of private land ownership (tribally owned lands would be gradually transferred to individual tribal members, full ownership occurring after a person had successfully cultivated their land for twenty-five years) and citizenship (Indians who accepted their individual land allotments would ostensibly be granted citizenship). Both of these themes were reflected in the pageants the students were given to perform on Indian Citizenship Day. Storylines traced the awakening of a savage land from its slumber with the arrival of Columbus. Indians were shown a better way of life through the feats of George Washington and other Revolutionary War heroes, and they were entreated to join the white man's march of progress. Bible verses were recited, the virtues of work were extolled, and farming was presented as a noble and unquestionably desirable vocation.

In addition to the pageants themselves, which were completely scripted, the performances were framed by the speeches of visiting dignitaries and by students' prepared oratorical contributions. These lent a personal touch to the Citizenship Day observances, and sought to impress upon students in the audience the idea that their learned peers and presumptive role models were embracing the gifts of citizenship offered by the Dawes Act. A student at the Hampton Institute, for example, led his classmates in a cheer by proclaiming, "Now we are citizens / We give him applause / So three cheers, my friends / For Senator Dawes!"[2]

While the author of this cheer seems to have been well indoctrinated with the ideas of private land ownership and civilization, ascertaining how most students responded to these early pageants is difficult. The reactions that were recorded in written form are those that were unwaveringly positive and would serve as good public relations material for the schools. One boy at Hampton in 1898 recounted the Indian Citizenship Day celebration in a letter to his family, enthusiastically describing the pageant and the day's events, and closing by explaining, "Well, I am going to tell you what is reason we do all that. Well, reason for celebrating Tuesday was the Indians are going to be citizens now and be free now, and take their lands and make a good farm for themselves and try to do what the white people do, and you are citizen now and I tell you all this because I thought you would like to know it if you didn't all hear it yet."[3]

Preserved by school officials to prove the progress they were making in transforming Indian hearts and minds, this account is unabashedly glowing. But if later responses to assimilationist propaganda in the boarding schools are any measure, students' responses likely ran the gamut: cynical, starry-eyed, skeptical, grateful, distrustful, excited, resigned, questioning, and even apathetic, sometimes all felt in turns by a single student. The pageants did succeed in their most general goal of imbuing the Dawes Act with deep symbolic meaning. Just how the early boarding school students regarded this meaning, however, can only be glimpsed in fragments.

Pageants that glorified the greatness of America and the values that were its undergirding—and, in the process, depicted Indians as savages desperately in need of the transformative mercies of civilization—continued unabated through the first fifty years of the residential school system's existence. Subtle changes may have occurred as reformers lost their early optimism that Indians could fully achieve the same successes in life as their white counterparts, but no fundamental shifts in pageantry occurred until 1928, following the release of the Meriam Report. With the revealing of schools' denigration of Indian culture and traditions, public outcry (bolstered by a growing interest in Native arts and crafts) sparked a new generation of officials in Washington, D.C., to direct boarding school personnel to value Indian cultures and incorporate them into the schools' curricula and campus life. Revising the pageants was one means by which this new valuation could be publicly achieved.

Many schools established Indian Clubs and Indian Dramatics Clubs, groups whose purpose was to encourage students' research on their tribal backgrounds, mythologies, and cultural expressions. The clubs would then plan performances, both on and off campus, where they presented their songs, dances, and stories to the public. While such expressions of "Indianness" had been resolutely banned by the schools for their perceived ability to undermine the school system's credibility as an efficient mechanism for assimilation, progressive reformers now sought ways of incorporating Indian people into mainstream society while preserving the traditional cultures they feared were disappearing.

According to the words of students who authored articles in their school papers and the reminiscences of those living alumni who still remember the Indian Clubs, student response to the clubs was overwhelmingly positive. Since the residential school system had been operating for a half century, decades of assimilationist laws, land "reforms" (i.e., dispersals), and compulsory education had pushed many cultural practices towards obsolescence. After generations of such cultural genocide, Indian Clubs emerged as a place where some students encountered their tribal traditions for the first time. A San Juan Pueblo student who attended the Santa Fe Indian School in the late '20s explains, "I don't think I appreciated my Indianness until I . . . became a senior in high school, when we had our Indian Club here, and I joined the Indian Club."[4] This process of recapturing and valuing one's Indianness became a positive trait of pageants—however mediated by school employees and policies—for decades to come, though school officials did not immediately understand the implications for building students' sense of worth. Georgia Davenport (Sac and Fox) directed pageants at Phoenix Indian School from 1958 to 1980, and came to champion the benefits of reclaiming one's background: "We could use their Indianness to develop the self-esteem . . . They had to do research on their background, on their tribal heritage, on their dress. It was interesting for me to learn that many of them did not know their tribal background. They had to work hard."[5]

Teacher Esther Horne (Shoshone) described similar responses, and her affirming experiences performing in pageants while a student at the Haskell Institute led her to direct pageants herself while working at the Wahpeton Indian School in the 1930s: "I encouraged my students to draw scenes related to their home environments . . . The creation of these reservation scenes evolved into a lot of after-school visiting in our room . . . I had gotten to know a lot of Indian families from across the United States through my friends at Haskell, and this created a bond between the students and myself. I tried to make Wahpeton a home away from home for these students."[6] This was during the worst of the Great Depression, when many parents could not afford to visit their children regularly. Horne allowed the students to name the pageants, and she regarded the pageants as vehicles for exploring the changes Indian people had gone through—without suggesting that Indian cultures or people would or should disappear.

Though the post-Meriam Report pageants usually showcased the cultural expressions of individual Indian groups, the process by which students prepared for the pageants together allowed for a pooling of memories and myths. In planning the pageants over subsequent years of living in community at a school, they developed what historian Alexandra Harmon characterizes as a "standardized lore that became a common heritage."[7] After all, the students found themselves in school together because the government regarded them all as Indians, and their interactions at school thus helped them to form a common Indian identity. By testing and acting out elements of this identity in public, in such events as the pageants, students had the opportunity to reflect upon and shape just what it meant to be Indian in their particular time and place. Like other schools in the system, Chemawa provided a site for this testing and fleshing out of one's Indian identity.

Extant documentation of Chemawa allows us to glimpse the campus life in the late 1920s, just before the Indian Office prompted a transition towards pageants that would gradually seek to affirm, rather than undermine, Indian cultures. As with early pageants throughout the boarding school system, themes tended towards the patriotic or the Christian. Pageants promulgated the values that would encourage Indian students' salvation, patriotism, and assimilation.

During the holiday season in late 1928, music instructor Gertrude Turney (née Brewer) staged a Christmas pageant at Chemawa. Accounts in the school paper suggest that this was not the first such Christmas pageant to be held at Chemawa, but that it was part of a recently established tradition: "On Sunday evening Mrs. Turney and her choir gave what has grown to be an annual program at Chemawa—what may be, for lack of a better name, called a pageant." Content was that of a Nativity play, with added music: "The various events attending the birth of Christ are featured in this program and Christmas carols are sung throughout. It always proves impressive and carries a lesson unlike anything else. There is an atmosphere about this pageant that cannot fail to assist in making one feel inclined to be a better man."[8] While this brief article was printed unsigned, the word choices and the emphasis on the pageant as a means of ennoblement suggest that the author was likely a faculty member, and possibly Mrs. Turney (who was both pageant director and newspaper manager) herself. Even more effusive post-pageant accounts appeared the following year, following a Christmas pageant that was larger and more elaborate: "The choir members covered themselves with glory last Sunday evening in presenting the Christmas pageant. The pageant is becoming traditional at Chemawa, as every year it is put on as Chemawa's part in commemorating the greatest of sacred dramas." More faculty collaboration was in needed to mount the larger production: "Miss Gunn was Mrs. Turney's assistant in putting on the pageant this year. The pageant was in every way a success. To provide the proper atmosphere Mr. H. A. Kunkel played Schubert's beautiful 'Ave Maria' as an introductory number, and he played it well . . . It was one of the 'high lights' of the evening."[9]

Concurrent with the rise of more elaborate Christmas pageants at Chemawa was an interest on the part of the faculty and the non-Native public in a passion play that was touring the country in the late 1920s. A passion play is a dramatic presentation depicting the trial, suffering, and death of Jesus; for some Christian denominations, including Catholicism, it is a traditional feature of Lenten observances. Chemawa faculty took trips to Portland to experience the play, and news of these excursions was shared in the school paper for the edification of the students: "During last week our bandmaster, Mr. H. A. Kunkel, had occasion to visit Portland. He was combining business with pleasure and while there he witnessed the wonderful 'Passion Play,' which is everywhere taking the country by storm." No mention is made of the possibility of students attending the play, and transportation costs for such a field trip may have been prohibitively expensive. Nonetheless, the writer who contributed these accounts to the school paper felt that evidence of faculty attending the play was relevant to the Chemawa community, perhaps as a means of modeling desirable adult behavior to the students. Attending the passion play would have conspicuously combined a zeal for the narratives central to Christianity with an interest in Western theater, a form of the performing arts deemed, if not highbrow, at least "civilized." Such public modeling was more possible in boarding schools than day schools, and school administrators sought to capitalize on the attributes that spoke to the advantages of the boarding school system: "We have reason to believe that a number of our people went to Portland during the week-end especially to witness the wonderful 'Passion Play'; we are informed that Miss Earlougher made the trip purely on account of this great production, and we believe that others did the same and were well repaid for their trouble and expense."[10]

While the students were not taken to Portland en masse to see the passion play, they were eventually treated to a cinematic version: "A movie of the 'Passion Play' was shown to our students last Saturday night. The picture was filmed in Europe and featured a cast of fine actors. From every standpoint it was a wonderful picture."[11] Student responses to such events were not typically printed in the school paper during the 1930s. Some might not have been as excited about the film; some may have found it entertaining and inspiring.

After the holiday season, students at Chemawa found another pageant opportunity close at hand in the form of a patriotic pageant produced by the junior high students each February. Timed to commemorate George Washington's birthday, it consisted of a series of episodes, songs, silhouettes, and music, all chosen for their rustic nationalism and potentially inspirational stories. A program from 1929 reveals a typical "Patriotic Pageant," directed by two teachers, Miss Gunn and Mr. Frost:

> Processional   Orchestra
> Prologue by Spirit of Patriotism
> Dramatic Silhouette: LORDS of the FOREST Music: Forest Echoes
> First Episode: PRINCESS POCAHONTAS Scene: A Small Indian Encampment
> Second Episode: FERRY FARM Scene: Plantation Scene at Ferry Farm
> Third Episode: WASHINGTON'S FORTUNE Scene: An Open Portion of Lord Fairfax's Estate
> Dramatic Silhouette: THE SPIRIT of '76 Music: Tenting on the Old Camp Ground To Thee, O Country
> Fourth Episode: ABRAHAM LINCOLN, RAIL SPLITTER Scene: The Lincoln Kitchen and Living Room
> Song: SECOND MINUET Grandma and Grandpa
> Recessional   Orchestra[12]

Soon after came the celebration of Chemawa's birthday, commemorating the day the school was founded. The events did not originally include a pageant, but rather consisted of a series of cheer contests in which the various high school classes competed against each other by creating verbal expressions of school spirit: "Chemawa's fiftieth anniversary is approaching—as usual we will have our annual song, poem and yell contest on Feb. 25th. This custom was originated by Mrs. Flora Iliff when she was principal at Chemawa. The classes are hard at work trying to think up something new and out of the ordinary."[13]

Unique to this school event was the degree of spontaneity the students were accorded. Though their cheers may have been monitored or screened by faculty advisors before being presented before the entire school, the competition was designed so that the students might engage themselves emotionally in reflecting upon and shouting the qualities that made Chemawa great. Thus the activities served a dual purpose of commemorating Chemawa's birthday and fostering student loyalty and enthusiasm, hopefully sealing a personal relationship between the students and the school. The very use of the term "birthday," rather than "anniversary" or "founder's day," works to instill a notion of the school as a living entity, a friend of the students rather than a cold, impersonal institution.

It bears noting that Chemawa students at this time had knowledge of Western theater traditions and were regularly called upon to participate in local productions. Sometimes their participation in off-campus theater events was initiated by school administrators, and other times they were invited by outside organizations; Chemawa students frequently joined forces with local high schools, colleges, and performing arts groups, particularly to augment their musical resources. In May of 1928, for example, the Chemawa orchestra played for two contrasting productions in Salem: *Pocahontas* and Ibsen's *The Master Builder*, the latter performed at the Capitol Theater by Willamette University students under the direction of Dr. J. O. Hall.[14] Individual Chemawa students who had developed special talents or skills were often allowed to join performing ensembles in the Salem community, and their accomplishments were publicly noted, both as good public relations material for the school and in hopes of inspiring other students. Students who excelled on their musical instruments were frequently in demand: "Verne Wilson is holding down two jobs: He plays first violin in the High School Orchestra in Salem and second violin in the Chemawa organization. Last Friday night he played in Salem for the High School production of a musical play."[15]

Chemawa students did not have to travel off-campus to pursue an interest in Western theater. Literary societies on campus provided an ostensibly informal yet actually structured and supervised setting in which students presented plays from the Western literary canon to their classmates. These societies, with lofty names coined during the Victorian period (e.g., "Excelsior," "Reliance," "Nonpareil"), were gender-specific, a practice common in public schools as well; students were presumed to have more freedom to plumb the emotional and intellectual complexities of literature in the context of same-sex groups. The largest literary societies on campus, Excelsior and Reliance, even had their own student bands that provided music at their meetings, plays, readings, and other special events. Newspaper accounts suggest that desirable student behavior at these events was spirited but orderly: "Lack of space prevents a more extended account of the Excelsior Society's open session program, as rendered on the evening of Armistice Day. It is reported to us that the boys put on a really creditable program—interesting, good and clean. 'Horse play' was absent." Group chants to engage school spirit were an integral part of the gatherings: "The other societies of the school were out in full force and there was the usual period of songs and yells in friendly rivalry. All in all it was a most pleasing affair, creditable alike to the Excelsior members and their critic, Mr. Stacy."[16] The "horse play" condemned in this article may have referred to a meeting held the previous month, which nonetheless had been favorably described in the school paper. The author lauded a "wild night" at Chemawa the previous Friday evening, with a joint "open session" for all of the literary societies. "The Excelsior orchestra and Reliance band were two musical organizations that provided music, and there were many vocalists on the bill, debates—and everything. It was great!"[17]

Although Chemawa was geographically removed from the governmental confines of Washington, D.C., it was obligated to respond quickly to BIA directives, and its actions were monitored regularly by visiting superintendents. Hence, after the 1928 release of the Meriam Report prompted an intense reassessment of the ways tribal cultures had been denigrated by the schools, Chemawa began to incorporate the music, crafts, and drama of the Indian population into its curriculum and extra-curricular activities. John Collier, founder of the American Indian Defense Association, fought vehemently against schools that were designed to "proselyte the child and shame him away from his tribal settings, his Indianhood."[18] When Collier was named Director of Indian Affairs in 1933, the new Office of Indian Affairs administration in Washington mandated the ways in which boarding school personnel would begin to value Indian cultures.[19]

This change in cultural valuation did not mean the outright discarding of existing Western drama and pageantry. The literary societies gradually increased in popularity, and reports from 1950 show no less than sixteen operating concurrently at Chemawa. Christmas pageants, too, continued as before, under the direction of Mrs. Turney until her retirement in 1941.[20] A brief account of the Christmas 1940 pageant reveals that the contents and staging of the holiday pageant had changed remarkably little over Mrs. Turney's thirty-year tenure at Chemawa: "The traditional Christmas Pageant by the choir was presented in the Auditorium under the supervision of Mrs. Gertrude Turney, Sunday, December 15th. The pageant portrayed the story of the birth of Christ, in singing and tableaux. The stage setting was strikingly beautiful." The children conveyed the Christmas story through topical songs and bodily movements: "The orchestra played a selection composed of several Christmas Carols, and Mr. Lovell sang a solo. For one of the scenes in the pageant, Marjorie Skahan recited the story of Christ's birth. The choir sang a medley of Christmas melodies, while scenes of the Christmas story were portrayed in pantomime."[21]

What did change fundamentally after the Meriam Report, however, was the nature of Chemawa's annual birthday celebration. Originally comprising song and yell contests, it had been a day dedicated to the honing of school spirit. After reformers' newly impassioned call to save and affirm Indian cultures, however, school officials re-oriented the observance into a celebration of Indian identity. To be sure, the resulting pageants were fabricated depictions that had more to do with white conceptions of Indianness than with actual Native lives and identities. Still, students were directed in the performance of songs and dances from their respective communities of origin, an original pageant—albeit with mildly didactic themes—was presented, and a queen was crowned in an elaborate ceremony.[22]

The pageants were particular to Chemawa, and were written in-house by staff members. For example, in the 1950s, girls' advisor Miss Alberta Challis wrote and narrated the pageants, while students acted out the scenes on the auditorium stage or the gymnasium floor. *Canoe Prophesies*, one of Miss Challis's creations, reveals a fusion of traditional culture and Euro-American education that was typical of pageantry in this period: "In the pageant, Red Eagle, a twelve-year-old Indian boy, on his quest, has seen important happenings of future years, among them, Chemawa's 1954 birthday celebration. On the stage, where the setting was a river scene with a fishing platform and a canoe, the part of Red Eagle was taken by Richard Thompson."[23] Miss Challis told the story while it was portrayed visually on the floor of the gymnasium. By re-imagining the tribal past and inserting into it a prophesy of Euro-American schooling methods, the pageant gave Chemawa officials a means by which they could publicly assert the validity of tribal cultures while positing the residential school's rightful place in the growth and education of Indian youth. Tribal cultures and residential schools were reconciled for public view. Native dances and ceremonies lent credibility and authenticity to this reconciliation, and the program of performers lists the various capacities in which dozens of students were employed in the pageant: chanters, chorus, Navajo corn-grinding ceremony, and twelve distinct dances.[24]

The following year's birthday celebration, Chemawa's "Diamond Jubilee," marking seventy-five years of operation from 1880 to1955, included a similar mix of events but on a larger scale. More publicity was directed at the off-campus community, invitations were extended to families and alumni, and visitors from across the Northwest attended the celebration. Following the big weekend, students' own accounts of the festivities were printed in the school newspaper, with each author identified.[25] Several commented on the pride they felt at the number of visitors. Emily Nightgun summed up: "Friends and relatives and special guests were there to help us celebrate our school's birthday. Among the guests were many former employees and students." Alvin Cultee took delight in being able to extend hospitality to the visitors: "There were many people at the birthday party. There were boys and girls from Warm Springs and from many other parts of Oregon, and more from Montana. It made me feel proud. The explorer scouts were ushers. We tried our best to do a good job." Younger student Ellery Broncho simply remarked, "I liked the visitors that came. I hope they will come again." The comments of the younger students are usually identifiable by their brevity and straightforwardness, and the newspaper managers sought to present positive quotations from the complete range of students at Chemawa. Young and old alike commented on the cake, which was a prominent part of the celebration. Primary school student David Alvarez declared, "The cake and the punch were delicious." High school student Lucetta Hahn elaborated, "It wouldn't seem like a birthday party if there were no cake. Thanks to Mrs. Augusta Sanders and students who helped bake the cake, Chemawa's birthday party was complete. The cake, which served nearly a thousand, was shaped like a star. It was decorated with white, fluffy frosting, and was topped with a small red and white C flag. Many pictures were taken of the cake." Clearly, the cake was central to the celebration.

Students, most of whom did not own cameras themselves, were very aware of the photographs that were taken during the various phases of the pageantry. One, Leah James, who was the queen chosen to reign over the evening's festivities, even counted the flashes that went off during different time periods: "It was most interesting to watch and count the flash bulbs while the dances were being performed. Three dances, the thunderbird, swan, and war dances, each had 36 to 40 flashes. The court had 41 flashes."

Some students took pride in the ways their dormitories and musical groups were able to perform exercises and songs that provided windows into Chemawa's past. Their written contributions reveal that they students had some knowledge of Chemawa's history, as well as a sense of the transformation that had taken place in recent decades. Harold Thomas explained, "A military drill was done by Mitchell Hall boys in representation of the years when Chemawa was a military school." And Benjamin Charles added, "The octet boys were given many compliments for their singing of the songs of long ago."

Other students were most struck by the pageant itself—by the stage setting, and the content of the pageant story. The 1955 pageant, *Through the Years*, was another product of Miss Challis, and it showcased inter-generational storytelling as a means of transmitting Chemawa's history. In the process, the school's early years—in which a couple of dozen students braved cold Oregon rains to construct the school's buildings and physical grounds—could be looked back upon as exciting and, at times, enjoyable. Student Joanna Meninick described the stage, recounting, "This year for Chemawa's birthday party the stage was decorated with fir trees, and there was a log cabin like one of the old days of 1885. The cabin was built by the Navajo carpentry class. In front of the cabin Grandfather was talking to his grandson." Her classmate Austin Phillips continued, "Johnny's grandfather was telling him about Chemawa. He told him about how it started, first at Forest Grove, Oregon, and then, in 1885, at the present site. He told of the hardships and of the fun." Pasquel Mullen took the part of Johnny, and the part of the grandfather was played by Randolph Wilson.

What meanings did the pageants have for younger students? Responses suggest that the younger students were particularly captivated by dance numbers. Even the briefest comments evoke the students' sincerity and their sense of connection with the dances. Margaret Wesley explained, "Included in the program were many Indian dances done by the Northwest and Southwest students," and Gloria Tendoy weighed in: "The dance I liked best was the eagle dance. The singing for the dances went real well."

The older students who participated in the pageant as dancers were often loaned regalia from people sympathetic to the school. Sometimes the regalia came from Indian families; other times, it came from costume collections that had supplied the movie industry in Hollywood. Marie Barr described her experience with the regalia loaned to her: "It was the first time I ever wore an Indian costume or participated in Indian dancing. The costume I wore was worn by the actress Coleen Miller in two Western movies. One of them was *Four Guns to the Border*, recently shown in Salem. The costume is complete, and everything matches." Students used their articles as an opportunity to publicly thank their costume donors, and Miss Marr graciously concluded, "I am indebted to Yvonne Muss Muss Toe for going to the trouble of bringing the costume down from Toppenish for me." Another high school student, Joan Harwood, quoted from her donor to explain the history of the regalia she had borrowed: "I got a letter from Mrs. Mary Grounds telling about the Indian costume I wore in the dances. Mrs. Grounds wrote, 'The red flannel, basket beads, and shells for the dress were all bought at the Sherburn store in Browning, about 1895. Mrs. Kayio, one of the old-timers on the Blackfeet reservation, made the dress. In those days the Indian men and women wore their Indian dress whenever some sacred woman made a medicine lodge. The costumes have been passed on, so I had the pleasure of getting this one from my great-aunt for a keepsake.' " Particularly poignant in these accounts are the testimonies of teenagers learning about their tribal heritage through the costumes that were sent to them, or in some cases, being afforded the opportunity to dance for the first time in their lives. However scripted or didactic the pageants may have been, the rewards of students encountering their tribal cultures were far-reaching and cannot be overstated. This annual practice of public pageantry—which engendered students' pride in their school and in their respective tribal histories, as well as increased self-understanding—would have been impossible before the reforms instituted as an eventual result of the Meriam Report.

In addition to the inclusion of Native dances, the target audience for the pageants shifted from a solely internal one—the student body—to a dual audience of the Chemawa campus and the public at large. The new prominence of the pageants necessitated more publicity, and organizers broadened the purpose of the pageants to include the advancement of public relations. Events were repeated over two days, with the first day designated as an internal day with the pageant presented to the students, employees, and their families. On the second day and evening, the pageant was presented to the public. Clearly, the scope and intent of the birthday observances had grown considerably, and the transformed celebration was no longer just a pep rally.

While new pageants emerged, others disappeared. The patriotic pageants formerly held on Washington's birthday no longer took place. No executive order seems to have halted the patriotic pageants; they likely fell away due to changes in staffing and the residential school system's shift in emphasis towards affirming students' tribal heritages. Indian Office circulars that had called for instilling national loyalty in the students by acquainting them with the mythologies of colonialism were no longer issued, and patriotic-themed pageants became infrequent. In their place, Washington's birthday was observed with a simple holiday from classes. In 1954, for example, students were allowed to sleep in until 7 a.m., and the day was programmed with a series of leisurely—albeit carefully supervised—activities. After breakfast and work details, the boys at McNary Hall attended a structured visit of Winona Hall, the girls' building. At 2:30 p.m. there was a basketball game at the gym between the McNary All Stars and the B squad, and after the game the students danced until 4:00. In the evening, they watched the musical *I Love Melvin*, starring Debbie Reynolds and Donald O'Connor.[26] The absence of patriotic activities is striking when compared with the Revolutionary War pageants that had marked Washington's birthday in the 1920s. Faculty and staff had re-directed their energies towards the increasingly elaborate Chemawa birthday celebrations, which happened to fall less than a week later.

One new pageant did emerge, held later in the school year during commencement week. A showcase of the students' cultural backgrounds and vocational work, the exhibition drew visitors from Salem as well as Indian communities scattered throughout the Northwest. The emphasis on Indian culture, rather than the Euro-American cultural system the schools had originally sought to transmit, is notable in descriptions of the pageant.

> Celebration! Pageant! That's what everyone is thinking about now that school is nearly over. The hustle and bustle of preparing for the celebration always brings a tinge of excitement to the students.

As we look around the campus we see a group of students practicing a scene for the pageant. Somewhere else we see boys putting up some scenery or helping someone put up a tepee. From the direction of the music room we hear strains of Indian music which lends a sort of enchantment to the setting. Then people begin to arrive. Crowds and crowds of people, who have come to see the results of days of practicing and work. They go from one building to another looking over the exhibits and voicing their opinions. In the evenings the lure of the days gone by grips the campus as the pageant is presented. Scene after scene is unfolded with girls and boys in beautiful costumes and singing enchanting melodies.

After the pageant and celebration are over and the students start leaving for their homes, the campus grows quiet as it awaits the coming of a new school year and another celebration.[27]

Apparently the end-of-year pageants were important to students and staff alike, both as a vehicle for the school to present itself to the public and as a great source of pride for the students. The commencement pageants were brief-lived, however, and took place only for a few years in the late 1930s through 1940. In 1941, the year after the glowing pre-pageant account above, the festivities were discontinued, in the era of economic restraint that would accompany World War II. The administrators at Chemawa may have been overwhelmed by too many visitors from surrounding reservations, and the dissolution of the pageants may have been a way to regain control at the close of the school year. A simple notice appeared in the May 2, 1941, *Chemawa American*: "NOTICE: There will be no pageant or celebration during the Commencement Week this year as has been the custom in the past. In view of this it is not expected that Indian visitors will come from nearby reservations. Therefore, no provisions are being made for accommodating the large number of visitors who have come to the school in the past few years."[28]

The same issue of the *Chemawa American* that included this notice also carried a description of a recent chapel service that was deemed "unusually interesting." The emphasis on Indian songs at this chapel service was atypical, and may have been planned as a token substitute for the cancelled commencement pageant: "The chapel service on April 20 was unusually interesting. Several Indian songs were sung by primary students, including an Indian Medicine song, a lullaby, and a war chant." The rest of the program was more typical of the Sunday pageants: "The choir sang two numbers, 'Behold the King' and 'Now the Day is Over.' The orchestra played the selection, 'In a Persian Market,' and Miss Cruise gave the themes of the song. Judge Rossman, of Salem, was guest speaker. He gave a splendid talk on the opportunities offered to youth."[29] The inclusion of these Indian songs at a chapel service—and their relegation to the primary, rather than upper-grade, students—was perhaps considered a safer, more controlled way of letting students sing their heritage without the guests, unpredictable in numbers and behavior, who had formerly attended commencement week pageants. Following the chapel service, the freshman class held a reception in honor of Judge and Mrs. Rossman, with a program that featured two "civilized" recital pieces, presented at Winona Hall: an Indian song by Roosevelt Supah, and an Indian poem, E. Pauline Johnson's "The Song My Paddle Sings," recited by Julia Landigreen.

The commencement week pageants never again rematerialized in the same form, though end-of-the-year powwows would emerge in the 1970s (see Chapter 8). Chemawa's birthday, however, observed each February, is still regarded by school officials as an appropriate time for students to celebrate their Indian identities and act as hosts to off-campus guests. But pageants to celebrate the school's birthday appeared only sporadically until the 1960s, when two Navajo staff members organized large-scale pageants that sought to celebrate traditional cultures while educating the public about the students' tribal backgrounds.

For a brief period in the 1960s, these pageants became an annual part of campus life at Chemawa. Though the new pageants flourished for just a few years, they were large, public events that left a profound imprint on the students enrolled at Chemawa at that time and on the greater Salem community. Many of Salem's older residents still hold perspectives of Indian people that were formed by their experiences of attending Chemawa's pageants in the 1960s.

Each pageant would run for three days: Friday, Saturday, and Sunday. There were enough students and dances that the pageants could have been week-long events, but the school administration would only allow them to be held on the weekend, so as not to interfere with the students' studies. Each evening would begin with a spoken introduction, explaining the songs' origins to the public; then, a series of dances was performed on the stage in the auditorium, with the dancers in full regalia and the stage prepared with a nature-themed set or backdrop, such as a mural of Mt. Hood.

The pageants were spearheaded by Reggie and Saide Begay, a Navajo couple who served on the staff at Chemawa for several years before they created the pageants. Though they both passed away in 2004, their daughter, Linda Begay, still lives in their Salem-area home and has clear recollections of her parents' life history, the pageants themselves, and the years the Begay family spent on the Chemawa campus while she and her brother were growing up. Linda explains, "Mom had gone to St. Michael, a Catholic boarding school in Gallup, New Mexico.

Then she went to secretarial school. My parents met at a Squaw Dance—now they call it 'Song & Dance'; it's a social gathering." [30] Linda's father came upon Oregon largely by chance: "Dad was in the military—he was in Australia, the South Pacific, Guadalcanal, and Iwojima. He was injured and shipped back to Alaska, then brought down to Puget Sound to recover. When he was well enough to go out for a couple weeks, he explored the area here, and decided this was a good place to live." The Begays' familiarity with music as cultural expression and as a vehicle for social gathering, their first-hand knowledge of boarding school life, and their sustaining of allegiances both to one's tribe and one's country were all experiences that would prepare the Begays for their later work at Chemawa. The added element of relationships—knowing the people of their clan and of the surrounding areas of the Navajo Nation—gave the Begays a knowledge base and credibility that enabled students to trust them with the preparation of songs and dances that require reverence for the sacred.

They joined the BIA in 1952, working at Concho School in Oklahoma, a place many Navajo students had been attending since the 1940s. Then a shift occurred in 1958, when most Navajo youths were enrolled at Chemawa. The Begays transferred there, staying until their retirements in 1986 (Reggie) and 1987 (Sadie). Linda recalls their varying job duties: "At first, Mom and Dad were in Guidance; they were like Matrons. They helped the kids, especially the Navajos. The school wanted the Native staff to live on campus, so they could translate and help the kids." Reggie would eventually train for a position in security: "Later, Dad worked as a head of security. Then, he went to Chemeketa [Community College], and the Police Academy, and worked more in a law enforcement capacity. He became a federal marshal."

One duty with which the Begays were entrusted was the recruitment of new students for Chemawa. Linda remembers this as hard work, and sometimes danger-ous: "Mom & Dad would recruit on the reservation in the summers. They knew the area. Other recruiters, they'd just go to the houses they saw on the paved roads, and they'd come back with a small pile of papers, but Mom & Dad would go out to other houses, and they'd come back with a thick pile of applications. Of course, they'd also both been shot at by grandfathers who didn't want their children to go to school."

The Begays organized the first pageant in 1961. The work of planning the dances and assembling the regalia fell entirely on them and was unpaid, an ar-rangement stipulated by their supervisors at Chemawa. Linda remembers the large amount of work the sewing entailed: "Mom made the girls' outfits. Twenty-eight skirts and blouses. She did it all on her own—there was no budget for it. Mom asked the supervisor if some Navajo girls, or some staff, could help her make the dresses. They said no, that she'd have to do it herself, on her own time, and with her own money." Initially, the blouses were tailored to fit each girl: "She made these velveteen blouses, and some with silk material too. She'd sew all through the afternoon, till ten o'clock. She could do six or seven outfits in that time, and they were made to fit; she'd get the girls' measurements first." Later, they switched to a universal top, and the sewing was much easier.

Reggie Begay managed the construction of the boys' regalia, using a variety of sources to procure fabrics and materials, some natural and some store bought. The making of the Navajo boys' regalia was labor intensive, involving beadwork and elaborate stitching. The boys learned to construct their own pieces, though, under Reggie's supervision. Linda recalls the beadwork as the time-consuming element that the boys took pride in: "With the boys, my dad helped them make their regalia. He'd get horse tails from a ranch in Canby. The boys bought some of their tops in town, at Meier & Frank. Then Dad would set up a table, at the top of McNary Hall. He taught the boys beadwork. They'd work for hours up there."

The Begays were able to design the Navajo students' regalia, but Alaska Natives would write home and ask their families to send parkas, shoes, and other traditional pieces they couldn't find or make in Oregon. Sadie Begay would help the students lock up their clothing for safekeeping, although Linda describes this as an extra precaution: "Theft really wasn't a problem at Chemawa in those days."

The amount of work the Begays contributed to the pageants—and the lack of assistance from other staff or faculty—speaks to the priority the pageants were given by the school administrators during the 1960s. With limited funds, the school could sustain a marching band and a chorus, but chose to rely on volunteer efforts for the public showcase of songs and dances that celebrated Indian identity. The school reaped the benefits of the pageants—improved public relations, combined with increases in the students' pride and confidence—without having to allocate any funds for their planning or presentation.

When new students arrived at Chemawa, each one's knowledge of traditional song and dance practices varied greatly. Even among students of a single tribe or nation, familiarity with forms of cultural expression differed markedly with a student's particular community of origin. In the Navajo nation, for example, where many clans are scattered over a wide expanse of land, each clan has developed its own characteristic ways of transmitting cultural knowledge to its youth. When these local differences are compounded by variations among households, families, and individuals, the traditional knowledge any given student will bring to boarding school becomes impossible to predict.

Linda Begay explains how the varying backgrounds of the students necessitated some planning to shape the pageants into coherent, polished events: "Some kids had the background and some didn't—it depends on what area they were from.

So, my mom & dad chose the dances. The kids had to attend practices. They knew they'd be warned if they missed one or two, and if you missed three, you could be asked to leave." On occasion, students attended practices initially, had their regalia assembled, and then for whatever reason chose not to attend the final practices. "Sometimes kids walked off, and that's when you'd end up with Eskimos being Navajos, and Navajos being Eskimos." Begay laughs in recollection, showing year-book and personal photographs that reveal the occasional student performing the songs and dances of a cultural group different from their own. Those who attended rehearsals regularly were usually willing to fill in when openings occurred, and did so with good humor. Audiences were none the wiser, and students were afforded the serendipitous opportunity to learn about each other's cultures experientially.

To showcase the breadth and vibrancy of the tribal cultures represented at Chemawa, the pageants included a variety of contrasting dances. Pageant photo-graphs in the 1962 yearbook showcase the Eagle Dance, Eskimo Motion Dance, Deer Dance, Horse Tail Dance, a Navajo Round Dance, the Apache Devil Dance, and a Hoop Dance by Maggie Chee. Photos from the 1964 pageant, "Drum Beats from the Past," include a War Dance, Ribbon Dance, Round Dances, Eagle Dance, Spear Dance, and a Yeibichai Dance.[31]

Yeibichai songs are part of the Navajo Nightway ceremony, an elaborate nine-evening healing ritual; the dance occurs on the final night. *Yé'ii-bi-chái* ("gods-their-grandfathers") refers to the ancestor deities who arrive to dance at Nightway. The complex re-enactment of the myth upon which the ceremony is based includes purification practices such as sweating and vomiting, prayer offerings, sand-painting rituals, competing dance teams that include a comic clown character, and hundreds of long chanted songs that feature elaborate texts of ritual poetry. During the Yeibichai segment, dancers wear masks to impersonate the gods who have the power to cure a sick person; these dances are performed in two parallel lines, with dancers moving in reel-like figures. The vocal style incorporates orna-mentation and tense falsettos similar to the sound of Plains songs, but the melodies develop through numerous variations and shifts in the rhythmic emphasis that render Yeibichai songs very difficult to learn.

The inclusion of this particular dance in a pageant is worth spotlighting be-cause it illustrates two key features of the pageants: 1) the dances were not easy, and the singing alone often demanded many hours of training; 2) the dances were often extracted from larger sacred ceremonies, sometimes raising questions of how to appropriately perform the extractions in a new context.

Regarding the complexity of the songs, and the amount of training involved, Linda Begay recalls, "My dad taught them to sing the songs. And they'd repeat them, and learn how to catch the rhythm." This technique—attentive listening followed by the repetition of gradually longer segments—is common today among singers who wish to learn traditional powwow and sacred songs in a thorough, intentional way. Singers listen to a song many times, join in on isolated phrases, and gradually "catch the rhythm" once they can anticipate the melody's twists and variations. As they learn the music, musicians in training can also glean lessons about tribal culture and lifeways. While explaining differences in learning processes that go beyond just those of oral versus written transmission, Linda Begay asserts, "There's an Indian way of teaching—it's not text-book. It's passed down. There are two different ways. It's a matter of how you use your philosophy."[32]

Regarding the extraction of songs and dances from their sacred contexts, students had a variety of opinions about which songs could or could not be performed at the pageants, and which might be performed in an altered fashion. The Begays wished to share the wealth and vitality of Native culture freely with the public, and this was shaped by dialogue with the students about which dances would be acceptable to perform, and how they could be presented to a non-Native audience without compromising the music's spiritual meaning. These varying stances on the appropriateness of public performance depended largely on the students' respective communities of origin. Alumnus Chet Clark (Navajo) recalls, "Sometimes they'd want us to do something we shouldn't, and we'd just tell them we couldn't do that one for the pageant."[33]

Different tribes had their own distinct histories of interactions with non-Natives, and this produced markedly different attitudes and actions on the part of the students. Linda Begay explains some of the general tendencies among Chemawa students in the 1960s: "There were Northwest ways of doing things. The tribes here have different ways, and they have a different history of interaction with the non-Natives." Specifically, "the Navajos tend to be quiet, reserved, more willing to work with the public. The Northwest tribes, they've had a lot of tensions and battles with non-Natives, and they're not so interested in the community [i.e., outside Chemawa, interacting with people in Salem]. This was because the Northwest tribes were in tune with what was out there, and how the white people treated Indians." During this era, there was a large Navajo presence at Chemawa, a smaller population of Alaska Natives, and a still-smaller contingent of students from Northwest tribes. The Northwestern students expressed the least interest in the pageants, performing only occasionally. Navajo and Alaska Natives had far greater rates of participation, due in part to the different relationships their home communities had with non-Natives. A number of different factors influenced an individual student's decision to perform in the pageants, however. When asked what she thought the students liked about the pageants, Linda Begay cited several aspects of the appeal: "to express themselves in public . . . to dance together,

Alaskans and Navajos . . . to show the public they weren't just a bunch of wild Indians. It was a way to say, 'This is who we are.' "[34]

The pageants were remarkable for the level of interaction they sparked between Chemawa and the greater Salem community. Boundaries between town and gown were more porous in the 1960s than today, and each year the pageants drew hundreds of people from Marion County and beyond. The low cost (three or four dollars for adults) made it possible for families to attend, and the open fields at Chemawa were quickly converted into parking lots that filled to capacity. Many of the attendees first learned of the pageants through a simple invitation that appeared in the Salem *Statesman*, with the gracious wording: "Chemawa Indian School cordially invites the public to see a pageant on their Native background." Dates, times, and directions were briefly noted.

The repercussions of the school's public exposure, while hard to quantify, were widespread and profound. New relationships were formed between the Chemawa community and the community at large, relationships that were often productive for the students. Families from local households and far-flung eastern Oregon ranches requested Chemawa students to live and work with them during the summer months, and social workers stepped forward to facilitate the increased popularity of this job program. Local churches sought to provide services to the Indian students. Public schools and civic organizations requested visits and performances from groups of Chemawa students.

An example of how the full effects of the pageants were not known for years, sometimes even decades, is the case of Mark Hatfield (1922-2011), former senator and governor of Oregon. Hatfield grew up in the Salem area and was brought to Chemawa pageants by his parents. He recalled growing up with little truthful knowledge of Indian people, except for what he learned at the pageants and from friends and acquaintances: "We did not have a great deal of specifics as far as Indians; the feds dominated the policies, the politics. We were more related culturally and through celebrations. I think we came to appreciate the Indian customs and the Indian traditions that at least came as a counter measure to the idea that we were going to lose them all through assimilation and termination." Viewing the songs and dances of the pageants as a testament to the culture of which the federal termination process sought to deny the very existence, Hatfield was later compelled to oppose termination policies. A life-long advocate for Indian rights, he helped lead the way for Grand Ronde's restoration campaign in the 1980s, continuing his life-long relationship with the Native people of Grand Ronde. Teaming up with House Rep. Les AuCoin and tribal leader Kathryn Harrison, he worked tirelessly to pass the Grand Ronde Reservation Act in 1988. In 1998, the Confederated Tribes of Grand Ronde announced the creation of the Hatfield Fellowship in honor of Senator Hatfield's accomplishments on behalf on the tribe; the Hatfield fellow serves as a liaison between a member of the Oregon congressional delegation and Oregon tribes on issues affecting Native Americans. Tribal member Brent Merrill remarked to Hatfield, "If there was ever a case for a non-Tribal member politician to be adopted into the Grand Ronde Tribe, I think you're it."[35]

In ways such as this, the long-term benefits of the pageants went beyond the students who participated, affecting the audiences, who gained an understanding of Native cultures and humanity, and sowing the seeds that could bring transformative changes in governmental policy and interethnic relations years later. Hatfield's experience of the "civilizing" campaign promulgated by the Indian schools led him to critique the discourse of civilization, and to question whether the federal government can authentically function as an agent of civilization. At a 2001 town hall meeting in Portland, he elaborated, "We've done a lot of de-civilizing in the world because we've used other countries as economic parties in which to sell our arms."[36] Former Senator Mark Hatfield's public career stands as one example of how a non-Native's experience of Indian culture—through musical gatherings, pageants, and other shared events—can later inform our national political discourse, commerce, and international relations.

During the early 1960s, the Chemawa pageants grew bigger and bigger each year, drawing increasing numbers of people from Salem and the surrounding countryside. The students' dances and regalia grew more elaborate, as did the sets and backdrops that bedecked the stage for the different dances. The publicity this provided for the school was consistently positive, and one would think that the school administration would have been expected to embrace the pageants enthusiastically and tout them as evidence of the richness and diversity of the tribal cultures of the students who were being served at Chemawa.

The administrative arm of the school, however, had been moved off-site from Chemawa to Phoenix, Arizona, in an attempt to centralize and streamline the operation of the shrinking residential school system. When the administrators in Phoenix learned of the Chemawa pageants, they informed the Chemawa staff that such events were inherently exploitative of the students and must be halted immediately. This was likely in response to a "mood for change" occurring within the federal power structure during the late 1960s and early 1970s, when the Indian bureau was characterized by turmoil and many rapid turnovers in leadership.[37] Despite students' protestations, no pageant was held in 1965, nor was there ever a pageant again at Chemawa.

For the next several years, the school's birthday celebrations still occurred but were increasingly subdued, designed more for the students than for the public. While troupes of students sometimes traveled off-campus to perform songs or dances at community meetings and events, there was no longer a campus-wide cultural showcase to which the public was invited. While the dissolution of the pageants did not immediately bring a closing-off of the boundaries between town and gown, it was a harbinger of the more distant, formalized campus-town relations that would coincide with the construction of the new campus in the mid-1970s. By then, Chemawa had begun planning and hosting powwows, intertribal events whose primary function was that of bringing Indian people together, rather than presenting students' song and dance traditions to non-Natives. On a national scale, the integrationist ethos that animated American society in the 1960s gradually gave way to the more separatist identity politics of the 1970s, and a performance form—powwows— that was rooted in individual tribes' performative contributions to intertribal gatherings better resonated with this shift. The era of pageants, as they had been known at Chemawa and in earlier forms throughout the residential school system, was over.

When music making (including such forms as theater and pageants) is regarded as social action, it becomes clear that the pageants served numerous purposes at Chemawa, and that they were performing various forms of cultural work. The assimilationist intent that rendered the earliest pageants powerful tools of hegemony was reversed by federal policy makers in the 1930s, allowing for much of the old patriotic thematic material to be supplanted by dance-and-regalia activities wherein students could explore their tribal heritages, albeit in safe, supervised settings. The 1960s saw these occasional pageants expanded even further into elaborate, multi-day public performances. These pageants held differing appeals for different students, and were particularly relevant for those living furthest from home: the Navajo and Alaska Native students, who delved into their own individual heritages but also encountered those of their peers. The pageants held profoundly different meanings for individuals situated in the various positions within the BIA school system as well, and a growing hesitation on the part of Native educators regarding "Indians on display" ultimately brought the pageants to an abrupt end. Succeeded in the 1970s by intertribal powwows, the pageants stand as a complex form of theatrical music making that began as a hegemonic device but ultimately allowed thousands of students to explore and publicly perform aspects of their Indianness.

Chapter 6
Dance: From Exacting Prohibitions to an Integral Part of Campus Life

"They were every Friday. Everybody had to go—some liked it; some didn't. A lot of guys were real shy. They taught us how to ask the girls to dance."

—Chet Clark (Navajo), recalling school dances at Chemawa in the 1950s[1]

The most virulent efforts to transform Native Americans involved Christianization campaigns and accompanying programs to suppress indigenous religious practices. Social reformers and government officials alike typically deemed Native religions and Christianity as incompatible, requiring that the former make way for the latter. This led to the growth of a bureaucracy dedicated to the "improvement" of Native Americans by abolishing their religious rites. Following the Indian Wars of the 1870s, Native dances and ceremonies where Indian peoples congregated were quickly targeted for eradication. When these targeted dances are considered for their actual meanings and functions, the government's attempts to eradicate indigenous dances highlight the conflict between the linear transformation endorsed by Christians and the Native cyclical principle of renewal, in which the cosmological forces that sustain the existence of all creatures must be re-affirmed through seasonal ceremonies and rituals.

Opponents of Indian religious practices depicted them as superstitious, cruel, and licentious. In 1883, the Secretary of the Interior informed the Commissioner of Indian Affairs that the Oglala Sun Dance was a heathen rite that hindered the civilization of the tribes and stimulated warlike passions. The commissioner responded by criminalizing ceremonial dances, medicine practices, and the exchange of property during funeral rituals.[2] At the same time, another religious movement, the Ghost Dance, was spreading across Indian Country. Fearful that the Ghost Dance might incite Indians to resist white control, in 1890 the federal government sent the cavalry and infantry to restrain the Sioux living on the Rosebud and Pine Ridge reservations. Soon afterwards, three hundred and fifty Miniconjou Sioux traveling to Pine Ridge with their leader, Big Foot, to work for peace were attacked by nervous soldiers armed with Hotchkiss cannons; in less than an hour, two hundred dead or wounded Sioux lay across the countryside around Wounded Knee Creek.

In 1902, the Commissioner of Indian Affairs issued a circular that became known as the "Short Hair Order." Designed to break up the cultural matrix of "Indianhood" that had retarded assimilation and land allotment, the circular pronounced that "the wearing of short hair by the males will be a great step in advancement," one that would "certainly hasten their progress towards civilization." The wearing of "citizens' clothing, instead of the Indian costume and blanket," was also encouraged. Facial markings used during dances and ceremonies were also targeted for elimination, allegedly for reasons of health: "On many of the reservations the Indians of both sexes paint, claiming that it keeps the skin warm in the winter and cool in the summer, but instead this paint melts when the Indian perspires and runs down into the eyes. The use of this paint leads to many diseases of the eyes among those Indians who paint." The facial markings were indicted for the loss of sight actually caused by trachoma and a variety of determinants: "Persons who have given considerable thought and investigation to the subject are satisfied that this [face painting] custom causes a majority of the cases of blindness among the Indians of the United States."[3] Letters explaining the Short Hair Order were sent to Indian agents and superintendents throughout the country, including school officials working in the Pacific Northwest.

In accordance with the circular, the Office of Indian Affairs issued new instructions in 1902 to the mostly Catholic staff at Grand Ronde School, thirty miles southwest of Chemawa: "The wearing of long hair by the male population . . . is not in keeping with the advancement they are making . . . in civilization. You are to induce your male Indians to cut their hair, and both sexes to stop painting. With some Indians, this will be an easy matter; with others, it will require considerable tact and perseverance." For Indians who did not obey the order, explicit punishments were suggested. "A non-compliance with this order may be a reason for discharge or for withholding rations and supplies . . . and if they become obstreperous about the matter, a short confinement in the guard-house at hard labor with shorn locks should furnish a cure."

Gatherings with communal dancing or feasting were perceived as particularly dangerous, and were often referred to with veiled sexual overtones: "Indian dances and so-called Indian feasts should be prohibited. In many cases these dances and feasts are simply subterfuges to cover degrading acts and to disguise immoral purposes. You are directed to use your best efforts in the suppression of these evils."[4] These directives reflect a preoccupation with long hair, face painting, and traditional dances as signs of dangerous behaviors, sinfulness, and depravity. In the Northwest, potlatches—gift-giving ceremonies practiced by Northwest coastal tribes including the Haida, Tlingit, Tsimshian, Salish, and Kwakiutl—provoked particular fear among non-Natives for their apparent renunciation of the tenet of personal property, a concept perceived as fundamental to civilization.[5] Indian people who continued to engage in such ceremonies and dances were functioning outside the control of white Christian society, and federal agents perceived them as a threat to assimilation and social order.

Soon after the Grand Ronde admonition, Harry Jones (Siletz and Grand Ronde-Mollala) enrolled at Chemawa Indian School. The school's ledger lists Jones as 5 feet 3 inches tall and 128 pounds when he arrived at the school in 1905 at age thirteen. Despite significant outbreaks of tuberculosis, cholera, and influenza (the last of which Jones himself sustained), he ultimately thrived at Chemawa and went on to graduate in June 1910 with the highest grades in the class. His valedictory address, entitled "The Outlook," reflects his complex understanding of tribal music and its implications for Indian-white relations.

> As the Indian was driven back, back, towards the setting sun, his hatred towards the white men increased. The hunting grounds which had been his were his no longer. The Great Spirit had forgotten the red man. The sadness of disaster predominated in the Indians' music—the weird, minor strains which were sung by the mothers to their little ones—colored the life of the Indian, and only gave place to the terrible war chant—the war cry—which their young men defiantly sang, in a despairing, futile hope of regaining the power of their ancestors. This hope died hard, but it—DIED.

Jones forthrightly acknowledges the potentially dangerous and destructive ways modeled by non-Native people: "No more will the Indian live his life as did his forefathers. This is generally understood by all Indians—even those who have been corrupted by the evil habits learned from the white man." He concludes with a request for help, not from the standpoint of an inferior but on a God-given equal footing with the white man:

> As the Indian was brought to bay, he looked around and saw the white man everywhere. He has submitted to the inevitable, and is now beginning to know that . . . the GREAT SPIRIT is the same as the White man's God—the UNIVERSAL FATHER—who calls all men His children, and intends that all men should be brothers. Instead of looking on the White man as an enemy, we turn to you for help. Will you be our brothers?[6]

While Jones's characterization of Indian music (with its "weird, minor strains" and despairing war cry) does not isolate dance specifically, it represents a Chemawa student's firsthand perception of Native music shortly after the turn of the century, and it reflects a modified understanding of the same tropes that whites had developed regarding Native music and dance: that it was acoustically weird or aberrational; that the war chant was terrible, defiant, and something to be feared; and that the Indians' music would ultimately share the fate of the Indian and, if not vanish, submit to the dominant culture.

This speech represents the words and sentiments Harry Jones chose to share with his classmates and teachers at his graduation ceremony in 1910. Jones had been born to Catholic converts who were both dead by the time he was six. Raised on the Grand Ronde Reservation, he left the church as a youth after witnessing malicious behavior on the part of the priests and nuns; this independence rendered him a misfit for the Grand Ronde School but led him to enroll at Chemawa. While his valedictory address uses musical description to allude to still-recent colonial conquests, Jones makes no apologies for being an Indian, and extends instead a disarming invitation for Indians and whites to work together. Even amidst language sympathetic to the cause of "civilization," Jones chooses not to relinquish his Indianness, but to locate it as a central feature of his identity. For Jones, music functions as a safe and useful rhetorical device to characterize the deeply painful transition taking place in Indian-white relations.

During and after the time that Harry Jones attended Chemawa, the commissioners of Indian Affairs each had specific strategies for attempting to manage the persistence of Indian dancing. Commissioner of Indian Affairs Robert G. Valentine (in office 1909-1913) contended that a situation mutually beneficial to Indians and assimilationists was available in the form of the Indian Fair, which would replace numerous summertime dances, feasts, and county fairs with a single large fair held after the fall harvest. Such an event could also promote farming by offering incentives for Indians to exhibit their crops, livestock, and domestic handiwork. American Indian Studies scholar Josh Clough characterizes the Indian Fair as "that rare example of a government program for Indians gone terribly *right*." The fairs quickly became the largest community gatherings held in many parts of Indian country. And yet, the fairs did not render other gatherings obsolete. Traditional dances and ceremonials continued to take place throughout the summer months. While Commissioner Valentine had allowed Indians to dance at the fairs to ensure their participation, his successor Cato Sells (1913-1921) regarded tribal dancing as patently offensive and deserving of no concessions. Sells quickly moved to ban traditional dances and sham battles, believing that both Indians and the non-Indian public alike should be satisfied with such proper amusements as "slow mule races" or "athletic contests involving feats of strength and skill";[7] the inclusion of athletic contests and band concerts became mandatory in 1913.[8] Most Indian people did not share Sells' vision of the fairs, and elected instead to dance for money at Anglo fairs or for privately sponsored events.

During the 1920s, dancing on reservations was severely repressed by Commissioner Charles H. Burke (1921-1929), who famously excoriated the residents of New Mexico pueblos as "half animals" because of their "pagan religion," ordering several leaders jailed for violating the religious crimes code he had implemented.[9] Of Burke's many edicts, the most notorious in Indian circles was Circular 1665, *Indian Dancing*. [10] The circular emphasized that morally "harmful" dances be considered "Indian Offences," with all the attending penalties: "On a number of reservations . . . the native dance still has enough evil tendencies to furnish a retarding influence and at times a troublesome situation which calls for careful consideration and right-minded efforts . . . when found so among the Indians we should control it by educational measures as far as possible, but if necessary, by punitive measures if its degrading tendencies persist." In vague and threatening language, the circular declares that the "sun-dance and all similar dances" would be subject to "corrective penalties."[11] A supplemental ban Burke issued in 1923 covered certain "degrading ceremonials," and was used to advocate for closer cooperation between missionaries and government officials, while banning gaming, giveaways, nighttime dances, and dancing by Indian people under fifty years of age.[12]

Despite these interdictions, Indian communities continued to practice dancing either clandestinely or in legal forms such as Wild West shows. Some tribes (e.g., Cherokee, Creek, Seminole) were able to continue dancing with little interference, while others (e.g., Lakota) were more closely monitored, rendering Wild West shows an appealing alternative. Traveling productions such as Pawnee Bill's Historic Wild West and Buffalo Bill's Wild West gave audiences a chance to indulge their curiosity about the "vanishing" Indians of the Western frontier. The performers gained income, travel opportunities, and friendships with members of different Indian groups. For some tribal communities such as the Lakota, this "Show Indian" tradition fostered honor and tremendous innovation in dancing.[13] While "Buffalo Bill" Cody maintained that his exhibition was for education rather than pure entertainment, he later teamed up with "Pawnee Bill" Lillie, who encouraged male dancers to "fancy it up," leading to the beginnings of modern Fancy Dance styles. Grand entries, where dancers enter the arena by groups according to their dance style, were another development of the Wild West shows that would later become adapted by Indian people for the powwow circuit.[14] As historian L. G. Moses has argued in his work on Show Indians, many of the performers were enriched by the experience, and had a good time playing themselves, finding in the Wild West shows a means to evoke and even celebrate their culture.[15]

Although the consequences for unsanctioned dancing included fines, jail time, and the withholding of food rations by Indian agents, dance culture flourished across the West in the 1920s. Indian people resisted the circular's prohibitions by speaking with newspaper reporters, corresponding with Burke or with OIA agents, mobilizing their communities, and publicly defying the order.[16] Even at the Haskell Institute Homecoming in 1926, Indian alumni used dance to revisit their identities and symbolically dramatize their resistance to white culture.[17] In Anadarko, Oklahoma, conversations between local Indian residents were underway that would soon lead to the first all-Indian managed cultural arts fair, the American Indian Exposition.[18] All the while, at off-reservation boarding schools, administrators implemented quietly repressive policies, wherein tribal ceremonies, when spoken of at all, were dismissed as purely antiquarian, wasteful of time and resources, and certainly not worthy of continued practice.

Whether as a consequence of Burke's regime or as part of the general social climate of non-Native America, the writings of staff and faculty at Chemawa in the late 1920s evince a high degree of anxiety regarding Native dance forms. Chemawa's school newspaper would occasionally carry articles about Native traditions, but dance was treated as a distant, exotic artifact from an earlier time. "Indian Karook," an article describing a Yakama observance for the dead, makes reference to the music, dancing, and "gaudy colors" of the costumes. An unsigned article, it was likely authored by a staff member, as was the convention of Indian school newspaper writing in 1920s. [19]

Students were encouraged to write articles with didactic messages, and those selected for publication almost always reinforced the school officials' policies and desired outcomes. Student Irene Diaz authored "The Ghost Dance," an account of a Ghost Dance as practiced by Indian people living in the Mohave Desert. Diaz explains that the Indians were warned not to waste so much time dancing. When they failed to heed the warning, floods followed, ruining their crops. All that was left was a circle of ghosts dancing; hence the name "Ghost Dance." She does not make clear whether her knowledge of the Ghost Dance is derived from research or from her personal experience, and the Ghost Dance she describes may be unrelated to the Plains Indians' Ghost Dance or may have been reworked in her mind into a lesson in productivity. What is clear is that Diaz likely had internalized repressive ideas about the Indian work ethic and an oppositional relationship between dance ceremonies and productivity.[20]

A recurring column in *The Chemawa American* during the late 1920s was "Arrows from the Long Bow," a series of quotations selected to encourage the students to study hard and apply themselves faithfully so as better to reap the benefits of civilization. The quotations were often taken from great authors or philosophers, but were occasionally "From Our Own Quiver," in which the ideas of Chemawa school officials were encapsulated in pithy sayings. These expressions often contrasted the old and new ways between which students must choose, and traditional music and dance were depicted as not only distracting but dangerous. To get the point across, language was often folksy or idiomatic, effectively parental and condescending: "Indians who prefer the dance horse and the tom-tom to the school and the plow are headed for Nemesis on the high speed clutch."[21]

On Saturday nights, school dances were held in the gymnasium, with music provided by orchestras composed of students and staff. Accounts of these events are replete with references to behavior, decorum, and efficiency, and the students' orderly behavior was an abiding concern of school officials. One described a Saturday dance in the gym as follows: "Two orchestras alternated in furnishing good music, exchanging places with hardly a pause in the program . . . The student body reached a 'new high' in conduct and efficiency at this social event, something for them to 'shoot at' in the future."[22] Overwhelmingly, the dancing allowed at Chemawa at this time consisted of Euro-American social dancing. Even visiting Indian musicians, such as the Sioux Indian band of Flandreau, South Dakota, were enlisted only to perform Euro-American dance music.[23] Accounts of traditional dancing are rare, the only instances being one-time, ad hoc events mounted for special visitors, such as a contingent of Nazi youth who passed through Oregon in the fall of 1932: "A band of young Germans . . . They were members of the youth movement of Germany similar to the boy scouts in our country. Disappointed a little at the lack of feathers and war-paint in evidence." Oddly, school officials responded by suspending their usual policy on Indian dancing: "Rather than have the German boys return home without having seen a part of the wild west our boys staged a war dance for their benefit."[24] Misunderstandings on all sides of the cultural divide notwithstanding, school officials placed a premium on public relations, and they were willing to depart from campus rules when an opportunity to promote the school's image presented itself. The inconsistencies of vilifying Indian dancing while actively staging some semblance of it for select visitors were never publicly reconciled, but may have stemmed from school officials' desire to impress their German visitors, or from a more mischievous sentiment of "They want Indians? We'll give 'em Indians!" on the part of school administrators.

After Charles Burke's oppressive reign and the brief era of Commissioner Charles J. Rhoads (1929-1933), a radical departure in federal Indian policy took place under the guidance of Commissioner John Collier (1933-1945). Having lost both of his parents as a teenager, Collier's subsequent search for meaning in his life prompted him to undertake wilderness retreats, and it was on one such retreat in the Appalachians that he experienced a vision wherein a bird appearing at sunset silently implored Collier to join his soul in "the immortal effort toward creation in which I, the bird, need you."[25] After studying at Columbia University and traveling to Europe to learn about labor and cooperative organizations, Collier returned to the United States and threw himself into the cause of social reform. Collier became well known in Washington, D.C., and in the national press when he sided with the Pueblo peoples against the dance ban, work that effectively launched his career in Indian Office reform and led to his 1933 appointment as commissioner of the OIA.[26]

While scholars have long regarded John Collier as the source of radical, progressive reforms in federal Indian policy, historian Tom Holm persuasively argues that these reforms reflected changes that happened *before* Collier, and can more accurately be attributed to the strength of what he has termed "Native peoplehood." The inevitability of complete assimilation touted by late-nineteenth-century reformers had failed when it did not transform the Indian identity into an American one; in effect, "the vanishing policy broke down before John Collier discovered Indians." Following the Great Depression and the shocking depiction of Indian school conditions contained in the Meriam Report, the 1930s saw a philosophical void in policy making that John Collier's ideas were able to fill. Attributing the resurgence of Indian culture solely to Collier's policies, however, perpetuates the analytical error of regarding "Native Americans as bit players in a Euro-American drama." The concept of Native peoplehood—a complex matrix of knowledge, symbols, relationships, and behaviors—is crucial for understanding the reasons underlying Native cultural resiliency. This matrix of peoplehood, even in instances where students and staff had incomplete knowledge of the complex meanings of traditional dance forms, would assist Chemawa students and Native staff in both reviving and continuing traditional dance forms that ran counter to the intentions of the "vanishing" policy.

Peoplehood in an off-reservation boarding school functions differently than it does in the more homogenous, cohesive setting of a tribal community. Students arrive with varying languages, religious practices, relationships to place, and cultural histories. Yet their experiences in boarding school—and quite pointedly in their involvement in dance activities—generated an interest in the aspects of Native peoplehood that could later be applied to the cultural practices of their own respective tribal communities. Students thus "developed a sense of themselves as 'Indian' that did not cancel out their tribal affiliation but cultivated instead . . . a repertoire of identities."[27]

One clear example of how the dynamics of peoplehood played out in a student's life is that of Kathryn Harrison (Grand Ronde) and her involvement in traditional dance forms while attending Chemawa in the early 1940s (see figure 15). At that time, Indian dance at Chemawa was manifested in two main forms: pageants and the girls' quintet, a group that would travel off-campus performing both Euro-American and Native-based songs and dances. In the pageants, the repertoire was standardized and remained fairly consistent from year to year. In the girls' quintet, the music teacher, Mrs. Turney selected the repertoire each year. Yet students recall being proud to be selected for participation, to don Native regalia, and to perform traditional music and dances. Harrison remembers dancing in the pageants: "We always had an Indian pageant, at the end of the school year. People would come from all over. It was called 'Thunder Mountain.' They performed a wedding, and did hunting scenes. There were dances—I remember being a part of the corn dance." Showing a photo of the corn dance from the school yearbook, she explains, "It was a beautiful thing—we'd be in a circle, we'd scatter the corn, and we'd pray. I always thought it was the neatest dance—we prayed for rain, after we scattered the seeds together. The Hoffman girls might have taught it; I'm not sure. We kind of did the same dances each year."[28] When Harrison speaks of the corn dance, it's clear that she found beauty,

(Left) Figure 15. Kathryn Jones (Harrison), Annabella Simmons, and Gladys Lane (Hudson), 1942. Building may be Brewer Hall, and the three students may be heading out to the football field. Photo courtesy of Confederated Tribes of Grand Ronde. (Right) Figure 16. Kathryn Harrison, ca. 2005. Photo courtesy of Kathryn Harrison.

meaning, and power in performing it. Her perspective springs from her particular life experiences—she came to Chemawa not directly from a tribal community but from a non-Native foster home—and cannot be assumed to represent all of her peers. Yet her ability to find truth and significance in the traditional dances of other tribes would later enable her to help reconstruct the cultural forms of her own people. Harrison went on to testify before the U.S. Congress regarding the persistence of Indian culture in western Oregon, successfully leading her tribe's campaign for restoration (see figure 16). This pattern—learning cultural forms of other Indian groups while at Chemawa and then returning home to further the cultural practices of one's own community—was common to many Chemawa alumni of Harrison's era.

The progressive reforms of Commissioner Collier's era represent more of a sea change than a single-handed achievement, and thus the full effects of Collier's policies were felt gradually. School officials did acknowledge that dance was a "natural" behavior for Indians, and they subscribed to newly popularized ideas about the everyday lives of Indian peoples being infused with art and music. The school paper quoted author Miss Olive Rush's assertion that "When the Indian baby learns to walk, he learns to dance" and elaborated that "This growing up with art makes art a part of life."[29] Still, Indian Affairs schools sought to channel the dance impulse into activities that would reinforce Euro-American social norms, and the school year at Chemawa was filled with a remarkable number of non-Native social dances. There was a Thanksgiving dance, a Christmas dance, and Chemawa's birthday dance. There were theme dances: an Irish dance, a hard-tack dance, a Sadie Hawkins dance, an old-time dance, a Halloween costume dance, a jitney dance, and a barn dance. There were dances held for various campus organizations: the Young Catholics' dance, the practice house students' dance, the beauty salon class dance, the ag. students' dance, and the Girl Scouts' dance. There were benefit dances, escort dances, and dances for each high school class. Ad hoc dances were mounted in the dormitories, students' birthdays were often occasions for dance parties, and sporting events were typically followed by dances. And all the while, there were the usual weekly or bi-weekly school dances held in the gymnasium.

Former biology and home economics teacher Floy Childers Pepper (Creek) recalls teaching social dance forms at Chemawa with her husband in the early 1940s: "So when we located to Chemawa, the kids all knew one dance and that was the two-step. And we decided that maybe they might have more fun if they could do more than one step. So we taught dancing—ballroom dancing—to the kids at Chemawa. And that was a lot of fun, 'cause the kids enjoyed it, and we enjoyed it." Childers attributes part of her success to the youthfulness of herself and her husband, Gilbert, and their ability to relate to the students: "We didn't have the usual problems of kids ducking behind the post and getting a smooch or whatever. They were interested in what we were doing and we were interested in what they were doing. And, even though we both looked young, and the students liked to flirt with us, they still respected us, and would do the kinds of things that we wanted, and so we felt pretty good about that."[30] The Peppers had both attended Fort Sills Indian School in South Dakota, and the fact that they had both experienced boarding school themselves no doubt informed their teaching methods and helped the Chemawa students to identify with them. Rather than outsiders mounting a top-down imposition of foreign dance forms, the Peppers were recent residential school graduates who were able to offer ballroom dance lessons from one young person to another, with students showing up voluntarily.

Dances provided the school with a natural opportunity for instilling Euro-American gender roles (such as male verbal assertiveness, which stood in stark contrast to the measured reticence that was valued in many tribal cultures), and the administration exploited this opportunity in ways both subtle and overt. Popular students were used to nudge other students towards desired behaviors, and to police those who fell out of line. The school paper featured articles on traits each gender found desirable in the other, with female contributors often including some variant of "I like a boy that can dance."[31] This served to reinforce the dance units that were taught in Chemawa's P.E. courses. Dance instruction always included lessons on social etiquette and behavior: "The gay little fresh-men are learning to dance. They are learning to [sic] rye waltz, waltz, glow worm mixer, and schottische. The 7th and 8th grade pupils have joined them in some of their lessons." Appeals were made to the new high school students' desire to fit in: "In order not to be found wanting, the freshmen practiced the correct ways to make introductions at the beginning of the school year. They find it comes as a very handy thing to know."[32] The anonymous authors played on the students' need for a sense of belonging ("in order not to be found wanting"), and were no doubt persuasive in a community where so many students were far from home, in an unfamiliar social environment. It bears noting that boarding school newspapers often acted as a means of domesticating the students by controlling the rhetoric that Native American youth produced.[33] Desired behaviors and ideals could thus be reinforced through indirect advice that students might perceive as peer to peer.

The transmitting of behaviors that were normative to Euro-American society stood to increase students' resiliency by expanding their capacity to adjust to novel social situations they might later encounter within non-Native society. For some students, such as the Navajo contingent, Euro-American social dance forms and even dances akin to square dancing were practiced in their home communities, and thus the imposition or reinforcement of these dance forms did not necessarily detract from students' awareness of their tribal traditions. For some students, tips on how to partake fully and effectively in the social bonding that dances could offer came as welcome words of guidance.

A critical component of dance etiquette was the guidelines for how to conduct oneself properly when dating, a particularly structured process at Chemawa. Students penned articles on dating tips, such as Joyce Bedah's "Things for a Girl to Remember About Dating," a list of seven pointers that express the awkwardness all teenagers feel in the early stages of dating. Bedah emphasizes how a girl might put a boy more at ease, offering such reminders as "Talk to the boy about something to make him happy."[34] Dating at Chemawa was formalized through strict guidelines set by the school. It was a privilege only granted to juniors and seniors, and the young couples were only allowed to meet in public, supervised locations. The school distributed the rules for dating to the students, and enforced them by using staff members to chaperone school dances and patrol downtown Salem on days when students were allowed into town. Although the guidelines were designed in order for students to "learn about the standards of boy-girl relations,"[35] repressive policies enforced without sufficiently compelling explanations often incite resistance in teenagers. The stories of alumni attest to students' ingenuity in getting around the rules. Minor infractions were sometimes handled by the students themselves, through the Boys' Council on Citizenship, which functioned as a sort of tribunal "to deal with cases of misconduct." Evidently, boys in the 1950s were more prone to misbehavior than were girls (who had no similar council themselves), and if a boy conducted himself poorly at the dining hall, a show, or a dance, he was sent to court to be tried by his peers.[36]

Other attributes that varied by gender included the types of dances that students preferred. While the upper-grade girls in Winona Hall[37] spent many of their free hours in the evenings listening to records and learning new steps, many boys were still loath to dance. When square dancing was incorporated into the P.E. curriculum in the early 1950s, boys embraced it as a type of dance that was accessible, easy to follow, and didn't require intimate physical contact with their partners. The square-dancing unit was a two-week period that broke up the usual routine of exercise and games, and it supported an additional weekly Thursday evening square dance that boys and girls could both attend.

The instructors presented square dancing holistically, with the proper music and clothing as critical components, and many girls sewed their own square dance skirts to wear at the Thursday dances and at weekly Wednesday meetings of the

Square Dance Club.[38] The older girls' interest in fashion was both encouraged by school officials as a means of fitting into the labor force upon graduation, and poked fun at by younger girls who were not yet so beholden to fashion's whims. Eleanor Foster and Annfusia Kenerzoff, two junior reporters for the school paper, jabbed: "WARNING: If you happen to hear the "click, click," don't think someone planted a time bomb near you—just look around and you will probably see a senior girl parading around just 'getting used to heels.' "[39] While proper dance attire was one arena wherein school officials could promote Euro-American standards, the constellation of body image issues that accompanied this agenda was complex, and particular physical features were sometimes acknowledged to be unattainable for Chemawa girls, or at the least very difficult to achieve. During World War II and in the postwar years, when changes in BIA leadership limited budgets, personnel, and the successful education programs of the 1930s,[40] Chemawa's agriculture and home economics students produced most of the school's food with great success. An account of the school's food-production system explained, "The bakery gives us the answer to the long sought $64 question, 'Why don't the Chemawa girls have those wasp like waist lines that give the new look?'"[41] What followed was a staggering description of the weekly output of cakes, buns, and cinnamon rolls from the campus kitchen.

Regardless of how their figures compared to the white ideal, many Chemawa students—especially females—loved to dance. In addition to the dozens of organized dances held on campus (some planned by the faculty and staff, other by the students themselves), students spent their free time in the evenings dancing to records. Other options for activities during free hours included cards and board games, ping pong, piano, reading, and crafts; still, the majority of students in the 1950s chose to dance. The school equipped the dormitories with phonographs, and allotted funds for the purchase of records that were selected by student officers. The students taught each other dance steps, and created routines to popular songs like "Ain't It a Shame" and "Seventeen." Younger students were occasionally allowed to watch the older ones dance, and male and female freshmen who recapped their experiences at the end of their first year of high school often mentioned dancing as the skill they were most happy to have learned. Just as many alumni attest that Chemawa students were and are "just like kids anywhere else," teenagers at Chemawa seem to have been engaged in the same early stages of rock-and-roll mania that were sweeping the rest of the country.

Alongside the perpetual array of high school social dances, Indian schools during Collier's era were directed to allow students to perform their tribal dance forms, and Chemawa was no exception. This radical departure from earlier policies banning tribal dances outright was implemented gradually and within safe, contained spaces of discourse. The Girls' Quintette and Septette [*sic*], which frequently performed off-campus with the school orchestra, began to incorporate Indian "costumes" and occasional hoop dancing. Eventually, three boys—Wilson Spencer, Willie Miller, and Roosevelt Suppa—were enlisted to "hold the interest of the audience with their intricate and clever war dancing."[42] The orchestra, then known as the Rhythm Chiefs, furnished popular music, jazz, and swing. This was no small feat considering that only seven years earlier, Chemawa had vehemently discouraged its students from performing or listening to jazz music, with staff members declaring, "We believe that 'Jazz,' so-called, represents a state of mind. If such is true, what an indictment of the American people."[43]

Off-campus performances were typically given at the invitation of such civic organizations as the Salem Women's Club, the Rotary Club, or the American Legion. As more Indian dances were incorporated into the performances, the attention given to the students' heritage was tempered with assurances of the students' civilizing school experiences in preparation for their futures as productive American citizens. The students presented popular songs that held currency with non-Native audiences—such as "Indian Love Call"— and the teachers or staff who chaperoned the excursions would give talks on the history of Chemawa and its current mission.

Another decade would pass before Chemawa would establish a club expressly for the purpose of researching and performing Indian music. The Indian Club formed in February 1946 under a mission statement more geared toward public relations than toward fostering students' wholeness: "The purpose of this club is to entertain groups that are interested in the Indians as well as Chemawa."[44] Just as earlier groups of students had performed off-campus for various civic organizations, the Indian Club was active every spring, performing at numerous western Oregon venues the songs and dances they had refined in the fall semester. What set them apart from earlier Indian dance efforts at Chemawa was that the students could focus solely on Indian dances and that the club could perform on its own, rather than in conjunction with a standard high school band, choir, or orchestra. It was especially popular with boys, and an account from student Willis Dixie attests to some tribes/groups being more represented than others: "Last night the boys in Indian Club practiced dancing. All the boys who participated in this are from Idaho. We have some good dancers in McNary Hall. More boys should join us."[45]

Interestingly, this comment dates from the Navajo period at Chemawa, in which Navajo students accounted for more than half of the school's enrollment. The Navajo program operated within a separate curriculum, however, and its students had a different slate of clubs available to them. One student, Ruth Long, explained, "All the Navajo students here at Chemawa belong to a club. The clubs are: square dancing, social dancing, singing, musical games, harmonica, wood carving, art, boys' cooking, and Navajo reading. We learn to do many things at the clubs. My club is square dancing."[46] Although five of the nine clubs involved music, Navajo students were regarded as having special needs distinct from the rest of the Chemawa student body and were not allowed to join the Indian Club at that time.

General school dances were open to everyone, and during the 1950s dances were held every Friday night at Chemawa. Attendance was required of high school students, and younger students were brought to the first hour of the dance, possibly to create an aura of excitement and desirability around the event. The younger students were taken back to their dorms while the night was still young, though, to keep their earlier bedtimes. Chet Clark (Navajo) recalls the orchestrated nature of the dances with mixed feelings that reveal the students' varying responses to the weekly event: "They were every Friday. Everybody had to go—some liked it; some didn't. A lot of guys were real shy. They taught us how to ask the girls to dance."[47]

From the school officials' standpoint, dances provided a perfect opportunity to teach the social etiquette that might help Indian students assimilate into non-Indian society. Acceptable clothing was carefully prescribed in advance. Boys were taught how to ask girls to dance, and girls were taught how to accept; students were shown didactic films that modeled these scripted conversations. Bodies were further managed as students were taught the standard social dances (waltz, fox trot, schottische) and, in a manner no doubt similar to what occurred in public schools across the country, discouraged from standing too close together. For some students, dances also offered a chance to interact with siblings who were also attending the Chemawa but, whether due to differences in age or gender, did not share common classes or extracurricular activities.

Boys and girls at Chemawa were kept segregated during many of their daily activities. Dee Pigsley (Siletz), who lived on the campus during the 1940s and '50s, recalls: "All boy-girl social time was *very* supervised. Even in the dining hall, the boys and girls sat on separate sides of the room. I think it was like this until they built the new campus, in the 1970s."[48] Dances, in contrast, offered a time to interact with freedom—to choose partners, or to talk with friends—albeit carefully monitored by the school workers and their families. Chet Clark further recalls: "If the boys were on their best behavior, they could walk the girls back to the dorms. There had to be lots of chaperones, though; the families [of staff] would go, and they'd even follow you outside, carrying flashlights." The stakes were high, and the potential existed for teen pregnancy or runaway students;

there was no room for error, and school officials could not allow students to move through the campus unsupervised, particularly during the nighttime hours.

The Chemawa Band would occasionally make an appearance at school dances; their primary function was that of icebreaker. As Dee Pigsley explains, "The band always started with a march, like a Sousa march. That's what got the kids mixed up, so the boys didn't all sit on one side of the room." The Chemawa students of the 1940s and '50s may have truly found the marches rousing, or they simply may have been happy for any opportunity for the sexes to mix. Alumni attest to a variety of sentiments regarding the Friday night dances. The main source of dance music, though, often was not the Chemawa Band—its repertoire did not include enough dance music—but a phonograph. As with public schools in general, budgetary circumstances did not often permit the use of live bands (particularly during the war years). Pigsley remembers, "I went every Friday night. We'd dance to records. It was always the same records—nobody spent any money on music then."[49] The fact that she remembers the dances fondly despite the limited musical selections suggests that, for a portion of the students, the dances offered a time for meaningful social interaction and relatively free body movement. As with many other activities at Chemawa, dances could be both mandatory and fun, invoking among the students many of the same responses (excitement, anxiety, apathy) that public high school students may have felt at the prospect of a social dance.

During the 1960s, students of residential schools were increasingly granted more personal freedoms. This was likely a response to the prevailing cultural climate in the United States as a whole, rather than a result of any progressive educational reforms initiated by the BIA; not until the Kennedy Report[50] in 1969 would off-reservation boarding schools embark on a fundamentally revised approach that put the needs of individual students, families, and tribal communities at its center.

Alumni who attended Chemawa in the 1960s report that at school dances, they danced the same popular dance forms that most other American teenagers enjoyed: the mashed potato, the twist, the workout, the watusi. What differed, however, was the public's perception of how Indian youth related to these dance forms. Still viewing Indian people through a lens of primitivism, local townspeople made conjectures relating the perceived wildness of modern dances to the Indian students' tribal cultures. In an article written ostensibly to promote Chemawa's upcoming annual birthday pageant, "Tales from the Moccasin Trail," a reporter for the *Salem Statesman* reporter penned, "The modern youth dances such as the watusi, swim, jerk and workout are nothing new for most students at Chemawa Indian School. Many of the movements and emotional expressions involved in the popular American dances resemble the tribal war dances of the Navajos from

New Mexico-Arizona, and the Thlingits and Athabascans from Alaskan Eskimo tribes, enrolled in the school north of Salem." He further asserts, "The main difference between the native tribal dances and the popular workout seems to be in costumes."[51] To highlight this difference in stark relief, a *Statesman* photographer staged two photos of dancing students. In each, we see the same six students, three boy-girl pairs in two lines. Their arms and postures approximate the same positions in both photos. But in one photo, the boys are dressed in suits and ties, and the girls in skirt-and-sweater sets, all with hair fashionably coifed (figure 17). In the other photo, the students are dancing in the same respective positions and postures, but are wearing different forms of Native regalia (figure 18).

The article depicts the Native dances as safe, non-threatening, infrequent, and presumably of superficial importance, since "without costumes it would be difficult to see any difference between the modern 'workout' dance and the same Chemawa Indian School student doing a tribal dance." Morrison does acknowledge that Chemawa students follow the same trends as other American youth, but underestimates and misrepresents the significance of their tribal dances, both for communities and individuals: "The Chemawa boys and girls follow the rock'n'roll tastes of the nation's youth, leaving the tribal dancing for special occasions such as the school anniversary program Feb. 25-26."

The students (who are not identified by name) did pose for the photographs, and most are smiling in both pictures. It is entirely possible that they understood the nature of the article their photos would accompany, and held no objections to

(Left) Figure 17. Chemawa students dancing the modern "workout" dance. (Right) Figure 18. Chemawa students practicing traditional dances for the annual pageant, February 1965. *Salem Statesman*, Feb. 20, 1965. Courtesy of Charles Holmes.

it. Awareness of the primitivism stereotype was in its infancy, and both Native and non-Native people alike were largely unaware of the ways this prejudiced attitude could be manifested. Beyond assumptions of primitivism, disregarding the sacred significance of tribal dance forms promotes the erroneous and dangerous notion that Native peoples have no religion—that they are "heathens." Early Christian settlers and reformers had used this very notion to justify their violent treatment of Native peoples, when in fact Native societies have always been deeply religious, with inherited beliefs of the sacred pervading innumerable aspects of their lifeways.

Not long after Chemawa students learned the youth dances that enjoyed national popularity during the 1960s, they also began producing the music themselves. Garage bands such as the Meteors (see Chapter 7) emerged on campus during the late 1960s, and part of their official *raison d'être* was to provide music for school dances. Max Lestenkof, guitar player and singer for the Meteors, recalls the contract that the band's faculty advisor, Mr. Blake, struck with the school's administration: "We had a contract with the school, and it stipulated that the band had to play for a school dance on Friday or Saturday. Then, we could take the other night to play a gig off-campus."[52] When asked what their influences were, former Meteors members referred to bands they had opened for, including the Monkees, Paul Revere and the Raiders, and the Young Rascals.[53] In short, the Meteors were a typical—albeit unusually successful—high school rock band of the time, complete with black lights and fluorescent-painted drums.

As Chemawa was in the process of planning the construction of a completely new campus, students and staff alike were looking to adopt new technologies to outfit classrooms and extra-curricular programs. Chemistry and physics laboratories were supplied with the latest equipment, as were the reading laboratory, math classrooms (which featured manual computers), and the printing and vocational shops. Girls dancing at the Junior-Senior prom were photographed with the latest compact personal cameras dangling from their wrists. This embracing of new technologies, when economically possible, does not imply a process of westernization or a discarding of Native ways so much as it speaks to the students' ability to coexist in different worlds and to integrate the material culture they encountered. As Chemawa entered the 1970s, the prom had particular significance as a threshold event in students' progression through high school, and it "signaled the end of another school year."[54] All the while, a growing resurgence of tribal dance forms and intertribal gatherings would soon render Chemawa's May pow-wow (see Chapter 8) a more potent signal of "the end of another school year."

Today at Chemawa, school dances remain an ongoing part of campus life. Their frequency has varied from weekly to biweekly to monthly, and attendance (which was compulsory as late as the 1950s) has long been elective. Still, a large portion of Chemawa students continue to attend the American youth ritual that is the high school dance. The school maintains numerous rules pertaining to the dances, stipulating appropriate behavior, proper dress, and who is allowed to attend. Some of these guidelines are typical of any high school, such as the rule regarding attendance: "Full day of school attendance is required to participate in extra-curricular activities (field trips, off-campus and evening activities)." Other guidelines are more particular to community life in a boarding school setting, as is evident in the Chemawa's list of "Student Responsibilities"[55]:

- Follow the Daily Schedule
- Maximize educational and social potential
- Carry student ID card at all times
- Complete details as assigned and maintain a clean/orderly living environment
- Attend scheduled dormitory and program meetings
- Follow established check-out/check-in procedures for on-campus and off-campus activities
- Use appropriate language; swearing and/or vulgar language is unacceptable
- Maintain acceptable standard in personal hygiene and care of clothing
- Displays of affection should be appropriate to the situation and environment
- Follow procedures regarding the cultural use of tobacco
- Keep all medical appointments
- Conduct yourself in a respectful manner to other students and staff
- Attend all scheduled classes and/or groups
- Complete all assigned homework and otherwise maintain the primary purpose of completing high school while at Chemawa

Confronted with problems of gangs and violence, most American high schools have grappled with implementing dress codes that are useful while not infringing too greatly on students' personal expression, and Chemawa is no different in this regard. The following prohibitions comprise Chemawa's "Personal Appearance and Dress Code":[56]

- Any clothing or jewelry, including buckle or items with gang symbols, nicknames, weapons, drug/alcohol references, profanity, or obscene language. Hairnets, skullcaps and bandanas of any color are not permitted. This does not prohibit use of these items for sports, as deemed appropriate by the individual coach.

- Clothing that is predominantly a solid color (particularly red and blue)—including shirts, belts, shoelaces and pants (blue jeans are ok).
- Apparel, jewelry, accessory, notebook or manner of grooming that, by virtue of its color arrangement, trademark or any other attribute, are specifically identifiable as belonging to a disruptive group or gang.
- Graffiti or gang-related symbols, including gang nicknames, drawings, or lettering on clothing, notebooks, backpacks, or assignments.
- Any clothing or item with racial put downs, sexually demeaning pictures, words, numbers or sexual innuendo.
- Pant legs should be worn evenly and not drag on the ground.
- Belts are to be worn in belt loops. No part of the belt should be left hanging.
- Clothing such as halter tops, tube tops, muscle shirts, sagging pants, backless tops/dresses, or revealing clothing that exposes inappropriate areas including undergarments.
- Chains such as security, wallet, and dog chains.
- Metal spiked clothing or accessory items are not permitted.
- Hoods are not to be worn on the head while in the building or in class.

If anything, these codes are more stringent and specific than those of a typical public school. This is in part because they can be (boarding school administrators are granted more latitude than regular public school administrators in devising and implementing policy), and because a sizable percentage of today's Chemawa students have a past history of gang affiliation, brushes with the law, drug use, and early sexual activity. Over the past thirty years, previous common reasons for attending Chemawa (e.g., a lack of public schools near their villages; family tradition) have been augmented by the increasingly acute reality of students from broken homes who come to Chemawa as a last resort.

Paradoxically, a guiding principle of Chemawa Indian School staff members is the maintenance of "a deep respect for individual differences." Strict dress codes aside, the Chemawa staff strives to utilize students' individual characteristics to further their authentic growth and development. The Kennedy Report found that Native students often dropped out of school because of cultural disintegration, and that the most common suggestion offered by students' parents was that "schools should pay more attention to the Indian heritage."[57] Thus the "individual differences" alluded to in Chemawa policies include tribal lifeways, and the school administration explicitly asserts that "through our own experiences, we realize that Indian culture has a long history of positively influencing our children's beliefs, values and goals."[58] Hence the policies of dress and behavior that might seem draconian can best be understood as part of a larger approach that seeks to keep the students safe, while honoring and utilizing the unique traits of the individual student.

As with any American high school, there are students who simply prefer not to attend school dances. They view the structured, supervised events as hokey, or they may have anxiety regarding the social norms implicit in school dances, or they don't like the styles of music represented. What differs at Chemawa, however, is that some students—those involved in traditional performing arts—consciously seek an alternative to school dances in the form of local powwows and intertribal gatherings. These students tend to have a combination of self-motivation, individuality, and friends who are similarly independent, and they view the powwows as an alternative, more genuine form of cultural expression that they can connect with at a deeper level. When a school dance approaches and the students learn of a concurrent intertribal event taking place off-campus, they petition their faculty advisor to request a school-sanctioned field trip that they might attend as an alternative to the school dance—an alternative social gathering that they find more meaningful and more fun.[59] Interestingly, school dances also facilitate bonding and resiliency among the students who choose *not* to participate. In devising alternative activities, these students develop a sense of their own independence, and in the process they create group identities that stand in playful yet real opposition to the dominant culture.

Part of Chemawa's mission and philosophy is to promote resiliency in its students, and it defines resiliency as the ability to adapt to changing environmental factors.[60] School dances help to build this resiliency by: 1) providing a social situation that is new to many students; 2) setting aside the space, time, and environment for facilitating relationship building between students, and between students and staff; 3) giving students with structured daily schedules a chance to relax in a less-structured environment. Alumni repeatedly cite school dances as a place where students can "blow off steam," and when one considers the fullness and unceasing regularity of the Student Daily Schedule, the regenerative potential of dances is readily apparent.

STUDENT DAILY SCHEDULE

Regular Wake-Up	6:00 a.m.
Dorms Close / Breakfast	7:30 a.m.
1st Period	8:00 – 9:05 a.m.
2nd Period	9:08 – 10:13 a.m.
3rd Period	10:16 – 11:21 a.m.
Lunch	11:25 a.m. – 12:25 p.m.
Advisory	12:30 – 1:15 p.m.

4th Period	1:18 – 2:23 p.m.
5th Period	2:26 – 3:30 p.m.
Activity Period	3:35 – 4:45 p.m.
Dinner	4:45 – 5:45 p.m.
Study Hour	6:00 – 8:00 p.m.
Curfew	9:00 p.m. (10:00 p.m. on weekends)
Lights Out	10:00 p.m. (11:00 p.m. on weekends)[61]

The 1965 *Salem Statesman* article comparing modern and tribal dance forms illuminates how the general public took comfort in the knowledge that Chemawa students engaged in the American ritual of the high school dance, with all of its concomitant social norms and behavioral expectations. This same audience might be surprised to learn that non-Native social dancing does not lessen students' sense of tribal identity or peoplehood. Rather, it facilitates bonding between students of disparate tribal backgrounds, and allows them to discover their commonalities, to identify with each other, and to learn about their respective cultural ways. In this manner, an institution that was originally implemented as a means of "domesticating" Native Americans has become, paradoxically, a site of Indian persistence.

Chapter 7
Rocking the Northwest: Chemawa's Garage Bands

"What is more American than the garage band?"—Lester Bangs[1]

In the late 1960s, Chemawa experienced the advent of student-run bands taking a form that has since come to be known as "garage rock." Now regarded as a specific genre that thrived during the period 1963-1967 and resurfaced in later incarnations, "garage rock" can also more loosely refer to the phenomenon of young, amateur musicians creating ensembles that would often rehearse in the family garage. Chemawa's premier garage band, the Meteors, fits both of these definitions, while complicating the commonly held stereotypes of garage bands as white, suburban, and middle class.

The 1950s through the 1970s was a period when popular musical performance was technologically simpler and less expensive than it is now, and young Native people were very active in promoting and exploring their own musical tastes through garage bands.[2] While the musical output of the Meteors was not generally infused with the strident political criticism that was increasingly prevalent in late-1960s popular culture, the band members exerted their voice individually and collectively through their actions more than their words. Forming a band on their own volition with minimal faculty guidance, maintaining a daily discipline of individual practice and group rehearsals, strategically crafting a public image, and seeking off-campus performance opportunities (and their accompanying freedoms) that were heretofore unknown to students of Chemawa—in actions such as these, the Meteors represent an important departure from the earlier student attendees of Chemawa, who did not have the instruments, training, or free time to develop a band that departed this much from the official school-sanctioned curriculum. Just how Chemawa became home to a successful garage band in the first place warrants further explanation.

As a genre, garage rock can be traced to California and the Pacific Northwest in the early 1960s. Along the California coastline, groups that resembled surf bands proliferated, with members wearing clean suits and playing Fender guitars while writing songs that revealed their cynicism and disillusionment with the politeness and inauthenticity they perceived in modern society. Further north, bands like the

Sonics (Seattle), the Kingsmen (Portland), and Paul Revere and the Raiders (Boise/ Portland) emerged with energetic, polysemic songs like "Louie Louie" (recorded by all three bands).

As a Pacific Northwest band that found success on both a regional and national level, Paul Revere and the Raiders bear special mention. Innovators in many ways, they were known for theatrical performances that sometimes bordered on anarchy, replete with goofy stunts and flamboyant costumes. Playing on Paul Revere's name, they presented themselves as the American response to the British invasion, complete with Revolutionary War uniforms. While their stage antics and coordinated appearance were sometimes at odds with the more hard-edged sound of their music, it was this keen sense of showmanship that helped them to achieve commercial success at the national level. In 1963 they became the first rock-and-roll band to be signed to Columbia Records, the largest record label in the world at the time. Soon afterwards, they became the first rock band to have their own television show, "Where the Action Is," a variety show that ran during 1965-1967 on ABC. It was followed by two other shows hosted by Paul Revere and Michael Lindsay, the band's lead singer: "Happening '68" (a Saturday follow-up to American Bandstand) and "It's Happening" (a weekday version that ran during 1968-1969).[3]

Many minor garage bands were primarily live bands, not actively engaged in recording. For those who did attempt to make records, recordings ran the gamut from extreme simplicity or crudeness to near-studio quality. In his characterization of garage bands as proto-punk, rock critic Lester Bangs attests that "virtuosity has nothing to do with the form" and that the ubiquity of the garage band stands as "the ultimate proof that rock & roll is the most democratic and all-American of art forms."[4] During the mid- to late-1960s, thousands of garage bands appeared throughout the U.S. and Canada, facilitated by accessibly priced electric guitars and motivated by the utopian dream of "everyman an artist."[5]

Several dozen of these bands produced recordings that achieved considerable commercial success. A sampling of garage band hits from 1966 reveals the variety of sounds encompassed by the ostensibly simple garage-band genre: "96 Tears" by ? [Question Mark] and the Mysterians, "Double Shot of My Baby's Love" by the Swingin' Medallions, "Psychotic Reaction" by the Count Five, "Kicks" by Paul Revere and the Raiders, and "Talk Talk" by the Music Machine. Lyrics often addressed the traumas of high school life, and since garage bands constituted a predominantly male genre, "lying girls" appeared frequently; the Castaways' "Liar, Liar" (1965) exemplified this wider trend.

For students at Chemawa, garage rock remained just as accessible (to perform and to attend) as it had been in the home communities from which they hailed. Garage bands had already formed in villages before the students knew they were coming to Chemawa, and when students who had played together arrived at school in Oregon, forming a modified version of their village band was natural. By remaining a constant activity even when the students' living environments had been radically altered, the garage band became an instrument of stability, tempering homesickness and facilitating social bonds—both new and old—between students.

The administration at Chemawa encouraged this bonding through music, allowing the bands to practice and perform on campus but stipulating that their activities must be supervised. Bands were assigned faculty members who acted as advisors or managers, and the school required that invitations to perform be carefully considered with due regard for propriety, the students' safety, and Chemawa's reputation. The faculty advisors functioned as liaisons between the bands and the school, as well as between the bands as potential clients, negotiating all aspects of off-campus performances including curfews, compensation, and adult supervision. When they were granted permission to perform off-campus, the bands in turn entered into written contracts with Chemawa, agreeing to perform for a comparable number of on-campus events as well.

As we have seen, the Chemawa group that consistently achieved the most public visibility and recognition during the garage band era was the Meteors. Active from the mid-1960s to early 1970s, the Meteors was a five-piece all-student band known for playing popular music that was current and danceable. The Meteors experienced several personnel changes as veteran members graduated from high school and other students matriculated in to replace them, yet the students' musical competence rendered them a strong public presence in Oregon throughout the lifetime of the band.

One of the band's key guitar players and singers was Max Lestenkof (Aleut).[6] Lestenkof was born on St. George, one of the Pribilof Islands in the Bering Sea, with a population of 102 as of the 2010 census. Soon after Max's birth, the family moved to the larger nearby island town of St. Paul (population 479), because his father, an Orthodox priest, needed airplane access for the traveling required for his work. Lestenkof remained in Alaska until 1966, when he entered Chemawa and attended school there continuously until his graduation in 1969 at age nineteen. He recalls that of the school's approximately one thousand students at that time, most were Alaska Natives and Navajos. When Lestenkof came to Chemawa, other students from his family and home community enrolled there as well. These included his younger brother Phillip, who would eventually take over as the drummer for the band.

Several bands were active at Chemawa at that time, including a Navajo band, a beginners' band that functioned as a feeder band for the Meteors, and the Meteors (see figure 19). The Meteors had already been established before Lestenkof's

Figure 19. The original Meteors: John Hensley on guitar, Alferd Andre on keyboard, Max Lestenkof on vocals with tambourine, Victor Lekanof on drums, Jack Alec on guitar, and Ted McGlashen on bass guitar. Courtesy of Max Lestenkof.

arrival, and because of his pre-existing relationships with the band members from St. Paul, Alaska, he was able to walk into the band upon his enrollment at Chemawa. Though he arrived knowing the guitar, the band already had a guitar player at that point, so Lestenkof gave himself a crash course on the drums and remained a drummer during his high school years. The instrumentation, typical for a garage band, consisted of drums, lead guitar, rhythm guitar, bass, and sometimes keyboards. Lestenkof sang the lead vocals, and other members supplied back-up vocals. The band members included four Aleuts and one Eskimo: Max Lestenkof on drums, guitar, or keyboards; Phillip Lestenkof later on drums; Lynn Jackson or Ted McGlashan on bass; Bert Merculief on guitar; and one more revolving guitar player. Others who were members of the Meteors in various years included Victor Lekanof (drums), Victor Merculief (guitar and lead singer), Jack Alec (guitar), John Hensley (guitar), and Alfred Andre (keyboards). The band was managed by one of Chemawa's faculty, Mr. Blake; the band was required to play for a school dance every Friday or Saturday but could take the other night off to play a gig off-campus.

The band played mostly cover songs, though Lestenkof wrote two original songs for them. The band members gave special attention to the visual aspects of their performances, and made collective decisions about their showmanship: fluorescent paint was applied to the drums, and black lights were employed to illuminate it. When playing at large, off-campus venues, the band performed in white pants, black boots, and silk Cossack shirts, which created a distinct style that resonated with their regional fan base. Their popularity increased as they competed against other garage bands in a large-scale Battle of the Bands contest, earning them TV spots, radio segments, and a sponsorship by 7-Up. Concert organizers sought them as an opening act for local bands and touring bands alike, and eventually they booked performances through EJD Enterprises, a company that promoted concerts in Portland. After forming a relationship with EJD, they opened for such groups as the Monkees, Paul Revere and the Raiders, and the Young Rascals. Even though they were based at a Salem boarding school, the opportunities for performance and public exposure that the Meteors found in Oregon far exceeded any prospects they might have found in Alaska.

Band members chose not to use their Indian identity as a selling point, preferring instead to rely on their musicianship skills and their rock-band showmanship. There was no attempt to hide or downplay their Indianness (a different tack from earlier Chemawa musician Spade Cooley; see Chapter 4); instead, the choice not to foreground their Indian identity was born out of the band members' strong focus on the music itself. When recalling the band today, Lestenkof dismisses the idea of employing Indianness for his stage presence, explaining, "I couldn't base it on what color I was, on being Native or anything." That said, Lestenkof did have a definite personal sense of his identity as an Aleut while at Chemawa, and of the unique historical position of the Aleuts that set them apart from such Native groups as the Navajos, who also featured prominently in Chemawa's population. He recalls the scarcity of traditional practices that the Aleut students brought with them to Chemawa: "The Navajos had their ceremonies. The Aleuts didn't bring much in the way of dances and rituals . . . they had been the slaves of the federal government, and they were just trying to survive." The U.S. government and various fur companies had long used the Aleut people for seal harvesting, relocating them at will and denying them access to sufficient food, clothing, and housing. When racial segregation was at its height during World War II, government officials moved the Pribilof Aleuts fifteen hundred miles away to Funter Bay, confining them to an abandoned cannery and mine camp. Though allegedly done to protect the Aleuts from the fighting taking place in Alaska's distant western islands, the relocation was conducted haphazardly, with a lack of provisions for health and sanitation that led to the deaths of one in ten internees. Those who did survive returned to their villages after the war to find their homes and churches looted and decaying from the elements.[7] Families today are still healing from the effects of this dislocation and assault, and many Aleut communities are now engaged in processes of deliberate cultural rebuilding. When Max Lestenkof attended Chemawa in the 1960s, however, attempts by the Aleut people to reclaim their traditional culture were just beginning, and many Alaska Native families were still focusing their energies on their basic survival.

Playing in the Meteors was life changing for Lestenkof for a number of reasons that were not always strictly musical. He recounts meeting his high-school sweetheart, Roseanne, who would later become his wife: "I met my first wife through playing in the band. She was Sioux, and she went to Sacred Heart—it was a Catholic all-girls school. She was on a committee to hire a band for a school event, and she heard the Meteors when we played at the Battle of the Bands. So she started sitting in on practices."[8] After they graduated from high school, Max and Roseanne went on to get married and have five children together. Eventually they divorced, but they still remain good friends today, both taking an active role in parenting their children, even now as the children enter into adulthood themselves.

Lestenkof believes that "You make a complete circle in life when you play music," and nowhere is this more evident than in his transmission of his craft to his son. Now in his late twenties, his son Max plays guitar in a Eugene, Oregon blues-rock band called Feel Good Remedy. After graduation from high school in Oregon, Max, Jr., moved up to Alaska for a period where he played gigs with his father, but he eventually returned to his home environs in Oregon to continue pursuing music. At age eighteen, he played as an opening act for well-known bands just as his father had, and Lestenkof supports his son's music endeavors enthusiastically.

Lestenkof (senior) still plays guitar today himself, for both paid and unpaid gigs, sometimes as a soloist and sometimes with a band. He has played for Alaska Federation of Natives events, University of Alaska at Anchorage campus gatherings, Chemawa alumni reunions, and on the general Anchorage club circuit. In addition to his live performances, which typically draw from a wide repertoire of cover songs, Lestenkof has written original pieces as well, and his work has appeared in films about Alaska's history and culture, including *Amiq: The Aleut People of the Pribilof Islands, a Culture in Transition*,[9] which chronicles the Pribilof Aleut culture in transition from sealing to fishing, and *Peter Picked a Seal Stick: The Fur Seal Harvest of the Pribilof Islands*,[10] an ethnographic film about the commercial fur seal harvest.

Lestenkof now works as the Community Wellness Advocate for the Aleutian Pribilof Islands Association; a nonprofit tribal organization of the Aleut people, it provides services related to cultural heritage, health, education, employment, vocational training, the environment, natural resources, and public safety. Lestenkof credits music with aiding his own recovery from alcoholism, and he uses it to promote wellness in the community, especially for elderly people. After having held a variety of jobs around Alaska and the Northwest, Lestenkof feels that this is the best job he has ever had, in part because it allows him to use his musical abilities to help others. By making music an integral part of his wellness and recovery work, Lestenkof again affirms his assertion that "You make a complete circle in life when you play music."

In several ways, Max Lestenkof's story is typical of other Chemawa garage band members of his era: he learned an instrument before attending Chemawa, honed his skills after enrolling at school by playing with friends, found opportunities for professional development that would not have existed in his community of origin, and continued to make music publicly long after his time at Chemawa. The Meteors' bass player, Ted McGlashan, followed a similar path.

Like Lestenkof, McGlashan (Aleut) has a connection to St. Paul Island, having been born there in 1948. McGlashan's family, however, soon moved to a much smaller community: Akutan, on the second island of the Aleutian chain, as the islands are counted from the east. With a population of about ninety people in the 1950s, and no radio or television in the village, McGlashan's early musical training came solely from old timers who played the accordion and the guitar. Ted picked up the guitar and played the music he heard around him, which consisted mostly of Scandinavian tunes, since whaling, fishing, and cannery operations had brought an influx of Scandinavian and other European fishermen in the early 1900s. Developing his musicianship skills within this soundscape, McGlashan spent his first jam sessions playing polkas and schottisches.

When he was old enough to attend high school, McGlashan applied to Mt. Edgecumbe in Sitka, a boarding school for Alaska Natives. Enrollment was full, so he decided to wait a year and apply again. When the following school year (1965) arrived and Mt. Edgecumbe was still full, the school informed McGlashan that the boarding school in Chemawa, Oregon, was accepting students. Having already missed a year of school, he decided to pack his bags and venture to Oregon.

His journey to Chemawa foreshadowed how he would stand out visually for his fair skin. He recalls leaving Akutan in late September: "It was pretty cold, so I had a new down parka—a warm one. Once I got to Anchorage, I flew from Anchorage to Portland, and [when I got there] it was like 90 degrees! I took off my parka. Then I sat in the terminal building for an hour and a half, almost two hours." McGlashan had been told to wait there for his ride to Chemawa. "There was a guy who was circling around, and eventually he approached me. He knew he was supposed to pick up an Indian kid, and he had been looking for someone darker skinned. The only reason he came up to me was because I was carrying my parka. I'd seen him walking back and forth, but I didn't know him from Adam."[11]

Once on campus, McGlashan soon connected with other students from the St. Paul area, and they asked him to play with their band, the Meteors. McGlashan characterizes the Meteors as essentially a four-piece band, with lead guitar, rhythm guitar, bass guitar, and drums. Most of their songs had vocals, and everybody sang. Initially, there was no bass player, and no one perceived a need for one. This would soon change, in response to developments on the national popular music scene. McGlashan explains, "At first, I played the six-string guitar. Then the Beatles came along, and the bass guitar was a big thing. In 1967, we all pitched in to buy a bass guitar, and no one wanted to play it." McGlashan was open to learning new skills. "So I picked it up, and I realized it was like a six-string, only with two of the strings gone, and instead of strumming chords, you'd just pluck one note at a time. And it just plays along with the beat of the drums. It gave us our full sound."

The band would sometimes include a fifth player in the form of a keyboardist—fellow student Alfred Andre played with the band briefly, but soon after joining, he fell in love. His priorities shifted, and he was eventually let go by the band in 1967. McGlashan speaks compassionately and empathetically of personnel changes, pointing out that many of the band members went on to form lasting relationships (often marriages) with girls they met at Chemawa: "We all eventually fell in love, and let our music slide a bit." It was during his time at Chemawa that McGlashan met another student, Rosemary, who would later become his wife. Rosemary recalls having an initial attraction to Ted's red hair: "One day I was at the place where kids would meet for sodas after school, and the sun was shining down on him, on that red hair. And I thought to myself, 'My god, that's beautiful!' I had never seen spun gold like that."[12] Both Ted and Rosemary credit Chemawa with their later successes, both personally and professionally; Rosemary went on to have four careers, in commercial fishing, secretarial work, helicopters, and certified caregiving, the last of which she has found the most rewarding.

McGlashan's career choices would be deeply influenced by his positive experiences playing with the Meteors while at Chemawa. After playing for many gigs in the area around Salem, including performing in the six-thousand-seat Salem Armory Auditorium, the Meteors were received well at the Battle of the Bands and proceeded to the Portland finals. McGlashan recalls, "It was in '67, or maybe '68, that the Battle of the Bands was in Portland. There were twelve or thirteen bands, and it was jam-packed. We were the fourth band up [to play]." The Meteors had one competitor in particular. "There was a band from Portland that was like our rival band; they were called 'Gentlemen Wild.' They won the Battle of the Bands, and then they went to the East Coast for the big Battle of the Bands, and they lost big time."

The exposure that the Meteors gained through playing at the Battle would lead to later engagements, including one on an area television show, *This Is It*.

The show featured a variety of dance bands playing for an enthusiastic throng of teenage dancers. McGlashan recalls how surprised the band was to find that the dancers would not be working live with them as the show was recorded: "We had gone up to Portland—it was kinda like *American Bandstand*, in those days. We went to the studio on a Thursday, and they taped us, and then had us lip-sync to our own music." There was no audience; a crowd was filmed later. "Then they taped a bunch of dancers, separately, about forty or fifty dancers, and combined the footage together, so it looked like it was all happening at one time. And it aired on a Saturday night."

The Meteors played some originals, but in the fashion of late 1960s garage bands, they played many cover songs, and they distinguished themselves by the sheer number of covers that they knew well. McGlashan describes their repertoire as "the Top 40 songs from the late '60s—now they call it classic rock, but as far as I'm concerned, it was the original rock music. We played things like 'Midnight Hour,' 'Gloria,' 'Mustang Sally,' 'Louie Louie'... We had a good repertoire of about fifty songs." In pursuing the repertoire they most enjoyed playing and felt an affinity for, the Meteors demonstrate how indigenous identity cannot be located simply in forms that outsiders recognize as distinctly Native or traditional. Anthropologist David W. Samuels has explored similar processes when describing garage bands of the San Carlos Apache Reservation. Samuels argues that ambiguity is crucial to an understanding of creative cultural expression, and that contemporary music forms such as country, rock, or reggae can enable Native people to perform and circulate contemporary music in ways that connect them to history, place, and each other.[13] In other words, Indianness can be marked by styles, customs, and music that are adapted from general American culture, rather than from stereotypic (or actual) pre-colonial lifeways.

There were various personnel changes during the life of the band; in addition to Max Lestenkof, McGlashan remembers Victor Lacana, John Hensley on lead guitar (he was the first to graduate, in 1966), John Aleck on guitar, Victor Merculief on rhythm guitar (he would later become the mayor of St. Paul and president of the Native Corporation), and Victor Merculief's younger brother, Bert, who later filled in on guitar. A new group of younger students tried to keep the band going after the key members graduated, but by the early 1970s the band had lost its edge, and could not land the high-profile gigs it once had. McGlashan explains, with humility, "We were a very tough act to follow, because of what we did for the school."

The public exposure and positive publicity that the Meteors gave to Chemawa is hard to quantify. In the late 1960s, overt anti-Indian prejudice was still rampant in Oregon's Willamette Valley, and many students first encountered racism while living at Chemawa, in their interactions with the Salem-area community. In McGlashan's experience, the prejudice he witnessed was not a part of the campus culture, but was a local phenomenon among some non-Indian youths: "Sometimes there'd be a special concert in town, and Mr. Matt would take us [the band] separately, in a car, and other kids would come too, in the school bus that said 'Chemawa Indian High School' on the side." The students in Mr. Matt's car would arrive first, before those traveling in the bus. "I remember standing in line [outside the concert venue], and hearing a bunch of white kids making Indian noises when the bus would pull up. That was the first time I encountered prejudice." Unlike McGlashan's home state of Alaska, Oregon had strident anti-miscegenation laws banning Blacks, Native Americans, Asians, and Native Hawaiians from marrying whites. These laws (one barometer of the severity of racism) were in effect from 1862 to 1951, only a decade before McGlashan's attendance at Chemawa. Despite the ugliness and potential harmfulness of such encounters as the school bus incident, McGlashan did not express having felt scarred by the encounter but rather conveyed a sense of sadness over the situation.

The saddening discovery of the stereotypes that many non-Natives had towards Indian peoples was counterbalanced by the numerous cross-cultural ties McGlashan formed while at school. The late 1960s was a time when Chemawa primarily focused on serving Navajo and Alaska Natives, and the coming together of disparate Indian groups represented at Chemawa was one of the school's strengths: "There were Navajo guys and gals there then, and I dormed with some Navajo guys. I asked them, 'What part of Alaska are you from,' because to me they looked like they were from Alaska, and they laughed. The Navajo kids, they pretty much kept to themselves. Overall they were pretty nice people; they just had their own thing, you know." McGlashan bears witness to the healing power of connections made with classmates: "It was sad to leave our parents at a crucial time in our lives. But [it was bearable] once I realized there were kids from Alaska there, and other kids from Unalaska . . . One thing I liked, there were kids from all over Alaska. So now, when I travel, I know people, whether it's in Bethel, or Point Barrow, or whatever village I go to."[14]

Ultimately, McGlashan chose to leave Oregon upon graduation and return home to train with the U.S. Weather Service. Marrying Rosemary right out of high school and starting a family, he worked as a weatherman for the next eleven years, stationed at intervals in Yakutat, Cold Bay, McGrath, Fairbanks, and Kodiak. In every town, he played in the weekend band, and he eventually quit the job to travel to Nashville, where he cut two country music records. When the band in which McGlashan was playing did not find professional success, the McGlashans returned to Alaska, where Ted embarked on a career as a professional musician, playing the nightclub circuit. His ex-wife Rosemary (the couple divorced in November of 1982) recalls this as a difficult time, but the family persevered, with Ted and Rosemary both raising their son and daughter. The children each grew up to pursue satisfying careers in Alaska, and both have delved into music as a hobby (their daughter with the violin, and their son with the guitar).

While supporting a family on a musician's income was not easy, McGlashan carved out a regular position for which he became legendary. It all started when he honed his vocal skills, began singing on stage more, and grew confident enough to start his own band. A gig opening up the Native Corporation bar in King Cove led to what would be a life-changing position in Unalaska, also known as Dutch Harbor. McGlashan recollects, "I had my own band in Dutch Harbor. I was a singer and bass player, and I hired three or four other musicians, and we stayed in a band trailer there. That's how my son learned guitar, and these guys knew a lot. I called the band 'Gentlemen Wild,' because I always hoped someone from our old rival band would call." The environment they played and lived in was coarse and colorful. "We played at the Elbowroom Bar—it was rated in some national article as the number two or number three roughest bar in the country, and we could never figure that out; the guys would get off the boats; they'd been out on the boats for a few weeks, and they were ready to fight. But the waitresses there, they were all women." The community at Dutch Harbor was eager for good live music, and they welcomed the band enthusiastically. "Before we came down there, they just had a jukebox. I talked to a friend who ran the bar about playing there, and we got there around one or two in the afternoon one day, pulled up with everything on a flatbed, and all the local folks were there, waiting to help us unload. We weren't going to play until later that night, but they wanted us to play right away, so we did a few songs right then. They loved it, and we ended up staying for ten years." The band's success no doubt stemmed from their ability to play the genres that were fitting for the disparate audience: "You get a great variety of people out there, working out there for crab season. There's young workers [and they like certain music], and then there's old skippers, and they always wanted country. We played all kinds of music—some old country songs, some ZZ Top, Steve Miller Band, even a couple polkas and schottisches."

Just as at Chemawa, the lack of urban diversions had a powerful impact on shaping the band's make-up, both in terms of personnel and with regards to the interpersonal dynamics between the band members. McGlashan went to great lengths to recruit versatile musicians, striving to include special instruments such as the mandolin, dobro, and fiddle. The lure of the fishing life has sometimes served as a distraction that gradually enticed band members away, but just as often it has served as an attractive force for musicians who chose to relocate to Dutch Harbor from the city. McGlashan hooked versatile string player Andy McCracken right away by taking him on a fishing excursion in his skiff, where they quickly landed a 180-pound halibut; McCracken then stayed with the band for more than six years. The unexpected events that can characterize harsh and beautiful areas such as Unalaska also helped make Gentlemen Wild a satisfying gig for musicians, and locals still recall island-escapist singer-songwriter Jimmy Buffet arriving incognito one weekend to do some fishing and then joining in with the band for a Monday night jam session.

McGlashan has brought his music to many remote parts of Alaska, but recalls few gigs more meaningful than returning home to play for Akutan Founders' Day: "I got a call from my hometown, and I went back to play for Akutan Founder's Day. My aunt runs the beer joint [The Roadhouse] there, and they were raising money for the local church." Getting to Akutan did not prove easy. "It was the Fourth of July, and all the planes had broken down that weekend, but we found an oil survey crew with a chopper and we talked them into giving us a ride. We had the drum set, our amplifiers, and all the instruments crammed into that thing, with us guys perched on top." During the course of the weekend, McGlashan was struck by how far life had taken him from his roots in Akutan. "It was a weird feeling, going back and not knowing any of the kids there. When I lived there, I was like one of those kids. There's an old song called 'There's A Stranger in My Hometown,' and I thought about writing a song called, 'I'm A Stranger in My Hometown.' " It had been a difficult journey home, but McGlashan deemed the reception the band received in the village to be well worth it.[15] A testament to the deeply embedding nature of local identity, McGlashan's strong feelings about bringing his music back to his hometown also show the power of convergent moments in a person's life, where the skills and experiences they have gained in other locations are integrated or synthesized with their relationship to their home community.

Just as he recalls with gratitude the relationships formed with other Alaska students during his time at Chemawa, McGlashan speaks of the relationships developed through his years of playing as one of the most important aspects of his career. Now living with emphysema, McGlashan plays less often, but he still does events for Native corporations, and he is considered a friend of crab fishermen throughout the far reaches of Alaska.

Of his high school days, McGlashan speaks openly about homesickness and not being overly excited about his studies. But his voice lightens when he speaks of practicing with the band: "We had a homeroom class that was from three to four p.m. The school would allow us to take that hour to play in the gym. They'd let us rehearse then, because of what we were doing for the school. Oh, I'll tell you, we couldn't wait for three o'clock to roll around! I loved music so much. That was the only thing that kept me going back there." It was this exuberance, competency, and stage experience that McGlashan would draw on for all his later work. By allowing a group of students to pursue their passion for music, Chemawa laid the foundation for such later professional successes as that lived out by Ted McGlashan.

Though the genre known as garage rock refers specifically to a style that was prominent in the mid-1960s, garage bands in the more general sense—ad hoc hobbyist groups whose raw sound sets them apart from the slickness and polish of commercially produced rock[16]—are again alive and well at Chemawa, after over twenty years where the Meteors had no comparable successor.[17] Though no subsequent band has matched the longevity or off-campus popularity of the Meteors, today's students continue to learn their favorite songs, play together, and occasionally write their own music.

Several similarities exist between Chemawa's first garage bands and the more loosely organized garage bands of today. Today's garage band musicians are still mostly male; this may be due in part to the continued preponderance of male musicians functioning as role models in the rock music industry. At Chemawa, this gender difference may be further pronounced due to the gender norms in some tribal communities—and in mainstream society—regarding appropriate forms of public behavior for females. School counselor Karen Graham points to the significance Native cultures accord to public speaking of any kind: "For Native American kids, getting up in front of people is really a big thing. They don't want to get noticed."[18] When these reservations about getting up in public are combined with non-Native society's restrictive constructions of female decorum, it's not surprising that most female students at Chemawa simply aren't interested in playing in a garage band.

As was true of the Meteors, the students who play rock music at Chemawa today are highly self-motivated, driven by their love of the music and the meanings they derive from it. Students alight on songs that resonate with the truth of their own life experiences, and performing arts instructor Warner Austin relates students' use of iPods and other electronic devices to pore over their favorite songs, listening to them repeatedly, learning the words, and figuring out the music by ear.[19] Though some sociologists contest the usefulness of rock as a functional site of political discourse,[20] many young people at Chemawa, coming from families and tribal communities that continue to suffer the profound effects of material and cultural dispossession, develop an abiding interest in counter-cultural messages that challenge the status quo. For these students, rock music styles continue to offer the possibility of authentic social opposition, particularly through the music of Native rock artists like Indigenous, Blackfire, and Casper Loma Da Wa. Moreover, students' ability to play and create the music themselves is a way to more stridently claim those messages as their own.

To the degree that today's student bands at Chemawa are not as organized, long lasting, or professionally successful as the Meteors, there are several differences between today's Chemawa students and those of the late 1960s: the amount of prior training, favored genres, and access to instruments. Current students are more likely to have grown up with substance abuse problems and/or with discontinuity in their living situations than those in previous generations; thus, while some do have mp3 players and portable stereos, students typically arrive at school with very little musical training and no instruments of their own. The plethora of genres in current popular music has made tastes and preferences more specific than ever, and there is no longer a single common repertoire of popular music with which all students become familiar during their time in high school. Also, as counselor Karen Graham explains, "Kids from reservations and small cities don't show up with instruments. Even if they've played instruments, they don't own them, and they don't have the money to buy them.[21] So, for whatever rock-music explorations students do want to make while at Chemawa, they are at the mercy of using a small selection of guitars that have been donated to the school.

Funding problems are a persistent issue at Chemawa, and support for music has occasionally been provided alternatively through the outreach efforts of local musical organizations. One recent collaboration involved blues guitarist the Original Snakeboy.[22] Brought to Chemawa through the Cascade Blues Association's Blues in the Schools (BITS) program, the Original Snakeboy led an interactive "blues evening" assembly and donated a guitar to the school, which guitarists on the Chemawa staff have used for tutoring sessions with interested students. The Cascade Blues Association has also provided a guest instructor, Mark Lemhouse, to give five ninety-minute instruction sessions on campus and to lead another assembly. Miguel Loredo Reyes, a Home Living Specialist at Chemawa, attests that the students responded enthusiastically, and photos from the first "Blues Evening" were posted on the BITS feedback website.[23] For the past three years, Emily Dickey, a recent graduate of nearby Willamette University, has facilitated the recording of Chemawa students at Willamette's recording studio and the production of Chemawa music CDs. Electric guitars have also been donated by the Native rock band Red Thunder, whose mission of promoting dignified images of Native Americans to the world at large has led them to support student-generated music in BIA schools. After Chemawa received the guitars in 2005, a Guitar Club developed, and it has become one of the courses offered by Chemawa during the final hour of the school day.[24] Guitar is again an official sixth-period elective, not because of the good publicity a successful student band is giving the school, but because of the combined efforts of concerned outside groups and a current school administration that recognizes the real personal growth and self-development that can come with musical competency.

When cultural studies theorists consider rock music performance and youth identity, they typically allow that youth is inflected by race, gender, ethnicity, sexuality, class, and spatial location, but they do not have the student rock musicians of Chemawa in mind, and they fail to address what forms a developing voice might take for Native youths specifically.[25] For Chemawa students, Native identity is likely to be manifested in the mood and feeling of contemporary music, and in a distinctive shared understanding of the music they develop with their peers. While Chemawa's garage band members may not articulate their interest in music in terms of politics, they are taking the first steps towards being political actors by finding their voices through creating collaborative student-generated music. If the alumni of the Meteors are any example, the focus, musicianship, self-knowledge, confidence, and public ease they acquire will be valuable for themselves as individuals and potentially for their tribal communities.

Chapter 8
Powwow: Chemawa Students Dancing, Drumming, and Hosting

"It's not enough to be able to sing a good song. You practice, develop your voice, you have dedication; it has to be quality. But it's important to *live* a good song . . . How to do this—that's the path of a singer."

—Arlie Neskahi, Chemawa counselor and musician, 2005 interview

In the years following World War II, when Indian groups welcomed returning veterans, the powwow assumed its modern form, and it has become one of the most popular and visible expressions of the cultural forces at work in Indian country.[1] Whether held on or off reservations and in urban or rural settings, powwows provide a vital way for Native peoples to gather with regularity. Most powwows combine both tribally specific and intertribal practices, and they are a means by which many groups construct and maintain their identities. More than any other form of music making at Chemawa, powwows have offered a healing counter-force to the generations of cultural hegemony imposed upon boarding school students, their families, and their tribal communities. By bringing people together and creating a space for shared ritual and honest conversation, powwows provide a way for the school itself to play an active role in healing and reconciliation.

One of the early comprehensive and insightful explorations of the function of powwows is Gloria Alese Young's unpublished dissertation on Oklahoma powwows, "Powwow Power: Perspectives on Historic and Contemporary Intertribalism" (1981). Young explains that the powwow is an event built on an overarching philosophy of "Indianness." Through this, it does the complex cultural work of integrating the members of many disparate cultures into, at a supra-tribal level, one identity; establishing symbolic boundaries between kinds of people (Indians/non-Indians, conservative/modern) and geographic regions; and raising the quality of life of its participants through improved mental health and social contacts.[2] The powwow's role in maintaining old ways and introducing new ones is critical to the interrelated processes of identity formation, cultural creation and preservation, and the promotion of personal wellness. Subsequent authors including Clyde Ellis, Luke Eric Lassiter, Loretta Fowler, and R. D. Theisz have confirmed Young's characterization of "powwows as identity performances," an approach that has come to replace earlier pan-Indianist methods that mistakenly assumed that sharing between cultures would necessarily eliminate tribal distinctiveness.[3]

The implications for off-reservation boarding schools are particularly important, as students forge and deepen friendships with classmates and visiting guests, build their on- and off-campus communities, cultivate their sense of self-worth, profit from mentor relationships, and develop their sense of "Indianness" and personal identity. For Chemawa specifically, powwows have offered the students critical opportunities to build supportive ties with local Northwestern Indian communities, including the Umatilla, Grand Ronde, and Siletz. This has allowed the tribes to monitor the students' well-being, and to provide resources for special needs that arise at the school. For example, it was not the BIA but the Affiliated Northwest Tribes who in 1976 decided that Chemawa needed a new campus infrastructure; the following year, they secured $10 million from the House Interior Appropriations Subcommittee to begin construction of the new campus.[4] More recently, the "Executive Order on American Indian and Alaska Native Education" signed by President Bill Clinton in 1998 has explicitly directed each agency participating in Indian education to consult with tribal governments on their education-related needs and priorities—including the transmission of tribal lifeways and forms of cultural expression.[5]

The earliest school-sanctioned "powwow" events consisted of gatherings that resembled actual Native powwows in name only. Students at Chemawa began attending events dubbed "powwows" in the early 1930s, shortly after the reforms recommended in the Meriam Report were implemented. As organized extracurricular activities, these trips were supervised by faculty or staff members and typically lasted a day or a weekend and included an overnight stay. The earliest evidence of such a trip dates from April of 1930, when Chemawa's Friendly Indian Club—a club designed by assimilation-minded school officials for the youngest male students to explore Indian culture in ways that were non-threatening to the greater public and to the schools' "civilizing" mission—attended a powwow at Camp Collins, a YMCA camp on the Sandy River, just east of Portland. This "powwow" may have been simply a youth gathering, not sponsored by any Native group, and something more akin to a Boy Scout camp. A faculty chaperone reported, "Some boy from Portland questioned whether we were all real Indians—a few freckles and blue eyes among us gave room for doubt."[6] Evidently, the boys of Chemawa's Friendly Indian Club were able to educate a segment of the non-Indian world about what real Indians can look like.

By the late 1930s, Chemawa faculty were organizing "powwows" for their students, though the term seems to have been used quite generally to cover any festive gathering held for relaxation and attended by Indian people. Accounts of the "Full Day Powwow" held to commemorate Chemawa's birthday in February of 1938 describe a social hour, athletic competitions, cake, and a dance.[7] It is not clear whether family members or representatives of nearby Indian communities attended this event.

Other off-reservation boarding schools took license with the term "powwow" as well, attesting to the administrators' continued anxiety about gatherings of Indian people and the need to render any such gatherings as safe and contained as possible. Flandreau Indian School in South Dakota held an annual Homecoming Indian Day that sometimes included a "powwow" as part of the day's festivities; also scheduled for the day were an inspection of the school, an Indian Day Parade, a welcome address, a concert by the school band, a program of Indian dances, and stunts. Nighttime events consisted of the homecoming game, an evening dance, movies, and parties.[8] Given this jam-packed schedule, the powwow may have been simply a social hour shoehorned into an already full day that was dedicated to welcoming alumni while promoting the school to the public.

Through the 1930s, '40s, and '50s, Chemawa offered its students opportunities to learn and perform Native song and dance traditions through the Indian Club (see Chapter 6, "Dance") and through school pageants, when Chemawa opened its grounds to the off-campus community (see Chapter 5, "Theater and Pageants"). Many of the hallmarks of traditional powwows, however—a Grand Entry, dancers coming from afar to participate, prayers and memorial songs, intertribal dances—were absent from these early celebrations. In effect, tribal dances as practiced at Chemawa took the form of performances, in which students prepared dances and performed them for each other and for off-campus guests. Chemawa's administration had not yet adopted the key collaborative element of opening the campus to guest dancers as equal participants in the powwow.

Chemawa finally began to welcome off-campus guests for powwows in an organized, intentional way in the mid-1970s when it hosted its first actual powwows. An outgrowth of earlier campus open-house pageants, the modern powwows became possible after a student group, the Northwest Indian Cultural Explorers, began working to help students retain their Indian culture in the face of a non-Native style of high school education. The Explorers also spawned Chemawa's first student drum, The Chemiwai Singers, led by staff advisor and Yakama traditionalist Leroy B. Selam[9] (see figure 20). By the time Chemawa's new campus was built in 1977, powwows were occurring annually at Chemawa, and over the years they have come to take place at several key times during the school year: a welcome-back powwow in September, Veterans' Day in November, the school's birthday in February, and at graduation in May.

Throughout Chemawa's long history of student involvement in powwows—including the events that scarcely resemble contemporary powwows—particular issues have persisted that have helped frame the meanings of powwows for students, faculty, and staff. For some people, these issues may be encountered primarily experientially, while others work with them very consciously or intentionally. Of paramount significance are issues of personal identity formation, intertribalism, and cultural revitalization.

Identity formation is a complex process wherein an individual responds to a variety of social events, pressures, and expectations, often progressing through a series of stages that lead to identity resolution. One formulation of identity stages has been articulated by Native American Studies scholar Devon Mihesuah.[10] In this understanding, an American Indian person moving through youth into adulthood might pass through stages of identifying with white culture, encountering their tribal history, grappling with becoming the "right kind of Indian," and developing an inner security about their racial heritage. Despite this apparent demarcation into enumerated stages, Mihesuah allows for a high degree of variability from person to person. No set order of stages is necessarily experienced, and even the final outcome is not always a point of resolution; some individuals may remain in a volatile state (e.g., Stage 3: Immersion-Emersion) indefinitely. There can also be additional complexities for multi-racial peoples, who may be pressured by family members or other communities to reject certain parts of themselves. For all individuals, a number of different forces are informing identity, both overtly and subconsciously; these forces can include: family members' own identity struggles; Native/non-Native relations in one's home community; regional culture; knowledge of one's tribal heritage; the perceived status and/or economic opportunities for different ethnic groups; and feedback from one's peer group/s.

The impact of powwows on identity formation is undeniable and complex, and can differ each time one prepares for, attends, and remembers such a gathering. To begin with, people participate for different reasons at different times in their lives, which in turn allows for changing perceptions and experiences. Dancer Derek Lowry (North Carolina Tuscarora) succinctly explained, "Why do we dance? Well, how many reasons you got? Sometimes it's for ceremony. Sometimes it's because I want to put on my getup and shake a leg. And sometimes it's because I want to remember my friends and family. And sometimes it's just *because*. You don't always need a reason, do you?"[11] At residential schools—where some students are seasoned powwow participants and some are engaging in the

Figure 20. The Chemiwai Singers and friends, on campus near Chemawa's iconic totem pole. From the cover of the album they released in 1974 on Canyon Records.

gatherings for the first time—powwows aid in identity formation by facilitating students' movements between identity phases, or students' repositioning of themselves within a phase. Many Chemawa students have grown up in their tribal communities, and thus have some familiarity with their tribal history and culture; some have had encounters with Natives or non-Natives that have complicated, intensified, or otherwise shifted their sense of their own Indianness. Most are engaged in some sort of identity formation, as are teenage people in the United States generally; powwows provide a site where different aspects of one's Indianness can be recognized, acknowledged, tested, and explored. Students at Chemawa who dance at powwows are often members of Chemawa's Performing Arts Club, and have arrived at school with much traditional knowledge, be it of songs, dances, regalia, storytelling, or other forms of culture expression.[12]

There are many ways in which powwows can provide students a safe (physically safe, though not completely free of social approbation) and rich, dynamic space to explore what being Indian means to them as individuals. Students participate in powwows of their own volition; attendance is not compulsory. A common sense of survivorship is acknowledged and celebrated through songs specific to the boarding school experience. As with any high school, peers can be supportive or critical; stereotypes based on skin color or historic tribal feuds can run rampant when students are grasping for security and belonging.[13] Biases regarding lighter or darker shades of skin are not as prevalent today at Chemawa, however, as they have been in the past or at other schools. Many students report being unaware of or unaffected by intertribal stereotypes, thus making school-sponsored powwows events where students can work out parts of their identity fairly free of belittlement and criticism. Through powwows, identity formation can happen organically and with minimal intertribal animosity.

Anthropologist James H. Howard's famous assertion that the powwow reflected a "process by which sociocultural entities . . . are losing their tribal distinctiveness and in its place are developing a nontribal 'Indian' culture"[14] posits that tribal distinctiveness is being lost to pan-tribalism, and that the modern powwow is largely to blame for this presumed cultural degradation. In the post-World War II era, Howard argued, Indian identity has become increasingly generalized, with the appearance of common powwow formats, cultural practices, and styles of clothing.

From Howard's hypothesis, it would follow that off-reservation boarding schools—with students gathering from a number of far-away Indian groups, removed from their tribal communities—would be particularly susceptible to cultural loss. And to be sure, a cursory look at Chemawa's powwows might yield outward signs of "a synthesis of related traditions that can articulate Indianness."[15] Widely shared practices of powwow format, clothing, categories of dance, and etiquette might superficially suggest the development of a new, generalized Indian culture. Yet when given thoughtful consideration, off-reservation boarding school powwows emerge as sites where students get in touch with their respective tribal heritages. Peer groups, teachers, staff members, and volunteers from the local Native community assist students in procuring and preparing their regalia, learning dance steps, and even making new songs within tribally specific traditions and idioms. Students who are the sole representatives of their tribal communities at Chemawa are paired up with other students or staff from culturally related Indian groups, helping to sustain their explorations of their tribal backgrounds. Cultural sharing that occurs between students of various Indian groups does not subsume the students' individual tribal identities. As William K. Powers asserted in 1990, "Although the idea that Pan-Indianism strives towards the creation of a new ethnic group, the American Indian, is novel and fascinating, it is unlikely that this definition can be regarded seriously, given what we know about the distinctiveness and variety of American Indian tribal cultures."[16] In keeping with Powers' characterization of the limitations of pan-Indianism, Chemawa powwows have provided fertile ground for the growth of tribally specific and community-specific aspects of identity as well.

Through their participation in school powwows, students at Chemawa often find themselves involved in the dynamic and somewhat uncharted process of cultural revitalization, a concept often invoked in the anthropology of religion literature but only beginning to be considered as a cross-cultural phenomenon.[17] This is particularly relevant for western Oregon tribes, all of which were terminated by the federal government in the 1950s.[18] Cultural revitalization has been gaining energy in the Northwest since tribes began to achieve restoration of their sovereign status in the 1980s. As numerous Indian groups work to bounce back from termination and rebuild their land, social structures, and forms of cultural expression, students at Chemawa have had unprecedented opportunities to learn songs, dances, and languages that can make significant contributions to the strength and vitality of their tribal communities.

One salient example is that of Chemawa's ongoing relationship with the nearby Confederated Tribes of Grand Ronde.[19] Officially terminated by Congress in 1954 under Public Law 588, the Grand Ronde Tribe saw the tribe's sovereign status and its members' individual rights dissolved. The tribe's young people left the Grand Ronde valley to find jobs in urban areas such as Portland, and the tribe's community assets dwindled to only a small trailer on a one-acre parcel of land. After years of struggle and concerted effort led by elders, the battle for restoration succeeded in November of 1983, when House Resolution 3885 restored federal recognition status to the Confederated Tribes of Grand Ronde. Since then, Grand Ronde has engaged in a conscious and intentional process of cultural rebuilding, trying to reclaim what had been lost after decades of dispersion and fractured community. Young people can now return to Grand Ronde and find employment, and comfortable housing is being built for elders. An immersion pre-school teaches Chinuk Wawa as a co-first language, elders' oral histories are being documented, drum-making and basketry classes are taught both at Grand Ronde and in Portland, cultural artifacts are being reclaimed from museums and private collectors, and rodeos and powwows are held throughout the year. Many tribal members have family ties to Chemawa, and have agreed to assist Chemawa's powwows in any capacity, be it helping students with their regalia, emceeing, finding funds for the special needs that arise, or simply dancing and being present. For students, unprecedented opportunities exist to learn languages that had been deemed extinct, dances that have fallen out of use, and songs that have not been performed in decades.

Similar processes of recovery are occurring for tribes from other regions as well, particularly smaller tribes and those that were severely affected by termination. If a student is the only representative of their tribe or band while at Chemawa, the staff seeks to connect them with students from tribes in close geographic proximity to their own, so that they might learn from related cultural traditions when applicable, and take this knowledge home with them to help their tribe. Students who are self-motivated to learn their tribal traditions often return home to assume leadership positions in their communities.

Many students recall their early childhood experiences of music as being particularly formative in their musical development, but they also attest that the interpersonal connections made as a result of attending Chemawa were what facilitated their involvement in music later in life. This has been true for Chet Clark, who attended Chemawa in the Navajo Five-Year Program from 1952 to 1957.[20]

When asked where he first learned drumming and singing, Clark said he couldn't remember. He then elaborated that it must have been very early, because he learned to walk by hanging on to the side of his father's drum. Clark noted that the Navajo use a different, smaller drum than the drums commonly seen at today's powwows. His father was a medicine man who composed many songs for individual sacred occasions (as is the Navajo tradition) as well as for social dances. Now called "Song and Dance," these secular events include Skip Dance and Two-step songs, danced in a large hall by couples wearing traditional costumes. Clark thus grew up exposed to a wide variety of both ceremonial and social music forms.

The youngest child in his family, he watched as each of his older siblings left their rural Arizona home to attend schools elsewhere, including the Sherman Institute in Riverside, which his older brother encouraged him to attend. Clark asked if he might also go to school, but his grandmother—with whom he lived—refused, saying, "Somebody's got to be here to watch the sheep." Unhappy that he could barely write his own name, Clark approached his father, who agreed to sign him up for school. Three weeks later they went into town to meet the bus taking students to the Sherman Institute, but it was full, so Clark could not go to Sherman, where his brother was enrolled. He did not want to return home, though, so they waited another day for a bus that was headed towards Chemawa. This bus was full as well, but Clark and two other boys got permission to board. From Klackateau to Flagstaff, 170 miles, they rode standing up or sitting on the floor in the aisle. They changed buses in Flagstaff and got seats, then continued westward, riding through Las Vegas at night and then across the desert. "I was homesick already. There was *nothing* out there," Clark recalls. The bus arrived at Chemawa about noon the next day, much to Clark's relief and excitement: "It was a pretty place, I thought—the buildings were huge."

Clark's participation in music at Chemawa included singing in a special pick-up choir for the Christmas programs, and singing traditional Navajo songs in the annual pageants in celebration of the school's birthday. He also recalls dancing to western bands, dancing to records in the gym during the Halloween carnival, and students' dancing to music played on the jukebox in the canteen at the general store. What left the greatest impact on his life as a musician, however, came after his school years, through connections he made as a result of his time at Chemawa.

Friends introduced Clark to some people from Oklahoma, who used a larger drum, played for 49s (late-night parties with a variety of dances), and knew lots of powwow songs. Locally, Clark connected with musician Arlie Neskahi, who had started working part-time at Chemawa while attending Willamette University in Salem. Clark remembers his own participation in powwow music as happening organically, as opportunities presented themselves to him: "Then Arlie came out to Willamette University and said, 'let's form a drum group.' Now I'm somewhere every weekend."

Now an active powwow singer, drum maker, and emcee, Clark keeps a busy schedule that includes drumming and emceeing around the Northwest and sometimes across the country. He has a keen sense of gratitude for his involvement in music, a gratitude rooted in his early childhood experiences and manifested in his relationship to the Native community: "Since I don't remember when I started singing or being around the drum, I say, 'I've been blessed by the Great Spirit.' I sing for the people: I sing for the elders, first; I sing for the warriors; I sing for the little kids. Drumming and singing's been real good to me." Clark drums at powwows, weddings, graduations, and a variety of occasions that mark turning points in the lives of individuals and communities. He recently sang at a groundbreaking ceremony at Chemawa, in honor of a new complex of student housing that had finally been funded and begun; Clark composed a new song in honor of that particular occasion.

In 1983, Clark made a song—"Chemawa Graduation Song"—to honor the students who had completed their time at Chemawa and were moving on to the world outside the school. It has been performed in the spring at many of Chemawa's graduation ceremonies, and Clark is invited back each year to sing and drum. the song is dedicated to all past, present, and future graduates. The text is in Navajo, and while a limited percentage of today's students speak the language, the presence of tribal languages in school ceremonies is appreciated by students and school officials alike. Lyrics stress the dual importance of the learning that takes place at school and the learning that takes place in one's home community, viewing both together as a source of strength and vitality:

"Chemawa Graduation Song"[21]

Young people what you have learned
Here in this place
And also the tradition of our elders

Long ago
Carry these with you
Whatever you endeavor to do in life
These will be your strength
These will be your strength

In addition to students and alumni, talented and caring faculty and staff have helped create space for powwow music at Chemawa. A particularly innovative example is that of Arlie Neskahi (Navajo), who has served Chemawa in a variety of capacities. A residential supervisor 1983-1984, a substitute teacher in 1984, an alcohol education specialist 1984-1987, Neskahi is well-practiced in the processes of drug and alcohol prevention, intervention, and treatment. The constellation of skills he assembled while earning his B.S. at nearby Willamette University, working at Chemawa, and during the years afterwards has included expertise in counseling, youth development, prevention, community building, and cultural diversity, all of which converged when Neskahi started bringing a drum to the students' dormitories in the evenings.

At first, he would simply bring the drum to the dorms and play powwow music from various tribes, including some songs he had made himself. The students started listening, and eventually Neskahi asked if they wanted to learn. Today he recalls some of the various reasons students were drawn to the drumming: "Some were involved in drug and alcohol support groups, and they wanted to emulate what they saw, as they looked for how to be involved in today's world while still connect with traditional culture. For some, the music was about reconnection; it served as a touchstone, something that let them feel what it was like to be connected to their culture again, even if it was just temporary." [22] Sometimes, students came to Chemawa with drumming experience: "Some were already involved in drums with their families. One boy was a Yakama who only knew stick game songs that he had learned from his family." While Neskahi didn't overtly push sobriety or designate the group as a "sober drum," he sought to model balanced living to all the students, knowing this would be of particular use to those with substance abuse problems: "Of the six strong members, two were involved with drugs or alcohol. Drumming was a good way for them to be involved in a healthy activity. And it has to do with modeling—they could see how I actually lived."

As the group coalesced and the students practiced regularly, the Chemawa Singers became strong, viable musicians, drumming at powwows both at home and on the road, as well as radio broadcasts, community functions, other schools, and Chemawa's own ceremonies. In time, the students came to know many songs, and the credits on their 1987 recording, *Intertribal Pow-Wow Songs*, reveal that some songs were made jointly by Neskahi and the students themselves. Neskahi describes the composition process as something that would occur only after a student developed a depth of knowledge of powwow repertoire and song forms: "Basically, it's a process of catching a song. After they'd learned many songs, they'd develop confidence." Neskahi listened to the students, creating space for collaboration: "Sometimes they'd come to me and say, 'I've got this idea, but I don't know what to do with it.' I'd sit quietly for a while. Then I'd start humming, and listen, and see how it [the music] forms. There'd be many parts [emerging]. It's a matter of chasing a melody—up, and down, and finding the joy of a balanced composition."

The tribes represented in the Chemawa student body typically number between thirty and fifty, and singers in the drum were from a variety of tribes— Navajo, Yakama, Blackfeet, Kootenai—and thus brought a diverse set of influences to bear on the group's repertoire. Their recording reflects this diversity by including a Horse Giving song, a Crow Hop/Foot Slide, Grass Dance songs, Circle Dance songs, and a variety of intertribal songs, both traditional and contemporary.[23]

Neskahi's own musical education had been deeply influenced by his mother and father, both of whom had attended Indian boarding schools. Born in 1957 on a reservation in northwestern New Mexico, Neskahi's earliest recollections of music are of Indian songs: "When I was just a very young child I remember my mother. She would never sing outright, but she would hum melodies to me. She had been taken as a little child and put into a Christian boarding school, and it was there that she was taught that anything that had to do with our culture was evil and wrong. She struggled with that, and so I never actually heard her sing when I was little, but I would hear her humming these melodies." Neskahi's father was more assertive in transmitting the traditional songs: "And it was my father then that, even though he was taken to boarding school too, his father—my grandfather—my dad's dad was a medicine man, and so he knew some of those songs, and he also was raised in the Native American church, and he used to sing songs then to me. And so some of the first songs that I learned were songs that my father taught."[24]

As for many Native Americans, the idea of walking in two worlds figures prominently in Neskahi's life, both in how he has modeled healthy living to his students and in his own upbringing, which included exposure to culture both Navajo and non-Native. He recalls growing up listening to the Fenders, a Navajo country and western band that was popular both on and off the reservation. The Fenders covered many famous country and western songs, and "they had a real strong Navajo accent when they sang." He also recalls as one of his fondest memories an afternoon out driving with his father: "When I was a really young boy we went into town, this little town next to the border there called Farmington, New Mexico, and we were driving in my dad's old car, and it had those push-button radios, AM radios, and he leaned over and he said, 'Go ahead, son, you choose what radio station to listen to,' and he made me feel so grownup." He still remembers the song he alighted on, and the formative role those early experiences had on his later musical taste: "And so I started pushing the buttons and I pushed it to this one station that I liked and the song that was coming over was: [He sings:] 'Walk right in / sit right down / baby let your hair hang down …' I'll never forget that! And I still have a wide taste in music—everything from rock'n'roll to grunge to jazz. I really enjoy music."[25]

Once in high school, Neskahi learned the powwow music tradition that he would later pass on to the students at Chemawa. This happened largely through chance meetings with other culture bearers, but his father's involvement in musical gatherings likely gave him an openness to the music and a conceptual framework for understanding it: "I learned the powwow style in high school, when I was a sophomore. I was president of the Indian Club. A Southern Cheyenne man would come and sing and teach us powwow dances. He did that for several weeks, and we had so much fun. Then the funding ran out and he stopped coming." The loss of the teacher did not ultimately mean the end of the music: "We were so sad at the next meeting. Then three of my buddies from the Ute tribe offered to bring a drum they had, and we kept up with the dances. They started singing the songs they knew, and they showed me the singing style that they had learned from their uncles." The students continued learning, largely self-directed. Arlie was aware of his own musical shortcomings, but he continued nonetheless: "I was very bad! [Laughs.] But I had a car, so I was a good resource for them, driving us to powwows. My dad was an emcee, and he gave us a name: the Red Sky Singers."

In passing the music on to students at Chemawa, Neskahi cites a similar openness on the part of the students as a chief reason for the level of skill achieved by the Chemawa Singers. He attributes their readiness to learn in part to the lack of technology at their disposal, explaining that before compact discs were inexpensive, accessible, and widely distributed, students were more interested in the context and origins of each song they learned. "Once the CD thing took off, a lot of homogenization took place. It was a different time then [in the 1980s]—students were willing to learn, to learn where the songs came from and who they'd been taught to." The students would learn the music by repeating small parts of a song, gradually adding more and more. Sometimes Neskahi would just repeat two verses, until the students caught on and learned it; then he would change or add to the music. He was struck by their motivation, and the quality they were able to achieve with fairly rudimentary equipment: "They loved the challenge of it. The cassette we made, we just recorded in the band room with a four-track cassette player." Expensive recording technology was not an option, and the students emphasized instead their musical competence: the ability to learn new songs, the unique challenges of different genres of music, the development of a large repertoire, and a familiarity with the music that was deep enough to enable students to make their own viable compositions.

Neskahi imparted more than just musical knowledge to his young singers, however. Modeling a holistic approach that integrated music into the rest of one's life, he shared teachings that would help his students in work, school, and their personal relationships. "It's not enough to be able to sing a good song. You practice, develop your voice, you have dedication; it has to be quality. But it's important to *live* a good song. When the time comes that you leave this earth, you want to have lived a good song. How to do this—that's the path of a singer. It's how you want people to remember you." Neskahi shared such teachings with his students both implicitly and out loud, not shying away from talking about personal challenges but also taking the tack that lessons are best taught by modeling rather than by preaching. He acknowledges, "Other drums take a different approach, like saying, 'This is a sober drum.' " For Neskahi, though, melding the music with life is of paramount importance. The drum then becomes a place where the singer's whole self is accepted. His description of his attitude at powwows shows an approach to personal identity that incorporates a range of human emotions. "When we sing at powwows, I'm not the pious one. I laugh, and I have a good time; it's an extension of myself. But there's a time for fooling around, and there's a time for being serious. [I can be serious ...] when we sing."

When asked what he got out of the experience of leading the Chemawa Singers, Neskahi articulates a wide spectrum of gifts. "I got to see the kids develop a sense of community, purpose, capability, values, ethics, and a way to express spirituality and prayer life. The students had a pure desire to learn what was there. When they do it [drumming], it blesses people. They do their other stuff—video games, their other music—but they can do this too." Neskahi learned much from the students, and he is keenly appreciative of their unique time together: "It reinforced the value of what was given to me, and helped me to firm up my ethics around the music. It taught me to take care of my self, my thoughts, and my actions. It was one of the true joys [in my life]—that window in time. Kids today have no direct connection to who made the song, or what it's about."

Neskahi observes a similar disconnectedness in adult musicians, as well. This occurs when Indian musicians pay little heed to their roots, and instead strive for a Native sound without knowledge of the existing tribal repertoires and practices. The most meaningful songs to learn can be those of one's own tribe or of other

Indian groups; the practice to be avoided is that of learning generic-sounding pieces that employ aural stereotypes and are not grounded in the traditions of any tribe. Neskahi notes that such simplicity only serves to support existing stereotypes of Native American music as simplistic and primitive: "There are Native musicians right now who have not studied the traditional singing arts who are trying to sing in traditional forms, and I don't think that's good. And there has been this perception for a long time that our music is simple and all it is is grunting kinds of sounds. White people call it 'hey how are ya' music." Neskahi demonstrates, singing on a perfect 4th: "Hey, how are ya / hey, how are ya / hey, how are ya …" He argues that the problem stems from a lack of knowledge of the traditions: "And some of these Native musicians who have not taken the time to study and learn traditional singing styles, that's what they're doing. They're making songs, and they're just going, 'Hey a ho / a ho …' And it's really not good." The solution, while requiring time and effort, lies in building one's knowledge of traditional music forms, becoming immersed in the idioms, and eventually allowing imaginative space for the creation of new songs. Neskahi notes that just as learning Western music takes time, so does learning the music of indigenous peoples: "What I wish these musicians would do is to find a singing person in their local area, go to them, offer them a gift, ask them if they could be taught these traditions and these singing styles, and that they be taught some songs, and that they take some time, just like the time it took them to learn how to play electric guitar or whatever instrument they did to discipline themselves—to learn some traditional style of music and then come back to this music and add that element to it." The alternative is culturally bankrupt, and does an injustice to the listeners and musicians alike. In this case, "what they are doing is playing into the stereotype that our music is just some simple, nonsense kind of syllables that are sung over and over, when in fact it takes a lot of years to develop a real strong vocal style."[26]

Neskahi's perspective and vision for the future have grown out of his career as a promoter of Native American music, as well as his family upbringing as the son of a lifelong musician. When recently asked where he thinks the Native American music scene is going, Neskahi responded by recounting the story of his father's death: "My father passed away in January [of 2005], and he was a very strong spiritual man. And he had been following what I'd been doing over the last several years, and the things that I'd been talking about, and things that I'd been experiencing. And in the last few days before he passed away he was talking to my sister—I wasn't able to go home for that; I just made it for the funeral." When Neskahi arrived home, his sister related to him something their father had said repeatedly during his final days: "There's a movement coming. It's gonna be here pretty soon. It's gonna happen pretty soon . . . It's gonna be really great for Native people. It's gonna excite the world, and the world's really gonna take notice. And the way it's gonna happen—is through music."

Neskahi interpreted his father's vision in terms of the transformative power of contemporary Native music for Native and non-Native listeners alike: "When people allow this music to be a part of their experience, there's gonna be a real strong re-centering of human being-ness, of peace and balance and respect. That's what our musicians are writing about. They're taking our people's philosophies and dreams and welding them together."[27] Just as Neskahi's father transmitted more than just musical knowledge to his son, so did Arlie Neskahi seek to pass on to his students at Chemawa this sense of dignity, assuredness of purpose, and awareness of one's self as part of a larger spiritual endeavor.

Today, the state of music instruction at Chemawa could be described as tenacious and Indian oriented. Western music classes such as choir, band, and music appreciation ended in the late 1990s with Hal Beyers' retirement (see Chapter 4). Just as in Oregon's public schools, a tightening budget has meant the sacrificing of many of Chemawa's arts education offerings. Academic Counselor Karen Graham explains that the "old thinking [about desirable course offerings for BIA schools] privileged math and reading" as a means of instilling the skills that students would need to survive in the outside world. Subjects seen as extraneous were eliminated. "To be honest, music has gone down that way too." The current BIA-mandated curriculum does include the Culture Cluster, a sequence of courses covering cultural expressions of the indigenous peoples of the United States. Graham acknowledges that meeting all the students' needs is a tall order: "It's difficult [teaching tribal traditions] here, for two reasons: not all faculty are Native, and there's not one tribe in the majority." With as many as fifty tribes represented in Chemawa's student body, attempts to address every student's heritage are necessarily tempered by an aversion to the superficiality that comes with a broad survey. Instruction in Native musics is more prevalent than Western music instruction at Chemawa for another reason as well: the socioeconomic backgrounds of the students. As Graham explains (see closing pages of Chapter 7), students from reservations and small towns don't arrive at Chemawa with instruments; even if they have played instruments at some point in their lives, they haven't had the money to buy them.[28] Consequently, the demand for instruction on Western band and orchestra instruments is virtually nil.

During the final hour of the school day, students attend a variety of elective course offerings, including the Performing Arts Club and the Powwow Club. The Performing Arts Club is available to students who want to pursue an interest in Native music forms. Both a class and a club, it has been run by Warner Austin

(Cherokee) for the past ten years. Membership typically fluctuates between eigh-teen and forty students, many of whom often connect with the club through other students from their area of origin, or from pre-existing family connections to music. The songs and dances the students choose to work on depend on the tribes that are represented in the club and at Chemawa, where trends in tribal representation fluctuate every few years (see figure 21).

For singers and dancers of a particular tribe to collaborate, a critical mass of students is needed, if not from one tribe then from nearby groups or areas with closely related cultures. The students seem to be particularly appreciative when the music of their own tribe is represented. Sometimes, a group of students will know their dances, but they don't have the necessary singers, and they're shy about dancing with a tape recording. One recent example is that of students from the Yuman tribes of the Colorado River basin. The tribes are related, and many do dances they call "bird dances." For several years, Chemawa had singers from the Yuman tribes. The students would recognize each other's songs as related, and they'd dance to each other's songs. Getting to know the students each year is criti-cal to engaging their potential. Once the singers are identified, the accompanying performing group comes alive again; different groups emerge at different times, in cyclical fashion. A similar process has happened with the Apache Crown Dancers and with Chemawa's contingent of singers and dancers from Alaska. The presence of an adult mentor from a particular area can particularly help a group coalesce.[29]

Students are drawn to the Performing Arts Club for a variety of reasons. Some are involved in their tribal culture before they arrive at Chemawa; for others, the club's initial appeal is that it offers a time to be with friends and attend off-campus events. Regardless of what animates them, students must seek out the club on their own and express an interest in membership. Some students arrive on campus looking for the club, asking their peers, "Where's it at?" Others, upon hearing that the club does trips off campus, come in and ask, "How can I sign up for that?" Because of the self-motivation students must possess to connect with the club, they evince a sense of ownership not found with all campus activities. Members who take a hiatus due to other activities (e.g., athletes who must use the sixth-period time slot for meets and practices for a season) continue to check in with the group, stopping by during free moments to assert that they're "still a part of the club," even if they can't take the class at that time. When the perform-ing arts group does cultural performances, students who belong to the club can be called out of their other sixth-period classes to perform.

Students have a free period later in the evening, from 8 to 9 p.m. and fre-quently use this time to work on club activities. This time is particularly useful for students who hold leadership positions in the club. With music not formally

Figure 21. Chemawa drum group during a recording session at Willamette University, 2013. Clockwise from front left: Alex Santos, Kaycee Wyatt, Jeremy Russell, Donreil Atene, Warner Austin, Tre'von Danforth, and Lucas Pease. Photo courtesy of Emily Dickey.

funded at Chemawa, the program is run on a volunteer basis, and Warner Austin shares many of the responsibilities with the student leadership, a group of four officers of whom he speaks with great respect.

Though the Chemawa campus is not sealed by a fence, students are only permitted to leave for school-sanctioned events and family emergencies; opportunities to perform off-campus, therefore, are regarded with anticipation and excitement. Like other adult club mentors, when Warner Austin receives an invitation to perform, he submits a request to the school, and negotiates the content and structure of the performance with the host party. Chemawa has an Activities Committee composed of faculty who meet every Tuesday to coordinate such requests; they handle the transportation, and make sure there are no schedule conflicts. The scope of the field trips varies. Sometimes, the inviting party only wants one or two singers. Other times, they've heard the club has storytellers also and can do a whole presentation, and they are eager to arrange a forty-five-minute or one-hour performance.

Some students prefer to participate in these performances over other school activities. In addition to events where the Chemawa Performing Arts Club presents the sole performance, actual powwows present other opportunities for club members to travel off-campus. Free time on weekends can be spent at powwows, which usually entail a day trip or, less frequently, an overnight stay. All Chemawa students have different options: on weekends, some students like to shop, or go to an organized activity, such as school dances held on Saturday nights; the performing arts students like to go to powwows. So Austin puts in requests for the club to travel, and he stays abreast of powwows occurring in areas near Chemawa, such as Salem, Portland, or Vancouver, Washington. Though any student can participate in the club—the main prerequisite is that they want to be there—students must meet academic and citizenship requirements to maintain eligibility for off-campus events, and Austin makes sure the students are aware of the criteria for traveling with the club. They know a school attendance official can board their bus to verify eligibility, and can pull students off before a trip commences. Austin uses this as a teaching opportunity to show students that their conduct reflects back upon their various communities of origin. For the most part, the students try to carry themselves with dignity. They learn that they don't just represent themselves, but also their family and their tribe, as well as the school.

The students' commitment to continuing indigenous performing arts has led them to build positive relations with off-campus communities, both Native and non-Native. In the interest of furthering the students' work, these outside parties support the club with large and small donations, which help cover the costs of materials and incidentals. Though money comes sporadically and from a variety of sources, the club, though not funded by the school, consistently manages to receive support and keep active. The club also raises money on its own, through honoraria from performances, and grants from the Confederated Tribes of Grand Ronde and Siletz. Sometimes a corporation or agency will make a sizable contribution; recent donors have included Portland Gas & Electric and the Bonneville Power Administration.

Being a part of a BIA school, the club is accorded freedoms that are absent from clubs in public schools. These freedoms extend into the realm of spirituality and its place in school. Particularly meaningful to the students is when they are asked to do an honor song, a song performed expressly to honor someone, such as an alumnus returned from war or the memory of a deceased relative. This can alleviate tensions and interpersonal conflicts, helping to right imbalances in the group psyche and leave the students feeling better. When students can openly acknowledge that their songs function as prayers, they can access more fully the music's transformative potential. Similarly, at a recent Chemawa graduation ceremony, the New Boys (more recently called the Red Nation Boyz) drum did an honor song, in a language of the Great Lakes region. The song was selected for its multiple meanings, appropriate for the graduating seniors, the school community as a whole, and the drum members' wish for one of their members. The song described an eagle, how it soars—and that it does more than carry the students' prayers; it prays along with them. Chemawa's young people, when graduating, are taking flight. Also, one of the boys was competing in a track meet the next day, and his classmates wanted him to take flight too. So the song was appropriate in multiple ways.

The Red Nation Boyz is one of two drums at Chemawa. Until recently, there was only one drum, its pluralistic membership reflected in its name: Chemawa Nations.[30] It's an intertribal group, with both males and females sitting at the drums. Normally, females wouldn't drum until they were older, but they are allowed to participate at school. The name of the Red Nation Boyz reflects the drum's different code of membership: some students come from tribes where females aren't supposed to sit at the drum, so these boys started a different drum. It was actually the females in their families—the mothers and the aunts—who enforced the gender distinction. Having two drums emerged as a solution to the needs both for inclusivity and for honoring the gender norms of students' tribal communities; both drums enjoy equal opportunities to participate at powwows on- and off-campus, and no resentment is bred between members of the two drums.

Family members attend powwows and also support their students during the year by sending regalia and by monitoring their student's activities from afar. School officials strive to honor requests from students' families and tribes so that students' participation in school programs is in keeping with their respective tribal traditions. For Warner Austin, this occasionally means conversations with family members to discuss the goings-on of the group; more often, the students themselves will let him know the preferred performance practices of their tribal communities. It also means the weekly sweats he leads on Sundays are only for male students. Some tribes don't believe in mixed-gender sweats, so the girls have their sweat lodge separately, on Saturdays. By advising the Performing Arts Club and running the boys' sweat lodge, Warner Austin creates the necessary space for the students' tribal traditions of song, dance, storytelling, and religion.

Another club, offered for students interested specifically in the production of powwows, is Chemawa's Powwow Club. Faculty advisor Chance May (Tsimshian/Haida; Chemawa alumnus, class of 2002) explains the Powwow Club's distinct function: "The Powwow Club really does the grunt work—they make sure the four powwows are up every year. They're working to put on a good event. They're dedicated. There's about twenty to thirty students; it's an after-school extra-curricular activity." The club has two designated advisors and three support staff, and operates with the funds earned from their previous powwows. There is also a stipend position designated for the powwow emcee, a job that Chance May has been doing since spring 2011. May now emcees all four of Chemawa's annual powwows, and he describes the work as fun, and largely "a management thing—making sure people keep moving, that we're not here till midnight."[31]

What makes for a good powwow? For the Powwow Club, it's all about participation. May explains, "For the most part, it has to do with the dance floor. If we have lots of dancers and drums, then it is a good powwow. Second, we look at the stands [to see how many people attend]."[32] Each powwow is a unique event that will never be duplicated in another place or time. Moreover, the number of drums that will be there is not known in advance, but rather is a matter of chance, with drums learning on their own about the powwows and deciding whether they want to attend. Because of this, a Chemawa powwow might include four drums, or it might have fifteen, but eight or nine is a typical number. The emcee works to make sure all the drums get their time, and stay in rotation. Certain drums may be picked to do certain songs. A powwow can be a good community-building experience whether large or small, but more drums often means more people, more connections, and a greater energy. Ethnomusicologist Tara Browner—herself a dancer of Oklahoma Choctaw heritage—asserts, "Because one of the primary purposes of a pow-wow is to bring Indian people together, an event's success is gauged by how many attend." She also notes that "for Indian people . . . specific dates and figures are not as important as the overall flow of events."[33]

For someone attending a Chemawa powwow, arriving on campus begins with a stop at the gatehouse, where a security guard checks your driver's license and records your visit. A large LED marquee visible from the road scrolls the powwow date, job openings, and philosophical tenets in alignment with the school, such as "Knowing yourself is the beginning of true wisdom." Proceeding towards the campus complex of buildings, you pass the school's emblematic water tower on the left, and the lush Pigsley Field baseball diamond on the right, followed by the football and track field, with large concrete bleachers. In the parking lot near the gym, food carts offer yakisoba and Thai noodles, espresso drinks, and Mexican food; Chemawa students have also set up a booth to sell fry bread. Inside the gym, the noise level increases, with sounds reverberating through a cavernous space framed by brick walls, a corrugated metal ceiling, and HVAC ducts and vents. Ceiling-mounted speakers, fluorescent lights, and six basketball hoops hang from above, and the mascots of nine other high schools in Chemawa's athletic conference adorn the back wall. Vendors at tables sell clothing, jewelry, blankets, regalia, and smoked salmon and sturgeon.

The powwows typically advertise a 1 p.m. start time on a Saturday, and the emcee strives to begin the Grand Entry at 1:15. Calls for "Five minutes, dancers ..." and then "Dancers, please line up" are integrated with an announcement that Chemawa is a drug- and alcohol-free campus, and that those wishing to use tobacco must go off campus to do so. The drums are set up on either side of the gym, at the base of the bleachers. Grand Entry can be followed by a Victory Charge, the posting of colors, and an invocation. Chet Clark (Navajo) is often called upon to do the opening prayer, and he speaks in Diné, and mentions that he's been coming to powwows at Chemawa for almost fifty years. If there is time allowed to honor veterans, the emcee then asks the veterans present to introduce themselves, dance or walk through one rotation, and stand to shake hands with anyone present who wishes to thank them (a majority of the people in attendance line up to do so). The reigning Miss Chemawa introduces herself, perhaps giving her tribal or clan lineage and a brief welcome speech. The emcee is introduced, and he does a roll call of the drums, to see which ones are present and at the ready. The powwow dances then proceed, with an opening intertribal followed by many of the popular dance forms, such as Fancy Shawl, Double Bustle, Jingle Dress, Grass Dance, Women's Traditional, and Men's Traditional. Special dances offered by Chemawa students include a Navajo Hoop Dance and the Apache Crown Dance. Small children in regalia join in many of the dances, and everyone is invited to join in the Intertribals—the emcee might say, "All nations, come on down . . . If all you can do is jitterbug, then come on down and jitterbug."

Brief breaks are taken for the benefit of the emcee and other participants, and a second Grand Entry typically happens around 6 p.m. Dancing continues till about ten in the evening. The idea that the powwow's success can be gauged both by the numbers of people attending and by the general flow of events is definitely borne out when participants discuss Chemawa's powwows. Indian newspapers covering the event typically feature headlines proclaiming the number in attendance; such was the headline that graced the cover of Grand Ronde's *Smoke Signals* the week after Chemawa's birthday in 2005: "Chemawa Pow-wow Celebrates The School's 125th Birthday—Nearly 300 filled the gym for the event."[34] The article and accompanying photographs emphasize the number of drums (eight), the geographic range of the participants (Washington, Idaho, Oregon, and Alaska), and the variety of the vendors' concessions (some made solely of horseshoe nails, others molded with "Alaskan clay found after an earthquake," and still other items—including the most popular: hand-crafted chess sets—made by tribal inmates, who comprise a disproportionately large segment of prisoners in federal and state prisons[35]).

Dancers who were interviewed for the *Smoke Signals* article—whether students, alumni, or guests having no formal affiliation with the school—typically commented on other markers for success, criteria more closely related to what Browner characterizes as "the overall flow of events." Tribal elders discussed the importance of renewing old friendships, and mentioned people they've run into whom they hadn't seen in years. A young mother talked about learning to make her children's regalia from her older sister. Older dancers commented on the changes in regalia, and in participation: "They keep getting better every year. The styles. And how young they start."[36]

Bob Tom (Siletz), who grew up on the Chemawa campus (see Chapter 3), and Chet Clark (Navajo), who attended Chemawa as a child, reveal more criteria that participants often take into consideration when appraising a powwow. Both Tom and Clark serve as emcees for powwows at Chemawa and around the Northwest, and their perspective is that of two elders who have watched powwows change over time.

Some of the issues Tom and Clark raise are not unique to Chemawa, but are issues about which any seasoned drummer or emcee might be concerned. They both share the pet peeve of powwows that don't adhere to the order of the drums; when they emcee, they strive to keep the drums in order, so that none are overlooked. "Otherwise, say you're the ninth drum, and they're on the seventh one but it's time for a break; then, after the break, they go back and the first one starts again."[37] They also discuss the tribally specific traditions they have observed at different powwows, and the importance of language—when to use English, and when to use tribal languages. Often tribal languages are used during the prayers that open or conclude a powwow; because powwows are inherently multicultural events, the tribal languages are often those of the host community. While Tom and Clark don't subscribe to the belief that knowledge of one's tribal language is necessary for salvation, they are aware of others who maintain that a person must know his or her language, or else when they go on to the next world, the Creator won't recognize them. "They're worried that they'll get there and nobody will know them."[38]

Other issues Tom and Clark raise, though, come directly from their experiences at Chemawa. They discuss how procedures for addressing the dropping of eagle feathers have become lax over time, and how they have even witnessed instances of the person who retrieved the feather taking the microphone and indulging in extended praise of the person who had dropped the feather. Both agree that the retrieving of eagle feathers is a somber occasion and *not* the time to praise the dropper; Tom recalls that in earlier times, feathers had to be picked up by a combat veteran, someone who had seen his comrades fall at his side.

This same easing of standards is manifested in the way some young people do not care properly for their regalia. Tom and Clark have both observed this development repeatedly at powwows, as young dancers are donning their regalia, dancing, and removing their regalia afterwards. When recently called by

Chemawa with a request for eagle feathers for a boy's regalia, Clark opted to give the boy turkey feathers instead, out of a desire that eagle feathers be treated with the dignity with which they've heretofore been accorded by Indian peoples. Clark felt that when the boy grew older, he would better understand the significance of the eagle feathers, and would have other opportunities to obtain some then.

Lamentations about the decline of traditional values among youth at pow-wows are common among Native elders throughout Indian country. Rather than simply decrying the declining morals of young people these days, however, Tom and Clark approach powwow culture with humility and freely share anecdotes about mistakes they themselves have made or times when they were unsure of how to proceed in a new situation. A recent and exciting addition to Chemawa's powwows has been a group of Apache Crown Dancers; as Siletz Tribal Chair Dee Pigsley notes, "they've really put Chemawa back on the map."[39] Crown Dancers are unique to the White Mountain Apache Tribe and they perform a visually striking dance that is not commonly seen at powwows. Also known as G'aan,[40] Crown Dancers represent mountain spirits, and they have an appearance mark-edly different from other powwow dancers. They have black-hooded faces, painted bodies, and harness bells, and the movements of Crown Dancers have been likened to marionettes as they swing their large headdresses from side to side and sometimes fling wooden swords. Symbols of lightning are sacred to the Apaches; these are placed on the Crown Dancers' bodies, in accordance with how the mountain spirits taught that the Crown Dance should be performed. The dance is a ritual for curing and healing.

Bob Tom recalls that one night when he was talking with a friend near the parking lot at a powwow, he noticed the Crown Dancers clustered around a van, putting on their regalia and special make-up. As Tom spoke with his friend, he casually glanced over at the van a few times, to watch how the dancers prepared. Once they were ready to dance, one of the Crown dancers approached Tom and explained, "you shouldn't have been watching us getting ready." Each dancer then had to walk over to Tom, address him, say a few words, and do a particular gesture to make things right for him. Tom thanked the dancers and reverently returned to the powwow. Today his respect for the Crown dancers stems largely from the dignity with which they approach their dancing. Tom explains, "These dancers take care of their regalia, and understand the importance of what they're doing."[41]

Despite their decades of experience and finely honed skills as drummers and emcees, Bob Tom and Chet Clark still exhibit a quality akin to "beginners' mind": a dedicated humility enlivened with an openness to learning new truths. Tom and Clark's actions and attitudes evince not only a respect for, but a curiosity about, different cultures and tribal traditions. This commitment to engage diverse cultures has been bolstered by participating in countless boarding school pow-wows, where the presence of students from far-flung communities, ever changing with the school's enrollment policies, is the norm.

In their celebration of pluralism, coordination with various Indian groups, and affirmation of Native personhood, powwows at Chemawa today stand as a powerful counterforce to decades of cultural hegemony. Even with the real concerns articulated by elders regarding the easing of standards and the loss of traditional practices of respect and reverence, most of the students who participate do aspire to learn and claim as their own their respective tribal heritages, including the right ways of behaving at powwows. When these gatherings are considered as social action, their power to interrupt stereotypes, employ traditional values to critique the present, and reflect indigenous modernity in its myriad forms is undeniable. Just two generations ago, the existence of such an open intertribal gathering at Chemawa would have been unthinkable. In providing a space where the past meets the present and students can forge identities that integrate both, the powwows represent the best of what can be achieved by collective music making at an off-reservation boarding school today.

Chapter 9
After School: Keeping the Music Going

"What goes right in childhood predicts the future far better than what goes wrong."

—George E. Vaillant, *Aging Well*[1]

Students who are resilient have acquired, at some point in their lives, the skills they need to navigate life's challenges.[2] When studies of off-reservation Indian boarding schools touch on the idea of resiliency, they often consider student shows of resistance as an indicator. In this approach, student agency is measured in the ways, whether subtle or overt, that students act out in opposition to the strictures imposed by the school on their bodies and their actions. A more expansive and accurate concept of resiliency, however, and one that reveals more about students' ways of being in the world, takes into account not only resistance to assimilation but also students' negotiation of the myriad ways a school or society can encourage a young Indian person to be true or false to his or her self—the self in all its complexity, fluidity, knottiness, and hybridity. The forces that would deny a student his or her humanity are those against which music making (initially a tool of assimilationism) can now offer unique possibilities for counteracting stereotypes and developing a strong personal identity that will serve and support a student into his or her adulthood.

Resiliency, while sometimes hard to quantify, presents itself in qualities or attributes that often exist outside of resistance, and it can most accurately be observed in the extent to which students can bounce back from adversities to be fully themselves: complex human beings who are liable to interrupt the stereotypes regarding the expected behavior for Natives and non-Natives. The collective, organized ways that boarding school students have used music making in the service of opposing limited or wrongheaded conceptions of Indianness reveal new alternatives to Brenda Child's characterization of resistance as individual rather than collective[3] and Basil Johnston's experience that passive resistance (e.g., dawdling) was "the one available means of defying authority."[4] Through such forms of music making as garage bands and powwows, students are able to cultivate resiliency in ways that are active and collaborative. When students find these modes of working together to be useful, they often find ways to continue their collaborations even after they leave Chemawa.

Alumni organizations, now a common feature of Indian boarding schools, have their roots in loose networks of former students that began to coalesce in the 1930s. The specific missions of such groups varied, but they often sponsored activities that were both social and philanthropic: raising funds for specific projects for their alma mater, recruiting future students, or simply raising awareness of the boarding school through public events and written discourse. The relationship of an alumni organization to the school itself was typically loose, consisting of occasional correspondence and updates on each other's recent activities.

What spurred former students to create such groups? They were moved by the power of their shared experience in the schools and the importance of forming and maintaining interpersonal connections. Boarding school alumni, though each had undergone his or her schooling individually, shared collective memories of the residential schools that were more intimate and far-reaching that those shared by alumni from a typical public school. The importance of maintaining connections to one's peers has been particularly salient in remote areas such as Alaska, where Chemawa alumni are scattered over a large region. In 1933, ex-students and graduates living in Metlakatla formed the Reliance Activity Club, which soon numbered over three hundred active members. Named for one of Chemawa's longstanding literary clubs, Reliance organized social gatherings and sought to maintain ties between its members as Chemawa began to phase out Alaskan students in the 1930s.

Because of the members' geographic dispersal, alumni wanting to see each other had to travel great distances, and music became one way the alumni could regularly reconnect and maintain a sense of group identity. Raymond Haldane, the club's treasurer, assembled an orchestra called the Chemawans. A seven-man band with piano, clarinet, saxophones, trumpet, guitar, and drums, the Chemawans was composed of recent alumni who had learned their instruments while at school in Oregon. The personnel included Haldane, pianist and director; Reno Booth, alto saxophone and clarinet; Terrance Booth (Reno's brother), tenor saxophone; Tony Haldane (Raymond's brother), baritone saxophone; Frank Hayward, trumpet; Al Fawcett, guitar; and Henry Chalmers, drums.[5]

Reno Booth, a graduate of the class of 1928 who had distinguished himself at Chemawa for his abilities as a musician and singer, had made his way back to Alaska after first trying to establish a professional career in Portland, initially through the medium of late-night radio. The school paper carried updates of his work and future plans: "Reno Booth, a member of our graduating class of last year, is now singing over the radio from Portland regularly. He sings over KOIN and

KXL. His regular night is on Tuesday, between 11 and 12 o'clock. This is known as the 'Varsity Hour.' On Thursday nights he is on from 10:30 to 12 with the Portland Tomcats. He is anxious to have request numbers sent in for that makes business for him." Booth tapped into his Chemawa network when special needs arose: "It should be mentioned that he expects to do some stage work pretty soon and is anxious to secure a genuine Indian costume for the work. If any one of our readers have something in that line to loan or sell they will favor Reno by addressing him at Portland, Oregon, general delivery."[6] We don't know what precipitated his move back to Alaska, but the Great Depression likely rendered it difficult to find steady work as a musician anywhere. Booth's eventual return to his family was typical of Alaska alumni in particular, as was the phenomenon of music as a family activity. The Chemawans, for example, included two sets of brothers.

Once established, the Chemawans quickly built up a repertoire and traveled to small towns around Alaska to play for dances. For those who could not attend the dances, the band was broadcast live on Saturdays at midnight over station KGBU out of Ketchikan. News from Chemawa was sometimes read on the radio, and the musicians elicited requests from their friends in Alaska and in Oregon.

Band members sent updates of their performance schedule and the doings of the Reliance Activity Club to the superintendent at Chemawa, who made sure that the accounts were published in the school paper. The articles sought to persuade current students that attending Chemawa was not just a transitory experience but a transformative process whereby the school would become part of a student's identity for life. An article submitted by Reno Booth, reporting the alumni club's continuance of Chemawa's Halloween carnival tradition, provides one example of this lifelong identification.

> The Reliance Activity Club of Metlakalta, Alaska, recently sponsored a very elaborate Hallowe'en carnival dance. The affair was a social highlight in these parts. The members sang good old Reliance songs which took us back to dear old Chemawa. Alaska's pride, the Chemawans, furnished the music (the best obtainable anywhere in this part of the country) for dancing. We are still upholding Chemawa in every way.[7]

An editorial decision on the part of the *Chemawa American* to introduce the article as "written by Reno Booth, a former student" suggests the intention to provide a testimonial that would highlight alumni loyalty to the school as an unforced, spontaneous, and grateful response to the good times they had at Chemawa and all the benefits their education had accorded them. And as music features prominently at many Native gatherings, so did it here at the alumni gathering, through the use of school songs and band music provided by these Chemawa-trained musicians.

Off-reservation boarding schools have altered the lives of many thousands of Indian people. During its 132 continuous years of existence, over thirty thousand students have passed through the doors of Chemawa alone. For countless young people, time spent in the boarding schools was traumatic, and resulted in the loss of cultural identity through the forced assimilation mandated by federal policies.[8] While families and communities are still recovering from these profound losses, the legacy of boarding schools is not simply one of victimhood, and the lives of Chemawa's musicians reflect this complexity.

Upon leaving Chemawa, some went on to become celebrated musicians, recognized nationally. These include Spade Cooley, whose teachers at Chemawa groomed him for life as a professional musician but failed to address the issues of alcohol misuse or personal identity that later contributed to his tragic and public downfall. They also include Will DePoe, who went on to make his living as a pianist and band leader; his appearances throughout the Northwest and in film gave him the relationships, perspective, and respect that ultimately allowed him to function as a tribal leader and cultural broker amongst Native and non-Native groups. Two more successful Chemawa musicians profiled in *Indian Blues* include Fred Cardin (Quapaw), who played first violin in Chemawa's Indian String Quartet, and went on to create several prominent all-Indian ensembles in the years following World War I,[9] and Joe Morris (Blackfeet), who played the trombone in Chemawa's Rhythm Chiefs and spent the rest of his life playing brass instruments in bands up and down the West Coast.[10]

Some students have continued on the paths begun at Chemawa by incorporating music into their later careers. These include Max Lestenkof, in his work as a wellness advocate, and Ted McGlashan, in his vocation as a guitar player and bandleader throughout the Alaska night-club circuit. Many Chemawa alumni have transmitted their love and knowledge of music to their children, and some have helped young people to better understand their tribal heritages by promoting traditional Indian musics. Chet Clark continues to write songs and make drums, Bob Tom maintains a busy schedule of emceeing powwows, Arlie Neskahi does extensive work in cultural maintenance and preservation, and Arlie's students such as Annie Evans (Blackfoot) have returned to their own tribal communities and begun leading music groups themselves.

Many alumni have continued to practice music for personal enjoyment, whether this takes the form of singing, such as for Millie Metcalf of Hooper Bay, Alaska (see Chapter 4), or through playing an instrument, as it did for Leah Tom's father, Sam Shoulderblades, who continued to play the fiddle after his years as a standout athlete at Chemawa.

Some have also used the public performance skills they gained as musicians at Chemawa to help develop their later roles as tribal leaders. Conspicuous examples include those of Kathryn Harrison (Grand Ronde) and her father, Harry Jones (Mollala), before her, as well as Dee and Don Pigsley (Siletz). Harrison especially exemplifies resiliency; she overcame being orphaned, suffering abuse from her foster parents and husband, and seeing the termination of her people; she stepped forward to lead the Confederated Tribes of Grand Ronde in a struggle for restoration that ultimately succeeded. Harrison helped propel the tribe's revival while paralleling it in her own personal life. The number of tribal leaders who have emerged from Chemawa is striking, and, for many of them, participation in Chemawa's musical ensembles was a means by which they acquired the skill sets that enabled their later service to their tribes. In these ways, Chemawa's musicians have gone on to demonstrate that particular quality of character that can often predict psychological wellness and social success later in life: resiliency.

Music at Chemawa has travelled a long and bumpy journey from its assimilationist beginnings to its current "by Indians, for Indians" inclusivity. As the many forms of music making that span the school's history demonstrate, music can be used sometimes in the service of hegemony and sometimes to counteract it. The hegemonic dominance that can be far-reaching within the confines of a "total institution" such as a boarding school has not proved to be the end of the story for Chemawa students. Students' responses to the music they encounter at school are varied and complex, often revealing their awareness of the issues surrounding identity formation, tribal heritage, and the acquisition of skills truly relevant for their lives after Chemawa. To this end, Chemawa's students have taken songs, instruments, and music ensembles and made them their own, through choices of repertoire, performance practice, and volitional interactions with the on- and off-campus communities.

How students make music merits more consideration than it has been accorded, for its ability to shed light on the most intimate encounters between different social spheres: students, their families, tribal communities, Chemawa staff and faculty, BIA administrators, the greater Salem-area community, and federal policy makers who shape and take cues from the national discourse regarding Indian peoples and social reforms. The complex encounters regarding Chemawa's music policies as lived out in the lives of its students reveal not just the trajectory of the assimilation campaign, but also the complex and personal nature of the campaign's successes and failures.

The legacy of music at Chemawa does not consist of a simple struggle between indoctrination and resistance. The results of hegemonic policies imposed by non-Native reformers for so many years are far more complicated, and are always contingent upon the particular situations, resources, and familial backgrounds of the individual students themselves. Music has always been important to Indian people, and students at Chemawa have used music to transform the tools of civilization into tools of Indianization, revitalization, and celebration. Today, the music instruction once aimed at capturing the hearts of Native students now serves to equip them with an array of skills for consciously navigating American society and becoming leaders in their tribal communities.

Bibliography

Adams, David Wallace. 1995. *Education for Extinction: American Indians and the Boarding School Experience, 1875-1928*. Lawrence: University Press of Kansas.

Adams, Evelyn C. 1946. *American Indian Education: Government Schools and Economic Progress*. Morningside Heights, NY: King's Crown Press.

Annual Report of the Commissioner of Indian Affairs. Var. Washington, D.C.: U.S. Government Printing Office. 1879-1917, 1921-1932.

Archuleta, Margaret L., Brenda J. Child, and K. Tsianina Lomawaima, eds. 2000. *Away from Home: American Indian Boarding School Experiences,* Phoenix, AZ: The Heard Museum.

Axtell, James. 1985. *The Invasion Within: The Contest of Cultures in Colonial North America*. New York: Oxford University Press.

———. 1981. *The European and the Indian: Essays in the Ethnohistory of Colonial North America*. New York: Oxford University Press.

Bailey, Donald Wilson. 1985. "Chemawa Indian School Art Education, 1880-1952." M.A. thesis, University of Oregon.

Baker, Ray Stannard. 1903. "The Day of the Run." *Century* (Sept.): 643-55.

Bangs, Lester. 1980. "Protopunk: The Garage Bands." In *The Rolling Stone Illustrated History of Rock & Roll*. Jim Miller, ed. New York: Rolling Stone Press, 1980. Pages 261-64.

Barry, Mary J. 2000. *Jack and Nellie Brown: Pioneer Settlers of Anchorage, Alaska*. Anchorage: MJP Barry.

Beaver, R. Pierce. 1988. "Protestant Churches and the Indians." In *History of Indian-White Relations*. Wilcomb E. Washburn, ed. Vol. 4 of *Handbook of North American Indians*. Washington, D.C.: Smithsonian Institution. 430-58.

Beavers, Helen Mary. *From Point Barrow to Chemawa*. New York: Carlton Press.

Becker, Judith. 2001. "Anthropological Perspectives on Music and Emotion." In *Music and Emotion: Theory and Research*. Patrick N. Justin and John A. Sloboda, eds. New York: Oxford University Press. 135-60.

Benard, Bonnie. 2004. *Resiliency: What We Have Learned*. San Francisco: WestEd.

Bishop, Randy. 2000. "Out Yonder, on the Edge of Things." *Christian History* 19 (2): 30-34

Bloom, John. 1996. " 'Show What an Indian Can Do': Sports, Memory, and Ethnic Identity at Federal Indian Boarding School." *Journal of American Indian Education* 35 (spring): 33-48.

Bonnell, Sonciray. 1997. "Chemawa Indian Boarding School: The First One Hundred Years, 1880 to 1980." M.A. thesis. Dartmouth College.

Briggs, Kara. 2002. "Reclaiming Tribal History." *The Oregonian*: B1. May 6, 2002.

Browner, Tara. 2002. *Heartbeat of the People: Music and Dance of the Northern Pow-Wow*. Urbana: University of Illinois Press.

———. 1997. " 'Breathing the Indian Spirit': Thoughts on Musical Borrowing and the 'Indianist' Movement in American Music." *American Music* 15 (3): 265-84.

————. 1995. "Transposing Cultures: The Appropriation of Native North American Musics, 1890-1990." Ph.D. diss., University of Michigan.

Burcham, Lena M. 1930. "A Study of the Student Activities, Discipline and Social Life of the Students at the Salem Indian School from the Point of View of Adjustment to American Life." M.S. thesis. University of Oregon.

Burns, Robert I. 1988. "Roman Catholic Missions in the Northwest." In *History of Indian-White Relations*. Wilcomb E. Washburn, ed. Vol. 4 of *Handbook of North American Indians*. Washington, D.C.: Smithsonian Institution. 494-500.

Cadman, Charles Wakefield. 1915. "The 'Idealization' of Indian Music." *The Musical Quarterly* 1 (3): 387-96.

Campbell, James Gavin. 2000. " 'A Higher Mission Than Merely to Please the Ear': Music and Social Reform in America, 1900-1925." *Musical Quarterly* 84 (2): 259-86.

Canadian Broadcasting Corporation. 2004. "A Lost Heritage: Canada's Residential Schools." <http://archives.cbc.ca/300c.asp?id=1-70-692>

Carey, Charles Henry. 1923. "Diary of Rev. George Gary." *Oregon Historical Quarterly* 24: 79-80, 84.

Chalcraft, Edwin L. 2007. *Assimilation's Agent: My Life as a Superintendent in the Indian Boarding School System*. Cary C. Collins, ed. Lincoln: University of Nebraska Press.

Charlton, Katherine. 2003. *Rock Music Styles: A History*. 3rd edition. New York: McGraw Hill.

Chavis, Ben. 1999. "Off-Reservation Boarding High School Teachers: How Are They Perceived by Former American Indian Students?" *The Social Science Journal* 36 (1): 33-45.

The Chemawa American. Var. School newspaper. Chemawa Indian School. Salem, Oregon.

The Chemawa Annual. Var. Chemawa Indian School. Salem, Oregon. 1962, 1964.

Chemawa Indian School Parent and Student Handbook. 2008. Volume 8. Chemawa Indian School. Salem, Oregon. Available at: <http://www.chemawa.bie.edu/Assets/documents/PSHandbook0910.pdf>

————.Volume 6. Chemawa Indian School. Salem, Oregon. Available at: <http://www.chemawa.bia.edu/Assets/documents/0708PSHandbook.pdf>

"Chemawa Pow-wow Celebrates the School's 125th Birthday." 2005. *Smoke Signals: A Publication of the Grand Ronde Tribe*. March 1, 2005. Page 6.

The Chief. Var. Chemawa school annual. Salem, Oregon. 1932, 1933, 1937, 1939, 1940.

Child, Brenda J. 1998. *Board School Seasons: American Indian Families, 1900-1940*. Lincoln: University of Nebraska Press.

Chilocco Indian School. 1938. School newspaper. Chilocco Indian School. Chilocco, OK.

Churchill, Ward. 2004. *Kill the Indian, Save the Man: The Genocidal Impact of American Indian Residential Schools*. San Francisco: City Lights.

Clark, Katerina, and Michael Holquist. 1984. *Mikhail Bakhtin*. Cambridge, MA: Belknap Press of Harvard University Press.

Clifford, James. 1997. *Routes: Travel and Translation in the Late Twentieth Century*. Cambridge, MA: Harvard University Press.

Clough, Josh. 2006. "A Victim of Its Own Success: The Story of the Cheyenne and Arapaho Indian Fair, 1910-13." *American Indian Culture and Research Journal* 30 (2): 35-61.

Colfer, Carol J. Pierce. 1975. "Bureaucrats, Budgets, and the BIA: Segmentary Opposition in a Residential School." *Human Organization* 34 (2): 149-56.

Colley, Carol. "Student Perceptions of the Chemawa Alcohol Education Center." Master's thesis. Portland State University.

Collier, John. *From Every Zenith: A Memoir*. Denver, CO: Sage Books.

Collins, Cary C. 2001. " 'Between Savagery and Civilization': The Memoir of Edwin L. Chalcraft, U.S. Indian Agent." Ph.D. diss. Washington State University.

———. 2001. "A Future with a Past: Hazel Pete, Cultural Identity, and the Federal Indian Education System." *Pacific Northwest Quarterly* 92 (1): 15-28.

———. 2000. "The Broken Crucible of Assimilation: Forest Grove Indian School and the Origins of Off-Reservation Boarding School Education in the West." *Oregon Historical Quarterly* 101 (4): 466-507.

———. 1998a. "Oregon's Carlisle: Teaching 'America' at Oregon's Indian School." *Columbia* 12 (2): 6-10.

———. 1998b. "Through the Lens of Assimilation: Edwin L. Chalcraft and Chemawa Indian School." *Oregon Historical Quarterly* 98 (4): 390-425. Cook-Lynn, Elizabeth. 2001. *Anti-Indianism in Modern America: A Voice from Tatekeya's Earth*. Urbana: University of Illinois.

Coreno, Thaddeus. 1994. "Guerrilla Music: Avant-Garde Voice as Oppositional Discourse." In *Adolescents and Their Music: If It's Too Loud, You're Too Old*. Jonathon S. Epstein, ed. New York: Garland Publishing, 189-224.

Cornell, Stephen. 1988. *The Return of the Native: American Indian Political Resurgence*. New York: Oxford University Press.

Cross, William E., Jr. 1991. *Shades of Black: Diversity in African-American Identity*. Philadelphia: Temple University Press.

Csikszentmihalyi, Mihaly. 1996. *Creativity: Flow and the Psychology of Discovery and Invention*. New York: HarperCollins.

———. 1990. *Flow: The Psychology of Optimal Experience*. New York: Harper & Row.

Daley, Patrick, and Beverly James. 1998. "Missionary Voices as the Discursive Terrain for Native Resistance." *Journal of Communication Inquiry* 22 (4): 365-84.

Dauenhauer, Richard, and Nora Marks Dauenhauer, eds. 1994. *Haa Kusteeyí / Our Culture: Tlingit Life Stories*. Seattle: University of Washington Press.

Davis, Julie. 2001. "American Indian Boarding School Experiences: Recent Studies from Native Perspectives." *Organization of American Historians Magazine of History* 15 (2): 20-22.

Dejong, David H. 1993. *Promises of the Past: A History of Indian Education in the United States*. Golden, CO: North American.

Devens, Carol. 2001. " 'If We Get the Girls, We Get the Race': Missionary Education of Native American Girls." In *American Nations: Encounters in Indian Country, 1850 to the Present*. Frederick E. Hoxie et al., eds. New York: Routledge. 156-71.

Dewey, John. 1934. "Art and Civilization." In *Art as Experience*. New York: Minton, Balch & Co. 326-30.

———. 1887. "Aesthetic Feeling: The Fine Arts." As reprinted in *John Dewey: The Early Works, 1882-1898*. Carbondale: Southern Illinois University Press (1968). 274.

Diamond, Beverley, M. Sam Cronk, and Franziska von Rosen. 1995. *Visions of Sound: Musical Instruments of First Nation Communities in Northeastern America*. Chicago: University of Chicago Press.

Douglas, Ann. 1977. *The Feminization of American Culture*. New York: Alfred A. Knopf.

Drinnon, Richard. 1997. *Facing West: The Metaphysics of Indian-Hating and Empire-Building*. Norman: University of Oklahoma Press.

———. 1984. "American Pastime: Rediscovering 'The Indians.'" *Massachusetts Review* 25 (1): 97-114.

Dvorak, Raymond Francis. 1937. *The Band on Parade*. New York: Carl Fischer, Inc.

Eddy, Sarah J. 1897. *Songs of Happy Life: For Schools, Homes, and Bands of Mercy.* Providence, RI: Art and Nature Study Publishing Co.

Eells, Myron. 1985. *The Indians of Puget Sound: The Notebooks of Myron Eells.* George Pierre Castile, ed. Seattle: University of Washington Press.

Ellis, Clyde. 2003. *A Dancing People: Powwow Culture on the Southern Plains.* Lawrence: University Press of Kansas.

————. 1996. *To Change Them Forever: Indian Education at the Rainy Mountain Boarding School, 1893-1920.* Norman: University of Oklahoma Press.

Ellis, Clyde, Luke Eric Lassiter, and Gary H. Dunham, eds. 2005. *Powwow.* Lincoln: University of Nebraska Press.

Emmerich, Lisa E. 2001. " 'Right in the Midst of My Own People': Native American Women and the Field Matron Program." In *American Nations: Encounters in Indian Country, 1850 to the Present.* Frederick E. Hoxie et al., eds. New York: Routledge. 143-55.

Farrow, Terry, and Gordon Oats. "Drop-Out Study of Chemawa Indian School." M.A. thesis. Portland State University.

Fear-Segal, Jacqueline. 2007. *White Man's Club: Schools, Race, and the Struggle of Indian Assimilation.* Lincoln: University of Nebraska Press.

Fife, Austin E., and Francesca Redden. 1954. "The Pseudo-Indian Folksongs of the Anglo-American and French- Canadian." *Journal of American Folklore* 67 (265): 239-51 and 67 (266): 379-94.

Fletcher, Alice C. 1900. *Indian Story and Song from North America.* Boston: Small Maynard.

Foster, Morris W. 1992. *Being Comanche: The Social History of an American Indian Community.* Tucson: University of Arizona Press.

Foucault, Michel. 1980. *Power/Knowledge: Selected Interviews and Other Writings 1972-1977.* Colin Gordon, ed. New York: Pantheon Books.

Fowler, Loretta. 2005. "Local Contexts of Powwow Ritual." In *Powwow.* Clyde Ellis, Luke Eric Lassiter, and Gary H. Dunham, eds. Lincoln: University of Nebraska Press. 68-82.

Fuchs, Estelle, and Robert J. Havighurst. 1972. *To Live on This Earth: American Indian Education.* Albuquerque: University of New Mexico Press.

Gaede, Jethro. 2009. "An Ethnohistory of the American Indian Exposition at Anadarko, Oklahoma, 1932-2003." Ph.D. diss., University of Oklahoma.

Gardner, Howard. 2000. *Intelligence Reframed: Multiple Intelligences for the 21st Century.* New York: Basic Books.

————. 1991. *Art Education and Human Development.* Los Angeles: Getty Trust Publications.

————. 1983. *Frames of Mind: A Theory of Multiple Intelligences.* New York: Basic Books.

Garrett, Michael Tlanusta, and Eugene F. Pichette. 2000. "Red as an Apple: Native American Acculturation and Counseling With or Without Reservation." *Journal of Counseling & Development* 78 (1): 3-13.

Garth, Thomas R., and Sarah Rachel Isbell. 1929. "The Musical Talent of Indians." *Music Supervisors Journal* 15 (3): 83, 85-87.

Garty, Judy. 2003. *Techniques of Marching Bands.* Broomall, PA: Mason Crest.

Giago, Tim A., Jr. 1978. *The Aboriginal Sin: Reflections on the Holy Rosary Indian Mission School (Red Cloud Indian School).* San Francisco: The Indian Historian Press.

Gilbert, Matthew Sakiestewa. 2010. *Education Beyond the Mesas: Hopi Students at Sherman Institute, 1902-1929.* Lincoln: University of Nebraska Press.

Gilbert, Matthew Sakiestewa, and Allan Holzman. 2006. *Beyond the Mesas*. A Film on the Hopi Boarding School Experience. 716 Productions and the Hopi Cultural Preservation Office.

Gonzales-Berry, Erlinda, Jun Xing, and Patti Sukurai, eds. 2007. *Seeing Color: Indigenous Peoples and Racialized Ethnic Minorities in Oregon*. Lanham, MD: University Press of America.

Goodrich, Frederick W. 1932. "Oregon Orchestra Music, 1868-1932." *Oregon Historical Quarterly* 33 (2): 136-42.

Gordon, Edgar B. 1956. "The Birth of the School Bands and Orchestras." *Music Educators Journal* 43 (2): 34-36, 43-45.

Green, Rayna. 1994. "The Image of the Indian in American Popular Culture." In *The Handbook of North American Indians IV*. Wilcomb Washburn, ed. Washington, D.C.: Smithsonian Institution Press. 587-606.

———. 1989. " 'Kill the Indian and Save the Man': Indian Education in the United States." In *To Lead and To Serve: American Indian Education at Hampton Institute, 1878-1923*. Mary Lou Hultgren and Paulette Fairbanks Molin, eds. Virginia Beach: Virginia Foundation for the Humanities and Public Policy. 9-13.

———. 1975. "The Pocahontas Perplex: The Image of Indian Women in American Culture." *The Massachusetts Review* 16(4): 698-714.

Grossberg, Lawrence. 1994. "The Political Status of Youth and Youth Culture." In *Adolescents and Their Music: If It's Too Loud, You're Too Old*. Jonathon S. Epstein, ed. New York: Garland Publishing, 25-46.

Haig-Brown, Celia. 2003. "Creating Spaces: Testimonio, Impossible Knowledge, and Academe." *International Journal of Qualitative Studies in Education* 16 (3): 415-33.

———. 1988. *Resistance and Renewal: Surviving the Indian Residential School*. Vancouver, B.C.: Tillacum Library.

Hall, Stuart. 1992. "The West and the Rest: Discourses and Power." In *Formations of Modernity*. Stuart Hall and Bram Gieben, eds. Cambridge, UK: Polity Press. 275-331.

Hansen, Richard K. 2005. *The American Wind Band: A Cultural History*. Chicago: GIA Publications.

Harmon, Alexandra. 1998. *Indians in the Making: Ethnic Relations and Indian Identities around Puget Sound*. Berkeley: University of California Press.

Harper, Earl E. 1955. "Music in American Education: Moral and Spiritual Values in Music Education." In *Music in American Education*. Hazel Beckwith Nohavec Morgan, ed. Chicago: Music Educators National Conference. 5-8.

Harper's Weekly. 1882. "Forest Grove Indian Training School." 27 May 1882. Vol. 26, No. 1327: 324-27.

Havinghurst, Robert James. 1978. *National Study of American Indian Education Research Reports*. Minneapolis: University of Minnesota.

Hazen-Hammond, Susan. 1997. *Timelines of Native American History: Through the Centuries with Mother Earth and Father Sky*. New York: Berkeley Publishing Group.

Henderson, Nan, and Mike L. Milstein. 2003. *Resiliency in Schools: Making it Happen for Students and Educators*. Thousand Oaks, CA: Corwin Press.

Higa, Jennifer Leilani. 2000. "Off-Reservation Boarding Schools in Contemporary Native American Education." B.A. thesis. Amherst College.

Holm, Tom. 2005. *The Great Confusion in Indian Affairs: Native Americans and Whites in the Progressive Era*. Austin: University of Texas Press.

———. 2003. "Peoplehood: A Model for the Extension of Sovereignty in American Indian Studies." *Wicazo Sa Review* 18 (1): 7-24.

Holston, Kim R., compiler. 1984. *The Marching Band Handbook*. Jefferson, NC: McFarland & Co.

Horne, Esther Burnett, and Sally McBeth. 1998. *Essie's Story: The Life and Legacy of a Shoshone Teacher*. Lincoln: University of Nebraska Press.

Howard, James. 1983. "Pan-Indianism in Native American Music and Dance." *Ethnomusicology* 71: 71-82.

———. 1955. "Pan-Indian Culture in Oklahoma." *Scientific Monthly* 81: 215-220.

Hoxie, Frederick E. 1984. *A Final Promise: A Campaign to Assimilate the Indians, 1880-1920*. Lincoln: University of Nebraska Press.

Hoxie, Frederick E., Peter C. Mancall, and James H. Merrell, eds. 2001. *American Nations: Encounters in Indian Country, 1850 to the Present*. New York: Routledge.

Huff, Delores J. 1997. *To Live Heroically: Institutional Racism and American Indian Education*. Albany: State University of New York Press.

Hultgren, Mary Lou, and Paulette Fairbanks Molin, eds. 1989. *To Lead and To Serve: American Indian Education at Hampton Institute, 1878-1923*. Virginia Beach: Virginia Foundation for the Humanities and Public Policy.

Hunt, Jesse D. 1993. "Social Behaviors of Chemawa Students: CAEC and CIBS Approach to Alcohol and Drug Intervention." B.A. thesis. George Fox College, Newberg, OR.

Hurtado, Aida. 1997. "Understanding Multiple Group Identities: Inserting Women into Cultural Transformations." *Journal of Social Issues* 53 (2): 299-327.

Hyer, Sally. *One House, One Voice, One Heart: Native American Education at Santa Fe Indian School*. Santa Fe: Museum of New Mexico Press.

Iliff, Flora Gregg. *People of the Blue Water: My Adventures Among the Walapi and Havasupai Indians*. New York: Harper and Brothers.

Indian Education: A National Tragedy, A National Challenge. Also known as "The Kennedy Report." Washington, D.C.: U.S. Government Printing Office.

"Indian Opera Seats On Sale." *Spokane Chronicle*, 19 July 1926.

"Indian Thespians Appear Tonight." *Spokane Chronicle*, 22 July 1926.

The Indian School Journal. 1914. School newspaper. Chilocco Indian School. Chilocco, Oklahoma.

International Resilience Project. 1998. Edith Grotberg, Director. University of Alabama. Summarized at: <http://resilnet.uiuc.edu/library/grotb97a.html>

Jackson, Curtis E., and Marcia J. Galli. 1977. *A History of the Bureau of Indian Affairs and Its Activities Among Indians*. San Francisco: E & R Research Press.

Jackson, Jason Baird, and Victoria Lindsay Levine. 2002. "Singing for Garfish: Music and Woodland Communities in Eastern Oklahoma." *Ethnomusicology* 46 (2): 284-306.

Jacobs, Margaret D. 2001. "Making Savages of Us All: White Women, Pueblo Indians, and the Controversy over Indian Dances in the 1920s." In *American Nations: Encounters in Indian Country, 1850 to the Present*. Frederick E. Hoxie et al., eds. New York: Routledge. 172-98.

Johnson, Al. 1995. "In Memory of White Wolf's Child." *American Indian Culture and Research Journal* 19 (3): 207-10.

Johnston, Basil H. *Indian School Days*. Norman: University of Oklahoma Press.

Jones, Dorothy Knee. 1982. *A Century of Servitude: Pribilof Aleuts Under U.S. Rule*. Lanham, MD: University Press of America.

Kaestle, Carl F. 1982. "Ideology and American Educational History." *History of Education Quarterly* 22:127-28.

Katanski, Amelia V. 2005. *Learning to Write "Indian": The Boarding-School Experience and American Indian Literature*. Norman: University of Oklahoma Press.

Kavanagh, Thomas W. 2008. "Powwows." In *Handbook of North American Indians*, Vol. 2 ("Indians in Contemporary Society"). Washington, D.C.: Smithsonian Institution Scholarly Press. 327-37.

Keene, James A. 1982. *A History of Music Education in the United States*. Hanover, NH: University Press of New England.

Keller, Jean A. " 'In the Fall of the Year We Were Troubled with Some Sickness': Typhoid Fever Deaths, Sherman Institute, 1904." *American Indian Culture and Research Journal* 23 (3): 97-117.

Kelly, Lawrence C. 1983. *The Assault on Assimilation: John Collier and the Origins of Indian Policy Reform*. Albuquerque: University of New Mexico Press.

Kenny, Michael G. 1999. "A Place for Memory: The Interface Between Individual and Collective History." *Comparative Studies in Society and History* 41 (3): 420-37.

Kienzle, Rich. 1996. Liner notes for *Heroes of Country Music, Vol. 4: Legends of the West Coast*. Rhino Records #72443.

———. 1977. "When a Country Star turns Murderer: The Strange, Tragic Case of Spade Cooley." *Country Music* 5 (10): 34-36, 38, 64.

LaCroix, Debbie Ann. 1993. "Indian Boarding School Daughters Coming Home: Survival Stories As Oral Histories of Native American Women." Ph.D. diss., University of Oregon.

La Flesche, Francis. 1963. *The Middle Five: Indian Schoolboys of the Omaha Tribe*. Madison: University of Wisconsin Press.

Lassiter, Luke, Clyde Ellis, and Ralph Kotay. 2002. *The Jesus Road: Kiowas, Christianity, and Indian Hymns*. Lincoln: University of Nebraska Press.

Lassiter, Luke. 1998. *The Power of Kiowa Song*. Tucson: University of Arizona Press.

Lemmon, Burton Carlyle. 1941. "The Historical Development of Chemawa Indian School." M.S. thesis. Oregon State College.

Leupp, Francis E. 1910. *The Indian and His Problem*. New York: Charles Scribner's Sons.

———. 1902. *Negro Self-Uplifting*. Tuskegee, AL: Tuskegee Institute Steam Print.

———. 1897. "Indian School Management. Reply to Attacks by Captain Pratt Upon the Introduction of Civil Service Reform Methods." *New York Evening Post*, February 1, 1897. Reprinted by the Indian Rights Association, Philadelphia, PA.

Levine, Victoria Lindsay. 2002. *Writing American Indian Music: Historical Transcriptions, Notations, and Arrangements*. Middleton, WI: A-R Editions.

Lieurance, Thurlow. "Stories of Famous Concert Songs: 'By the Waters of the Minnetonka.' " *Etude* 50 (6): 396, 449.

Lipsitz, George. 1999. *Time Passages*. Minneapolis: University of Minnesota Press.

Lomawaima, K. Tsianina. 2006. *To Remain an Indian: Lessons in Democracy from a Century of Native American Education*. New York: Teachers College Press.

———. "Tribal Sovereigns: Reframing Research in American Indian Education." *Harvard Educational Review* 70 (1): 1-21.

———. 1996. "Estelle Reel, Superintendent of Indian Schools, 1898-1910: Politics, Curriculum, and Land." *Journal of American Indian Education* 35 (spring): 5-31.

———. 1994. *They Called It Prairie Light: The Story of Chilocco Indian School*. Lincoln: University of Nebraska Press.

———. 1993. "Domesticity in the Federal Indian Schools: The Power of Authority Over Mind and Body." *American Ethnologist* 20 (2): 227-40.

Longden, Tom. 2008. "Logan, Frederic Knight." *The Des Moines Register*. Available at: <http://desmoinesregister.com/apps/pbcs.dll/article?AID=/99999999/FAMOUSIOWANS/41221035>

Luthar, Suniya S., ed. 2003. *Resilience and Vulnerability: Adaptation in the Context of Childhood Adversities.* New York: Cambridge University Press.

Macleod, Beth Abelson. 1993. " 'Whence Comes the Lady Tympanist?': Gender and Instrumental Musicians in America, 1853-1990." *Journal of Social History* 27 (2): 291-308.

Malone, Bill C. 2002. *Country Music, U.S.A.* Second revised edition. Austin: University of Texas Press.

Malone, Jacqui. 1996. *Steppin' on the Blues: The Visible Rhythms of African American Dance.* Urbana: University of Illinois Press.

Mankiller, Wilma, ed. 2004. *Every Day Is A Good Day: Reflections by Contemporary Indigenous Women.* Golden, CO: Fulcrum Publishing.

Mark, Michael L. 1982. *Source Readings in Music Education History.* New York: Schirmer.

Marken, Jack W., and Charles L. Woodard, eds. 2001. *Shaping Survival: Essays by Four American Indian Tribal Women.* Lanham, MD: Scarecrow Press.

Martin-Breen, Patrick, and J. Marty Anderies. 2011. "Resilience: A Literature Review." Commissioned by The Rockefeller Foundation.

Matt, Jesse. 1971. "A Pictorial Portfolio of Chemawa Indian School." Album #3 in series. Unpublished chronicles of campus life at Chemawa, with photographs and captions.

Mayo, Rev. A. D. 1873. "Methods of Moral Instruction in Common Schools." *The Addresses and Journal of Proceedings of the National Educational Association.* Washington, D.C.: National Education Association. 21-22.

McAllester, David P. 1984. Descriptions of Navajo music in "North America / Native America." In *Worlds of Music.* Jeff Todd Titon, ed. New York: Schirmer. 28-66.

McAnally, J. Kent. 1996. "The Haskell (Institute) Indian Band in 1904: The World's Fair and Beyond." *The Journal of Band Research* 31 (2): 1-34.

McBeth, Sally J. 1983. *Ethnic Identity and the Boarding School Experiences of West-Central Oklahoma American Indians.* Washington, D.C.: University Press of America.

McKeehan, Patrick Michael. 1981. "The History of Chemawa Indian School." Ph.D. diss. University of Washington. McMullen, Ann. 2004. " 'Canny About Conflict': Revitalization and Reality in Native Southeastern New England." In *Reassessing Revitalization Movements: Perspectives from North America and the Pacific Islands.* Michael E. Harkin, ed. Lincoln: University of Nebraska Press.

Mercier, Chris. 2001. "Hatfield Townhall Meeting in Portland." *Smoke Signals: A Publication of the Grand Ronde Tribe.* December 1, 2001. Page 2.

Merrill, Brent. 2001. "Hatfield Interview: Memories, Truth, and Insight." *Smoke Signals: A Publication of the Grand Ronde Tribe.* December 1, 2001. Pages 1 and 3.

Meyer, John M., ed. 2002. *American Indians and U.S. Politics: A Companion Reader.* Westport, CT: Praeger.

Mihesuah, Devon Abbott. 2003. *Indigenous American Women: Decolonization, Empowerment, Activism.* Lincoln: University of Nebraska Press.

———. 1998. "American Indian Identities: Issues of Individual Choices and Development." *American Indian Culture and Research Journal,* Vol. 22, No. 2: 193-226.

———. 1993. *Cultivating the Rosebuds: The Education of Women at the Cherokee Female Seminary, 1851-1909.* Urbana: University of Illinois Press.

———. 1991. " Out of the 'Graves of the Polluted Debauches': The Boys of the Cherokee Male Seminary." *American Indian Quarterly* 15 (Fall): 503-21.

———. 1991. "Too Dark to Be Angels: The Class System Among the Cherokees at the Female Seminary." *American Indian Culture and Research Journal* 15: 29-52.

Mitchell, Tony. 1993. "Treaty Now! Indigenous Music and Music Television in Australia." *Music, Culture, and Society* (15): 299-308.

Morris, "Indian Joe". 2001. *Alcatraz Indian Occupation Diary: Nov. 20, 1969 – June 11, 1971. Also, Early Life on Blackfeet Reservation, and Linda C. Morris' Tragic Love Story*. Private printing.

Morrison, Allen. 1965. "Indians Find Modern Steps Like War Dances." In *Salem Statesman*, Sat. Feb. 20, 1965. Sec. 1, page 5. Photographs by John Ericksen.

Moses, L. G. 1999. *Wild West Shows and the Images of American Indians, 1883-1933*. Albuquerque: University of New Mexico Press.

Mursell, James L., and Mabelle Glenn. 1938. *The Psychology of School Music Teaching*. New York: Silver Burdett Company.

Nabokov, Peter. 2002. *A Forest of Time: American Indian Ways of History*. New York: Cambridge University Press.

———, ed. 1991. *Native American Testimony: A Chronicle of Indian-White Relations from Prophecy to the Present, 1492-1992*. New York: Viking.

National Educators Association. 1909. *Journal of Proceedings and Addresses of the Forty-Seventh Annual Meeting*. Winona, MN: National Educators Association.

National Public Radio. 2000. "Indian Boarding Schools." "All Things Considered," Dec. 17. <http://www.npr.org/features/feature.php?wfId=1115656>

———. 2002. Neal Conan interviews Nan Henderson, President of Resiliency in Action. "Talk of the Nation." July 16. Available at: <http://www.resiliency.com/htm/streaming.htm>

Olson, Kristine. 2005. *Standing Tall: The Lifeway of Kathryn Jones Harrison*. Portland: Oregon Historical Society Press.

Parezo, Nancy J., and John W. Troutman. 2001. "The 'Shy' Cocopa Go to the Fair." In *Selling the Indian: Commercializing and Appropriating American Indian Cultures*. Carolyn Jones Meyer and Diana Royer, eds. Tucson: University of Arizona Press. 3-43.

Parham, Thomas A. 1989. "Cycles of Psychological Nigrescence." *The Counseling Psychologist* 17 (2): 187-226.

Patman, John Logan. 1942. "The High School Marching Band and Its Place in the Instrumental Music Curriculum." M.A. thesis. University of Oklahoma.

PBS Video. 1991. *The American Experience: "In the White Man's Image."* WGBH-TV Boston, MA and WNET-TV New York.

Pearce, Roy Harvey. 1953. *Savagism and Civilization: A Study of the Indian and the American Mind*. London: University of California Press.

Philips, Stephen. 1965. "The Challenge to the Marching Bands." *Music Educators Journal* 51 (4): 96, 100.

Philips, Susan Urmston. 1983. *The Invisible Culture: Communication in Classroom and Community on the Warm Springs Indian Reservation*. New York: Longman Inc.

Pisani, Michael V. *Imagining Native America in Music*. New Haven: Yale University Press.

Powers, Ramone. 1971. "Why the Northern Cheyenne Left Indian Territory in 1878: A Cultural Analysis." *Kansas Quarterly* 3 (fall): 72-81.

Powers, William K. 1990. *War Dance: Plains Indian Musical Experience*. Tucson: University of Arizona Press.

Pratt, Richard Henry. 1964. *Battlefield and Classroom: Four Decades with the American Indian, 1867-1904*. New Haven, CT: Yale University Press.

Program Handbook. Ottawa, Canada: Aboriginal Healing Foundation.

Prucha, Francis Paul. 1979. *The Churches and the Indian Schools, 1888-1912*. Lincoln: University of Nebraska Press.

————. 1976. *American Indian Policy in Crisis: Christian Reformers and the Indian, 1865-1900*. Norman: University of Oklahoma Press.

————, ed. 1975. *Documents of United States Indian Policy*. Lincoln: University of Nebraska Press.

Public Radio International . 2006. "Sound & Spirit." Episode: "Native Americans.". Interview with Arlie Neskahi, 2 April. Transcription available at: <http://www.wgbh.org>

Putney, Diane Therese. 1980. "Fighting the Scourge: American Indian Morbidity and Federal Policy, 1887-1928." Ph.D. diss., Marquette University.

Rader, Benjamin G. 2004. " 'The Greatest Drama in Indian Life': Experiments in Native American Identity and Resistance at the Haskell Institute Homecoming of 1926," *Western Historical Quarterly* 35 (Winter): 429-50.

Reddick, SuAnn M. "The Evolution of Chemawa Indian School: From Red River to Salem, 1825-1885." *Oregon Historical Quarterly* 101 (4): 444-65.

The Red Man. 1896. Carlisle Indian School. Carlisle, PA.

Reel, Estelle. 1906. *Teaching the Rudiments of Cooking in the Class Room: Primary Methods and Outlines for the Use of Teachers in the Indian Schools*. Washington, D.C.: Government Printing Office.

————. 1905. *Nature Study and Gardening: Primary Methods and Outlines for the Use of Teachers in the Indian Schools*. Washington, D.C.: Government Printing Office.

————. 1901. *Uniform Course of Study for the Indian Schools of the United States*. Washington, D.C.: Government Printing Office.

Report of the Secretary of the Interior. Var. Washington, D.C.: U.S. Government Printing Office. 1892, 1893.

Reyhner, Jon, and Jeanne Eder. 2004. *American Indian Education: A History*. Norman: University of Oklahoma Press.

Reyhner, Jon Allan and Jeanne M. Ovawin. 1989. *A History of Indian Education*. Billings: Eastern Montana College.

Rice, Timothy. 2003. "Time, Place, and Metaphor in Musical Experience and Ethnography." *Ethnomusicology* 47 (2): 151-79.

Righter, Charles Boardman. 1945. *Success in Teaching School Orchestras and Bands*. Minneapolis: Schmitt, Hall & McCreary Company.

————. 1941. *Gridiron Pageantry: The Story of the Marching Band, for Bandsmen, Directors and Football Fans*. New York: Carl Fischer.

Riney, Scott. *The Rapid City Indian School, 1898-1933*. Norman: University of Oklahoma Press.

————. 1998. " 'I Like the School So I Want to Come Back': The Enrollment of American Indian Students at the Rapid City Indian School." *American Indian Culture and Research Journal* 22 (2): 171-92.

Roddis, Louis H. 1956. *The Indian Wars of Minnesota*. Cedar Rapids, IA: Torch Press.

Roleff, Tamara L., ed. 1998. *Native American Rights*. San Diego: Greenhaven Press.

Rollings, William Hughes. 2002. "Native Americans and Christianity." In *Blackwell Companions to American History No. 4: A Companion to American Indian History*. Neal Salisbury and Philip J. Deloria, eds. London: Blackwell Press. 121-38.

Ross, Thomas E., and Tyrel G. Moore. 1987. *A Cultural Geography of North American Indians*. Boulder, CO: Westview Press.

Rothkopf, David . 1997. "In Praise of Cultural Imperialism: Effects of Globalization on Culture." *Foreign Policy* (June 1997) <http://bss.sfsu.edu/fischer/IR%20305/Readings/cultural.htm>

Salem U.S. Vocational School. 1921? A promotional pamphlet printed at Chemawa under the leadership of Supt. Harwood Hall. Salem, Oregon. Date unknown.

Samuels, David W. 2004. *Putting a Song on Top of It: Expression and Identity on the San Carlos Apache Reservation.* Tucson: University of Arizona Press.

Scales, Chris. 2007. "Powwows, Intertribalism, and the Value of Competition." *Ethnomusicology* 51 (1): 1-29.

Schultz, April. 1990. " 'The Pride of the Race Has Been Touched': The 1925 Norse-American Immigration Centennial and Ethnic Identity." *Journal of American History* 77 (4): 1265-95.

Schurz, Carl. 1881. "Present Aspects of the Indian Problem." *North American Review* 133 (July): 16-17.

Senier, Siobhan. 2001. *Voices of American Indian Assimilation and Resistance: Helen Hunt Jackson, Sarah Winnemucca, and Victoria Hunt.* Norman: University of Oklahoma Press.

Senior Class Number. 1928. Year-end retrospective. Chemawa Indian School. Salem, Oregon.

Sevetson, Donald J. 2007. "George Atkinson, Harvey Scott, and the Portland High School Controversy of 1880." *Oregon Historical Quarterly* 108 (3): 458-73.

Shanks, David, ed. 1997. *Human Memory: A Reader.* London: Arnold Publishers.

Shaw, Anna Moore. *A Pima Past.* Tucson: University of Arizona Press.

Simonton, Dean Keith. 2000. "Creativity: Cognitive, Personal, Developmental, and Social Aspects." *American Psychologist* 55 (1): 151-58.

"Sitting Dog A Proud Boy—First Indian Lad to Wear a Boy Scout Uniform." 1921. *Spokesman-Review*, 28 October 1921.

Smith, James Alan. 1993. "To Assimilate the Children: The Boarding School at Chemawa, Oregon, 1880-1930." M.A. thesis. Central Washington University.

Spack, Ruth. 2002. *America's Second Tongue: American Indian Education and the Ownership of English, 1860-1900.* Lincoln: University of Nebraska Press.

Spade Cooley's Western Swing Folio. 1945. New York: Hill and Range Songs, Inc. Includes liner notes.

Standing Bear, Luther. 1928. *My People the Sioux.* Lincoln: University of Nebraska Press. Reprinted in 1975.

Steward, Irene, and Doris Ostrander Dawdy. 1980. *A Voice in Her Tribe: A Navajo Woman's Own Story.* Socorro, NM: Ballena Press.

Swisher, Karen Gayton. 1998. "Why Indian People Should Be the Ones to Write about Indian Education." In *Natives and Academics: Researching and Writing About American Indians.* Devon A. Mihesuah, ed. Lincoln: University of Nebraska Press. 190-99.

———. 1991. "American Indian / Alaska Native Learning Styles: Research and Practice." *ERIC Digest,* ED335175. Available at: <http://www.ericdigests.org/pre-9220/indian.htm>

Szasz, Margaret Connell. 2001. *Between Indian and White Worlds: The Culture Brokers.* Norman: University of Oklahoma Press.

———. 1999. *Education and the American Indian: The Road to Self-Determination Since 1928.* Third edition, revised and enlarged. Santa Fe: University of New Mexico Press.

Tapping, Tim. 1992. "Wild Gentlemen Keeps 'Em Hopping in Dutch." *Fisherman's Journal*, later subsumed by *National Fisherman*.

The Teepee. Chemawa school annual. Salem, Oregon.

Theisz, R. D. 2005. "Putting Things in Order: The Discourse of Tradition." In *Powwow*. Clyde Ellis, Luke Eric Lassiter, and Gary H. Dunham, eds. Lincoln: University of Nebraska Press. 85-109.

————. 1987. "Song Texts and Their Performers: The Centerpiece of Contemporary Lakota Identity Formation." *Great Plains Quarterly* 7 (2): 116-24.

Thomson, William. "The Author Replies." *Music Educators Journal* 53 (9): 21.

Tick, Judith. 1986. "Passed Away Is the Piano Girl: Changes in American Musical Life, 1870-1900." In *Women Making Music: The Western Art Tradition, 1150-1950*. Jane Bowers and Judith Tick, eds. Urbana: University of Illinois Press. 325-48.

Toelken, Barre. 1991. "Ethnic Selection and Intensification in the Native American Powwow." In *Creative Ethnicity: Symbols and Strategies of Contemporary Ethnic Life*. Stephen Stern and John Allan Cicala, eds. Logan: Utah State University Press. 137-56.

Townsend, Kenneth William. 2000. *World War II and the American Indian*. Albuquerque: University of New Mexico Press.

Trafzer, Clifford E., and Jean A. Keller, eds. 2006. *Boarding School Blues: Revisiting American Indian Educational Experiences*. Lincoln, NB: Bison Books.

Trennert, Robert A. 1988. *The Phoenix Indian School: Forced Assimilation in Arizona, 1891-1935*. Norman: University of Oklahoma Press.

Troutman, John W. 2009. *Indian Blues: American Indians and the Politics of Music, 1879-1934*. Norman: University of Oklahoma Press.

————. 2004. "Indian Blues: American Indians and the Politics of Music, 1890-1935." Ph.D. diss, University of Texas at Austin.

Tucker, Sherrie. 2000. *Swing Shift: "All-Girl" Bands of the 1940s*. Durham, NC: Duke University Press.

Vaillant, George E. 2002. *Aging Well: Surprising Guideposts to a Happier Life from the Landmark Harvard Study of Adult Development*. Boston: Little & Brown.

Vander, Judith. *Songprints: The Musical Experience of Five Shoshone Women*. Urbana: University of Illinois Press.

Vanderpool, Tim. 2002. "Lesson No. 1: Shed your Indian identity." *Christian Science Monitor*. Tuesday, April 2, 2002. 14-15.

Warner, Sam L. No'eau. 1999. "Kuleana: The Right, Responsibility, and Authority of Indigenous Peoples to Speak and Make Decisions for Themselves in Language and Cultural Revitalization." *Anthropology & Education Quarterly* 30 (1): 68-93.

Werner, Emmy. 1995. "Resilience in Development." *Current Directions in Psychological Science* 4 (3): 81-85.

————. 1993. "Risk, Resilience, and Recovery: Perspectives from the Kauai Longitudinal Study." *Development and Psychopathology* 5 (4): 503-15.

————, and Ruth S. Smith. 2001. *Journeys from Childhood to Midlife: Risk, Resilience, and Recovery*. New York: Cornell University Press.

————. 1992. *Overcoming the Odds: High Risk Children from Birth to Adulthood*. New York: Cornell University Press.

————. 1982. *Vulnerable but Invincible: A Longitudinal Study of Resilient Children and Youth*. New York: Adams, Bannister, & Cox.

Whitehill, Charles D. 1969. "Sociological Conditions which Contributed to the Growth of the School Band Movement in the United States." *Journal of Research in Music Education* 17 (2): 179-92.

Williams, Robert A., Jr. 1990. *The American Indian in Western Legal Thought: The Discourses of Conquest*. New York: Oxford University Press.

Winship, A. E. 1905. "The Mission of Music in the Public Schools." *Journal of Proceedings and Addresses of the Forty-Fifth Annual Meeting*. Winona, WI: National Education Association. 630-33.

Witalec, Janet, ed. 1995. *Smoke Rising: The Native North American Literary Companion*. Detroit: Invisible Ink Press.

Wong, Deborah Anne. 2004. *Speak It Louder: Asian Americans Making Music*. New York: Routledge.

Woody, Elizabeth. 2002. "Singing." *Frontiers: A Journal of Women Studies* 23(2): 16-18.

Wright, Bobby. 1988. " 'For the Children of Infidels?': American Indian Education in the Colonial Colleges." *American Indian Culture and Research Journal* 12: 1-14.

Wright, David E., III, et al. 1998. *The Politics of Second Generation Discrimination in American Indian Education: Incidence, Explanation, and Mitigating Strategies*. Westport, CT: Bergin & Garvey.

Young, Gloria Alese. 1981. "Powwow Power: Perspectives on Historic and Contemporary Intertribalism." Ph.D. diss., Indiana University.

Young Bear, Severt, Sr., and R. D. Theisz. 1994. *Standing in the Light: A Lakota Way of Seeing*. Lincoln: University of Nebraska Press.

Notes

Introduction

1   *Atlanta Constitution*, 16 Jan. 1879: 2. For a more detailed explanation of the Fort Robinson massacre, see Ramon Powers' "Why the Northern Cheyenne Left Indian Territory in 1878: A Cultural Analysis." *Kansas Quarterly* 3 (fall 1971): 72-81.

2   For analysis of the impact Standing Bear's arrest, trial, and subsequent lecture tours had on the American public, see Frederick E. Hoxie, *A Final Promise: The Campaign to Assimilate the Indians, 1880-1920* (Lincoln: University of Nebraska Press, 1984), 3-9.

3   Susan Hazen-Hammond, *Timelines of Native American History: Through the Centuries with Mother Earth and Father Sky* (New York: Berkley Publishing Group, 1997), 186.

4   David Wallace Adams, *Education for Extinction: American Indians and the Boarding School Experience, 1875-1928* (Lawrence: University of Kansas Press, 1995), 8-9.

5   Carl F. Kaestle, "Ideology and American Educational History," *History of Education Quarterly* 22 (summer 1982): 127-28.

6   Adams 1995: 19. Adams notes that some reformers did not share Morgan's optimism that Indians could be uplifted to the level of whites within the time span of a single generation but that these views were in the minority.

7   Carl Schurz, "Present Aspects of the Indian Problem," *North American Review* 133 (July 1881): 16-17.

8   Cary C. Collins, " 'Between Savagery and Civilization': The Memoir of Edwin L. Chalcraft, U.S. Indian Agent" (Ph.D. diss., Washington State University, 2001), xxi-xxii.

9   For the history of schools run for Indians by the early colonists, see James Axtell, "Dr. Wheelock's Little Red School," in *The European and the Indian: Essays in the Ethnohistory of Colonial North America* (New York: Oxford University Press, 1981), 87-109. See also James Axtell, "The Little Red School" in *The Invasion Within: The Contest of Cultures in Colonial North America* (New York: Oxford University Press, 1985) 179-217.

10 From the 1938 *Chilocco Indian School Journal*. Reprinted in Archuleta et al. 2000.

11 Letter from Inspector McConnell to Secretary Hitchcock, 31 Oct. 1899, as quoted in Diane Therese Putney, "Fighting the Scourge: American Indian Morbidity and Federal Policy, 1887-1928" (Ph.D. diss., Marquette University, 1980), 10-11.

12 Adams 1995: 224.

13 Annual Report of the Commissioner of Indian Affairs, 1901: 382.

14 Flora Gregg Iliff, *People of the Blue Water: My Adventures Among the Walapai and Havasupai Indians* (New York: Harper and Brothers, 1954), 236-37.

15 Annual Report of the Commissioner of Indian Affairs, 1893: 211-12.

16 From an interview in K. Tsianina Lomawaima, *They Called It Prairie Light: The Story of Chilocco Indian School* (Lincoln: University of Nebraska Press, 1994), 152.

17   From Irene Steward's autobiography, *A Voice in Her Tribe: A Navajo Woman's Own Story*, Doris Ostrander Dawdy, ed. (Socorro, NM: Ballena Press, 1980).

18   David Wallace Adams 1995: 116.

19   Anna Moore Shaw, *A Pima Past* (Tucson: University of Arizona Press, 1974), 133.

20   Records of the Office of Indian Affairs, National Archives, Record Group 75. Letters Received, No. 22506. Enclosed in a letter from Agent E. H. Plummer to the Commissioner of Indian Affairs, 8 June 1894.

21   National Archives, RG 75, BIA, Flandreau. Letter from parent, L Plant SD, 27 Nov. 1913. Reprinted in Child 1998: 70.

22   National Archives, RG 75, BIA, Flandreau. Letter from parent, Okreek SD, 6 Oct. 1913. Reprinted in Child 1998: 70.

23   National Archives, RG 75, BIA, Flandreau. Letter from student, Porcupine SD, 13 Aug. 1913. Reprinted in Child 1998: 23.

24   Rayna Green and John Troutman link the advent of Indian Clubs to John Collier's term as Commissioner of the Bureau of Indian Affairs, 1933-1945. See *Away from Home: American Indian Boarding School Experiences, 1879-2000*, Archuleta et al., eds. (Phoenix, AZ: The Heard Museum, 2000), 77-78.

25   Sally Hyer, *One House, One Voice, One Heart: Native American Education at Santa Fe Indian School*. (Santa Fe: Museum of New Mexico Press, 1990).

26   Throughout this book, I use the term "traditional" advisedly. Scholars such as John Troutman have aptly noted that "traditional" can imply cultural stasis, rather than change, and reversion, rather than innovation. I wish to retain the usefulness of "traditional" in referring to tribally derived musical practices, be they centuries-old song cycles or contemporary powwow dance styles.

27   "About Us." Mission statement on Chemawa Indian School's official website. http://www.chemawa.bia.edu/AboutUs.html

Chapter 1

1   Carolyn Kenny, "The Haida story of the Raven," as told in "Our Legacy: Work and Play." Keynote presentation. Proceedings of the annual conference of the American Association for Music Therapy, "Connections: Integrating Our Work and Play," 1994. Reprinted in *Voices: A World Forum for Music Therapy* 4, no. 2 (2004).

2   Charles Henry Carey, "Diary of Rev. George Gary," *Oregon Historical Quarterly* 24 (1923): 79-80, 84. See also Bobby Wright, " 'For the Children of Infidels?': American Indian Education in the Colonial Colleges," *American Indian Culture and Research Journal* 12 (1988): 1-14.

3   For a well-researched account of Chemawa's early history, see SuAnn M. Reddick, "The Evolution of Chemawa Indian School: From Red River to Salem, 1825-1885," *Oregon Historical Quarterly* 101, no. 4 (winter 2000): 444-65.

4   Francis Paul Prucha, ed., *Documents of United States Indian Policy* (Lincoln: University of Nebraska Press, 1975), 73-75.

5   In 1869, President-elect Grant announced a new policy regarding Native Americans. Ostensibly, Indians willing to live on reservations, where they were expected to farm and become Christians, would be left in peace. For all other Indians, Grant ordered "a sharp and severe war policy." To this end, he established an all-white Board of Indian Commissioners to monitor the handling of Indian affairs by the Department of the Interior.

6   Annual Report of the Commissioner of Indian Affairs, 1879: 112.

7 The Catholic Church founded the St. Francis Regis Mission School near Fort Colville as an industrial boarding school (i.e., a school dedicated to work training) in 1877; in addition, the federal government established a boarding school at Fort Spokane in 1899 under the leadership of Superintendent Frank Avery. At Priest's Point near the Tulalip Reservation, a school established by Rev. E.C. Chirouse in 1857 was operated by the Sisters of Providence until it became a federal facility in the winter of 1900-1901. Destroyed in a fire soon after, the school was replaced by a newer and larger federal facility on the shores of Tulalip Bay in 1905.

8 Annual Report of the Commissioner of Indian Affairs, 1891: 292.

9 Annual Report of the Commissioner of Indian Affairs, 1893: 211-12.

10 The prisoners had surrendered at the end of the Red River War. in the school in Hampton, Virginia had been established twelve years earlier as a freedmen's school. Pratt charted their academic progress and convinced Congress to appropriate funds for a new Indian-only school to be established in the unused military barracks at Carlisle, Pennsylvania, in 1879.

11 Linda F. Witmer, *The Indian Industrial School, Carlisle, Pennsylvania, 1879-1918*, 3rd ed. (Carlisle, PA: Cumberland County Historical Society, 2002): 19.

12 Standing Bear, Luther, *My People the Sioux*. (Lincoln: University of Nebraska Press, 1928). Reprinted in 1975.

13 Francis La Flesche, *The Middle Five: Indian Schoolboys of the Omaha Tribe* (Madison: University of Wisconsin Press, 1963).

14 Robert Redfield, Ralph Linton, and Melville J. Herskovits, "Memorandum for the Study of Acculturation," *American Anthropologist* 38 (1936): 149.

15 See Cary C. Collins, " 'Between Savagery and Civilization': The memoir of Edwin L. Chalcraft, U.S. Indian Agent" (Ph.D. diss., Washington State University, 2001). See also Flora Gregg Iliff, *People of the Blue Water: My Adventures Among the Walapai and Havasupai Indians* (New York: Harper and Brothers, 1954); and Esther Burnett Horne and Sally McBeth, *Essie's Story: The Life and Legacy of a Shoshone Teacher* (Lincoln: University of Nebraska Press, 1998).

16 RG 75, Box 1, "A 2 Letters." Commissioner's Report 1881. 190.

17 RG 75, Box 1, "A 2 Letters." Commissioner's Report 1881, 157-\71.

18 Louis H. Roddis, *The Indian Wars of Minnesota* (Cedar Rapids, IA: Torch Press, 1956), 285.

19 *The Teepee* (Salem, OR: Chemawa Indian School, 1930).

20 Henry Zenk, "Notes on Native American Place-names of the Willamette Valley Region." *Oregon Historical Quarterly* 109 (spring 2008): 6-33.

21 "Chemawa Happy Home Video." <http://www.chemawa.bie.edu/HappyHome.html> Created Spring 2010.

22 RG 75, Box 2. Book 6: June 21, 1887 to March 18, 1889. Letter to the Commissioner, September 1887: 39.

23 Until the 1930s, boarding schools were run on a half-day schedule, with students only in the classroom a few hours a day to allow for farming and vocational training in the afternoons. As Superintendent Estelle Reel explained in her *Uniform Course of Study for the Indian Schools of the United States* (1901), the schools' goal was to train the Indian child to meet "the demands of active life, making him a willing worker as well as an inquiring learner."

24   Changes in Chemawa's service area are described by Cary C. Collins in "Oregon's Carlisle: Teaching 'America' at Chemawa Indian School," *Columbia* (summer 1998): 6-10.

25   Collins 1998: 9.

26   See the song sheet cover for "From the Land of Sky-Blue Water," where Charles Cadman set a poem by Nelle Richmond Eberhart to a tune based on an Omaha song transcribed by Alice C. Fletcher. Dozens of other Indian-themed popular songs touted themselves similarly, with song sheet covers featuring striking headdresses, moonlit canoes, and claims of authentic Indian source material.

27   This concept is developed fully in Jacqueline Fear-Segal's "The Man on the Bandstand at Carlisle Indian School: What He Reveals about Children's Experiences" in *Boarding School Blues*. Trafzer et al., eds. (Lincoln: University of Nebraska Press, 2006).

28   John W. Troutman, *Indian Blues: American Indians and the Politics of Music, 1879-1934* (Norman: University of Oklahoma Press, 2009), 147, 185.

Chapter 2

1   For Richard Henry Pratt's recollections of the early school bands at Carlisle, see his *Battlefield and Classroom: Four Decades with the American Indian, 1867-1904*, as well as his article in Carlisle's school newspaper, *The Red Man* 13, no. 7 (Feb.1896).

2   Sam L. No'eau Warner, "Kuleana: The Right, Responsibility, and Authority of Indigenous Peoples to Speak and Make Decisions for Themselves in Language and Cultural Revitalization," *Anthropology & Education Quarterly* 30, no. 1 (March 1999): 68-93.

3   Interview with Dee Pigsley, Siletz Tribal chairwoman. March 2005.

4   See *The Red Man* 13, no. 7 (Feb. 1896): 6. The band soon traveled the United States and Europe performing in concerts and dress parades, including the Chicago World's Fair and the Columbian Exposition Parade in New York City.

5   Report of Ed McConville, superintendent of school at Fort Lapwai, Idaho. "Report to the Commissioner of Indian Affairs," in U.S. House, 52nd Congress, 2nd Session. *Report of the Secretary of the Interior, 1892.* H.Ex.Doc.1, Pt. 5, Vol. 2; Serial Set 3088 (Washington: Government Printing Office, 1892): 662-64. In the same report, McConville's superior noted, "The brass band is also an interesting feature of the school; the semi-military drill and marching of the scholars to and from their meals and to and from the chapel were good features." 1287-95.

6   Lucetta Hahn, "Band Serenades in Broad Daylight," *The Chemawa American* 55, no. 8 (April 15, 1955).

7   For a more detailed explanation of how World War I jumpstarted school bands, see Whitehill 1969: 180-82.

8   Historian John Troutman has skillfully profiled Chemawa student violinist Fred Cardin, with a focus on Cardin's experiences traveling the Chautauqua Circuit, in *Indian Blues: American Indians and the Politics of Music, 1879-1934*: 217-28. Troutman also includes a colorful chronicle of later Chemawa student and jazz trombone player Joe Morris (Blackfeet); see *Indian Blues*: 228-33.

9   For more on the Indian String Quartet, see Philip J. Deloria, *Indians in Unexpected Places* (Lawrence: University Press of Kansas, 2004) 207, 209. See also John William Troutman, " 'Indian Blues': American Indians and the Politics of Music, 1890-1935" (Ph.D. diss., University of Texas at Austin, 2004) 261-78.

10 The Meriam Report, requested by and submitted to Secretary of the Interior Hubert Work in 1928, recommended the abolition of the "Uniform Course of Study" and argued that the Indian Service should provide Native Americans the tools to adapt both in their own traditional communities and American society.

11 *The Chemawa American* 29, no. 31 (May 9, 1928).

12 In *The Chemawa American*, descriptions of Kunkel are plenteous and favorable. He is mentioned forty-six times between Nov. 14, 1928, and Oct. 10, 1934, including several updates following his departure from Chemawa in September 1930. Vosburgh is mentioned only in the issue dated Sept. 10, 1930, and he appears to have held the bandmaster position only briefly.

13 Interview published anonymously in Sonciray Bonnell, *Chemawa Indian Boarding School: The First One Hundred Years, 1880 to 1980* (M.A. thesis, Dartmouth College, 1997), 49.

14 *The Chemawa American* 30, no. 23 (April 3, 1929).

15 *The Chemawa American*, April 1929, Sept. 1932, and May 1930.

16 "Favorable Mention," *The Chemawa American* 31, no. 2 (Sept. 1929).

17 Nora Marks Dauenhauer and Richard Dauenhauer, eds., *Haa Kusteeyí, Our Culture: Tlingit Life Stories* (Seattle: University of Washington Press, 1994), 73, 143, 653.

18 Dauenhauer 1994: 143.

19 Whitehill 1969: 179.

20 Donald J. Sevetson, "George Atkinson, Harvey Scott, and the Portland High School Controversy of 1880," *Oregon Historical Quarterly* 108, no. 3 (fall 2007): 458-73.

21 Frederick W. Goodrich, "Oregon Orchestra Music, 1868-1932," *Oregon Historical Quarterly* 33, no. 2 (1932): 136-42.

22 Richard K. Hansen, *The American Wind Band: A Cultural History*. Chicago, IL: GIA Publications, 2005.

23 "Jazz," *The Chemawa American* 31, no. 26 (March 12, 1930).

24 Thomas R. Garth and Sarah Rachel Isbell, "The Musical Talent of Indians," *Music Supervisors Journal* 15, no. 3 (Feb. 1929): 83, 85-87.

25 Charles Wakefield Cadman, "The 'Idealization' of Indian Music," *The Musical Quarterly* 1, no. 3 (July 1915): 387-96.

26 This delayed shift in genres appears clearly in the band performances that are described in *The Chemawa American* and in programs from commencements and special events from the 1920s through the 1950s.

27 "Local," *The Chemawa American* 31 (Sept. 1929).

28 See "Christmas," *The Chemawa American* 30 (Jan. 1929); "Band Celebrates," *The Chemawa American* 52, no. 5 (May 1952); and 1954-1955 accounts by Pat Carlson, Thamer Perry, Florence Hall, Evelyn Brahman, and Joan Harwood, among others.

29 New music and an enhanced bandstand are described in *The Chemawa American* 29, no. 31 (May 9, 1928); a new music room is characterized as "commodious" and "ideal" in *The Chemawa American* 30, no. 1 (Oct. 24, 1928); a succession of new band uniforms appears in photographs in issues of the school annual, *The Chief*. New bleachers constructed for the band by V. J. Matt's carpentry class in 1951-1952 featured a special design to allow room for larger instruments and band paraphernalia, as described in *The Chemawa American* 52, no. 3 (January 1952).

30 Interviews with Bob Tom and Chet Clark. Salem, Oregon. February 2005. See also "Chemawa Represented in Parade," *The Chemawa American* 55, no. 4 (Dec. 15, 1954).

31 "G.A.A. Is Active," *The Chemawa American* 55, no. 4 (Dec. 15, 1954).

32 The February 1954 issue of *The Chemawa American* describes the special feat: "The band is being complimented for a nice stunt they put on between halves at the Gervais-Chemawa basketball game. The band marched out on to the gym floor and formed a trombone."

33 "Melody Lane," *The Chemawa American* 50, no. 5 (March 1950). "Passing of the Red Man," composed by Karl L. King in 1916, is a short overture that musically depicts the interplay between Indian and white forces on the frontier in the nineteenth century. Stereotypical Indian characteristic music is gradually taken over by music represent-ing the white man. The piece was reportedly a favorite of Buffalo Bill Cody, and the composer dedicated the piece "To my esteemed friend, Col. Wm. F. Cody, 'Buffalo Bill.'"

34 "Band Celebrates," *The Chemawa American* 52, no. 5 (May 1952).

35 "Band Gives Concert," *The Chemawa American* 53, no. 3 (Jan. 1953).

36 "Pep Band Assists in Placement Program," *The Chemawa American* 54, no. 6 (April 15, 1954).

37 "Band Concert," *The Chemawa American* 55, no. 5 (Jan. 1955).

38 Beginning in the late 1940s, the editorial board for the school paper took great pains to have the paper be student-generated, and articles that were written by students were attributed to their respective authors whenever possible.

39 "All-Girl Band," *The Chemawa American* 55, no. 6 (Feb. 1955).

40 For rich historically grounded chronicles of the careers of these female swing musi-cians, see Sherrie Tucker, *Swing Shift: "All-Girl" Bands of the 1940s* (Durham, NC: Duke University Press, 2000). Whereas these women recall male club owners who would seek to replace a band member because she "doesn't smile enough, or is too fat, of her hair doesn't look just so," female band members at Chemawa were evaluated on the basis of their musicianship.

41 Compare the band as described in *The Chemawa American* 42, no. 2 (Nov. 7, 1941) with the band as photographed in *The Chemawa American* 52, no. 3 (Jan. 1952).

42 "Fifty-Four in Band," *The Chemawa American* 51, no. 3 (Feb. 1951).

43 In an effort to forcibly assimilate Indians into mainstream society and end the special relationship between tribes and the federal government, the government terminated recognition of a total of 109 tribes and bands as sovereign dependent nations between 1953 and 1964. Oregon was hit particularly hard by termination, with 61 of the termi-nated tribes residing in Western Oregon.

44 Telephone interview with Betty Pearson. April 2005.

45 *Ibid.*

46 See caption of band photo in *The Chemawa American* 52, no. 3 (Jan. 1952); see also "Band Items," *The Chemawa American* 50, no. 5 (Mar. 1950).

47 Telephone interview with Dee Pigsley, March 2005. One of Dee's brothers is Joe Lane, who went on to lead a western swing band, the West Coast Ramblers. Joe Lane was a logger by trade, but the band would travel to different towns on Friday and Saturday nights, and the Ramblers were known all around the Northwest.

48 Stephen Philips, "The Challenge to the Marching Bands," *Music Educators Journal* 51, no. 4 (Feb.-March 1965): 96, 100.

49 William Thomson, "The Author Replies," *Music Educators Journal* 53, no. 9 (May 1967): 21.

50 Funding for the new campus was enabled in part by the Kennedy Report's call for a much greater financial investment in Indian education. Released in 1969 as *Indian*

Education: A National Tragedy, A National Challenge, this report of the Special Senate Subcommittee was a milestone in the effort for tribal sovereignty and self-determination. Shortly after the Kennedy Report, two other projects—the NAACP's *An Even Chance* (1971) and the National Indian Leadership Training project—pointed out further weaknesses in the mechanisms of federal funding, and helped trigger fundamental changes in the ways funding for Indian education is administered. See Szasz 1999: 181-87.

51 Telephone interview with Dee Pigsley. March 2005.
52 Bonnell 1997: 111-13.
53 Telephone interview with Hal Beyers. November 2002.
54 Interviews with Ted Mack and Karen Graham, at Chemawa. May 2006.
55 Chemawa Indian School Parent and Student Handbook, Vol. 8 (July 2009): 15. Available at <http://www.chemawa.bia.edu/Assets/documents/PSHandbook0910.pdf>
56 See Karen Swisher, "American India /Alaska Native Learning Styles: Research and Practice." ERIC Digest, ED335175. May 1991. Available at <http://www.ericdigests.org/pre-9220/indian.htm>

Chapter 3

1   Woody 2002.
2   Such animal-themed songs were derived from both art music, such as "Welcome, O Birds" (Rossini), and folk music, with light songs like "Frog Went A-Courtin'." Cowboy songs ("Goodbye, Old Paint") and didactic songs portraying fables ("The Busy Bee") came to figure prominently in primary school songbooks.
3   Mihesuah 1993: 31, 35.
4   Annual Report of the Commissioner of Indian Affairs, 1897: 334.
5   Letter from Supt. Estelle Reel to the Commissioner of Indian Affairs, December 28, 1906. Incoming Correspondence from Estelle Reel, 1904-1907, Box 8, Special Series A, Office of Indian Affairs.
6   "Oregon Indians Buy Opera," *Talking Machine World* (August 15, 1920): 163.
7   "The Chemawa Indian School—Courses," *The Chemawa American* 29, no. 25 (March 28, 1928).
8   "Supt. Lipps Made the Address," *The Chemawa American* 30, no. 13 (January 23, 1929).
9   This was especially common in art music, both in the form of art songs and in character pieces. Arthur Farwell's Wa-Wan Press was a notable proponent of such "authentic" works.
10 Michael V. Pisani, *Imagining Native America in Music* (New Haven: Yale University Press, 2005). Pisani borrowed this idea from Browner's earlier work. For more on "Indianist" composers' different responses to Native musics, see Tara Browner, " 'Breathing the Indian Spirit': Thoughts on Musical Borrowing and the 'Indianist' Movement in American Music." *American Music* 15, no. 3: 265-84, as well as Browner's Ph.D. diss., "Transposing Cultures: The Appropriation of Native North American Musics, 1890-1990" (University of Michigan, 1995).
11 Sheet music for "Full Moon" can be viewed online at the Lester S. Levy Collection of Sheet Music maintained by Johns Hopkins University. Box 156, Item 159a. <http://levysheetmusic.mse.jhu.edu/>
12 Logan allegedly obtained the tune for "The Missouri Waltz" from orchestra leader John Valentine Eppel of Fort Dodge, Iowa, who recalled hearing it from a Black

man in Missouri. See Logan's entry in the *Des Moines Register*'s series, "Famous Iowans":   <http://desmoinesregister.com/apps/pbcs.dll/article?AID=/99999999/ FAMOUSIOWANS/41221035> Whether Logan also employed this method of musical borrowing in the writing of "Pale Moon" is unknown.

13   To see one popular cover illustration for "Pale Moon," which featured the silhouette of a lone Indian brave playing the flute before a smoldering campfire next to a solitary pine above a lagoon, see the concert edition in the Levy Sheet Music Collection, Box 156, Item 159a.

14   Sheet music for "By the Waters of Minnetonka" can be viewed online at the Lester S. Levy Collection of Sheet Music maintained by Johns Hopkins University. Box 155, Item 049a. <http://levysheetmusic.mse.jhu.edu/>

15   Lieurance gives his history of the song's inception in "Stories of Famous Concert Songs: 'By the Waters of Minnetonka,'" *Etude* 50, no. 6 (June 1932): 396, 449. The legend is partially recounted in Pisani 2005: 268-72, and corroborated by Victoria Lindsay Levine in *Writing American Indian Music: Historic Transcriptions, Notations, and Arrangements* (Middleton, WI: A-R Editions, 2002), 263.

16   Taken from the recital edition, for high voice, in the Levy Sheet Music Collection, Box 155, Item 049a.

17   "By the Waters of Minnetonka," *The Chemawa American* 30, no. 6 (November 28, 1928).

18   John W. Troutman, *Indian Blues: American Indians and the Politics of Music, 1879-1934* (Norman: University of Oklahoma Press, 2009): 4.

19   "Local," *The Chemawa American* 30, no. 17 (February 20, 1929).

20   "Local," *The Chemawa American* 31, no. 31 (April 16, 1930).

21   "Local," *The Chemawa American* 30, no. 16 (February 13, 1929).

22   "Local," *The Chemawa American* 30, no. 22 (March 27, 1929).

23   "News Notes," *The Chemawa American* 35, no. 8 (January 17, 1934).

24   "Girls' Music Club," *The Chemawa American* 36, no. 4 (November 21, 1934).

25   Sponsored by the National Federation of Music Clubs, National Music Week is traditionally celebrated each year in the first full week of May. It began in 1915 as a National Week of Song, and by 1924 had developed into a large-scale nationwide observance, with President Calvin Coolidge serving as the first honorary chair.

26   "Local," *The Chemawa American* 35, no. 1 (October 11, 1933).

27   "Melody Lane," *The Chemawa American* 50, no. 4 (February 1950). An article entitled "Music for All" later affirmed, "Two kinds of classes are held, one for those who are in the performing groups, and another for recreational singing and listening." [*The Chemawa American* 54, no. 1 (November 1953)] It is not mentioned to what extent the classes were selected by the students or applied for on an audition basis.

28   "Chemawa Students Sing," *The Chemawa American* 52, no. 2 (December 1951).

29   Basil Johnston, *Indian School Days* (Norman: University of Oklahoma Press, 1989), 57.

30   Conversation at Chemawa Alumni Reunion. Anchorage, Alaska. October 2002.

31   *The Chief* (Salem, Oregon; Chemawa Indian School, 1932).

32   Mrs. Gertrude A. Turney, the former Gertrude Brewer and a former Chemawa student, had been involved in Chemawa's music program for more than thirty years as an accompanist, piano teacher, and director of pageants and operettas.

33   *The Chief* (Salem, Oregon; Chemawa Indian School, 1937).

34   "Student Briefs," *The Chemawa American* 56, no. 8 (April 15, 1956).

35   Pictured in the 1940 yearbook, with girls wearing regular school clothes. Kathryn Harrison is in the middle.

36   Dorothy Jones later married Roy Track (Assinaboine Sioux), who played the trumpet for Chemawa's premier dance band, the Rhythm Chiefs.

37   Pictured in the 1939 yearbook, with girls wearing matching Indian dresses. The girls' ensemble was first organized in 1937, the year after the director, Mrs. Turney, received her master's degree in music.

38   Interview with Kathryn Harrison. Grand Ronde, Oregon. October 2006.

39   "Serenaders." Text accompanies photo in Chemawa's 1937 yearbook, *The Chief*.

40   Devon Mihesuah, *Cultivating the Rosebuds: The Education of Women at the Cherokee Female Seminary, 1851-1909* (Urbana: University of Illinois Press, 1993), 77-78.

41   Interview with Bob Tom, Feb. 2005.

42   Margaret Connell Szasz. *Education and the American Indian: The Road to Self-Determination Since 1928*. (Santa Fe: University of New Mexico Press, 1999), 106-9.

43   *The Chief* (Salem, Oregon; Chemawa Indian School, 1932).

44   *Ibid.*

45   Chemawa also was home to Sigma Phi Delta, a sorority that functioned as an honor society. Its handbooks include a battery of secret ceremonies and rituals, replete with music. Pamphlets are preserved at the archives of the Confederated Tribes of Grand Ronde.

46   "Local," *The Chemawa American* 34, no. 4 (October 26, 1932).

47   "Boys' Music Club," *The Chemawa American* 32, no. 3 (November 7, 1934).

48   "Club Notes," *The Chemawa American* 48, no. 4 (February 1948).

49   "Indian Service News," *The Chemawa American* 34, no. 9 (January 4, 1933).

50   Brenda J. Child, *Boarding School Seasons: American Indian Families, 1900-1940* (Lincoln: University of Nebraska Press, 2000), 94-96.

51   Billed as a "musical comedy," *Paul Revere* was preceded by an orchestral suite and accompanied by descriptive pantomime. "Indian Thespians Appear Tonight," *Spokane Chronicle* (July 22, 1926).

52   "Indian Opera Seats on Sale," *Spokane Chronicle* (July 19, 1926).

53   "Spotted Dog a Proud Boy—First Indian Lad to Wear a Boy Scout Uniform," *Spokesman-Review*. (October 28, 1921).

54   "Indian Opera Seats on Sale."

55   The music (a march in F major) was composed by Henry Bernard Murtagh, a theater organist popular along the West Coast during the silent movie era. The lyrics were written by John Andrew Buchanan, a prominent state judge from Astoria, Oregon.

56   1928 *Senior Class Number*.

57   *The Chief* (Salem, Oregon; Chemawa Indian School, 1940).

58   Words by Jeremiah E. Rankin (1928-1904), music by William G. Tomer (1833-1896) in 1902. An alternate version also in use at the time retained Rankin's text, but was set to the tune "Randolph" by Ralph Vaughan Williams (1872-1958) in 1906.

59   Interview with Kathryn Harrison. Grand Ronde, Oregon. October 2006.

60   From an interview with Kristine Olson, for *Standing Tall: The Lifeway of Kathryn Jones Harrison* (Portland: Oregon Historical Society Press, 2005).

61   For an exploration of the various ways Native American peoples have adapted elements of missionaries' belief systems to their own values and ceremonies, see William Hughes Rollings's "Native Americans and Christianity," *The Blackwell Companion to*

American Indian History, eds. Neal Salisbury and Philip J. Deloria (London: Blackwell Press, 2002) 121-38.

Chapter 4

1   National Archives, Record Group 75. BIA, Flandreau, letter from parent in Trail City, South Dakota (Sept. 26, 1913).

2   "The Chemawa Indian School—Courses," *The Chemawa American* 29, no. 25 (March 28, 1928).

3   Annual Report of the Commissioner of Indian Affairs (1886), 447.

4   See C.H. Forbes-Lindsay's "Shaping the Future of the Red Man" in *World Today* (March 1907) 290-92, and his "Making Good Indians" in *Harper's Weekly* 52 (Oct. 31, 1908) 12-13. Frederick E. Hoxie offers further examples in *A Final Promise: The Campaign to Assimilate the Indians, 1880-1920* (Lincoln: University of Nebraska Press, 1984), 95.

5   Ray Stannard Baker, "The Day of the Run," *Century* (Sept. 1903): 643-55.

6   Mollie V. Gaither, essay penned in Umatilla, Oregon (1897). See Child 1998: 78.

7   Estelle Reel to Commissioner of Indian Affairs, August 1904: 290. Incoming correspondence from Estelle Reel, 1904-1907, Box 8, Special Series A. Records of the Office of Indian Affairs, National Archives, Record Group 75.

8   John W. Troutman, *Indian Blues: American Indians and the Politics of Music, 1879-1934* (Norman: University of Oklahoma Press, 2009), 143-44.

9   Anonymous alumnus ("Bob") interviewed by Sonciray Bonnell, "Chemawa Indian Boarding School: The First One Hundred Years, 1880 to 1980" (Master's thesis. Dartmouth College, 1997), 66.

10 Correspondence via Marjorie Waheneka of Tamastslikt Cultural Institute, Pendleton, Oregon (August 19, 2002).

11 Photographs of the Mandolin and Guitar Club appear in the pamphlet *Salem U.S. Vocational School, Chemawa, Oregon*. While the pamphlet is not dated, it was printed in-house at Chemawa's print shop some time during the leadership of Supt. Harwood Hall. Across the country, mandolin clubs were wildly popular from the late 1890s until the Great Depression. The mandolin's small size, inexpensive price, and ease of playing were central to its appeal.

12 Red Thunder member Robby Romero has recently founded Native Children's Survival, a children's advocacy program that uses music and film to improve the physical health and educational futures of indigenous children throughout the country.

13 Recollections from William H. DePoe, Jr., are taken from a July 2005 interview.

14 "Local" columns, *The Chemawa American* 29 (April 25, 1928; May 2, 1928).

15 Helen Mary Beavers, *From Point Barrow To Chemawa* (New York: Carlton Press, 1970), 34.

16 Text preserved by Mississippi State University's "Trophies of Honor" program.

17 "Siletz Tribal Leader Chief DePoe Dies at 84," *The Oregonian* (January 13, 1997).

18 Inside notes from *Spade Cooley's Western Swing Folio* (New York: Hill and Range Songs, Inc. 1945).

19 "Local," *The Chemawa American* (November 21, 1928).

20 "Local" columns, *The Chemawa American* (November 28, 1928; December 5, 1928; April 17, 1929).

21 "Local," *The Chemawa American* (May 8, 1929).

22   "Local," *The Chemawa American* (Sept. 18, 1929).

23   "Local," *The Chemawa American* (Oct. 9, 1929).

24   "Local," *The Chemawa American* (Feb. 5, 1930).

25   Letter from Sharon R. Mote to Mr. Bent, Mr. Downie, Mrs. Brickell, and All Others Concerned. April 22, 1930. Student case file, "Cooley, Clyde Donald," in Chemawa section, NARA-Seattle, Record Group 75.

26   *Spade Cooley's Western Swing Folio.*

27   Cooley would eventually go on to act in thirty-eight films, spanning from the late 1930s to the mid-1950s. He occasionally played himself, and contributed to additional films as a story writer, composer, and producer. See "Spade Cooley" filmography on Internet Movie Database. <http://www.imdb.com/name/nm0177622/>

28   Rich Kienzle, liner notes for *Heroes of Country Music, Vol. 4: Legends of the West Coast* (Rhino Records #72443, 1996), 8.

29   Bill C. Malone, *Country Music, U.S.A.* (Austin: University of Texas Press, 2002), 200-201.

30   "Thrills," *The Chemawa American* 47, no. 2 (Jan. 1947).

31   Rich Kienzle, "When A Country Star Turns Murderer: The Strange, Tragic Case of Spade Cooley," *Country Music* 5, no. 10 (July 1977): 36.

32   Kienzle 1977: 36.

33   Telephone interview with Bob Tom, February 2005, and conversations with other Chemawa alumni. Some alumni of that era also report being unaware of Spade Cooley's later conviction. This might be due to their geographic distance from the trial, which occurred in southern California, or simply due to their preference to remember Spade Cooley's more positive legacy as a musician and performer.

34   Kienzle 1977: 38.

35   Jason Ankeny. "Spade Cooley." Article about Spade Cooley, with discography. <http://www.allmusic.com/artist/spade-cooley-p31043/biography>

36   Jeff Gordinier, "The Transoceanic In-Flight Playlist," *Fortune* 139, no. 12: 56.

37   Telephone interview with Hal Beyers of Aurora, Oregon. November 2002.

38   Nan Henderson, President of Resiliency in Action, in an interview with Neal Conan on National Public Radio's "Talk of the Nation," July 16, 2002. Also, as Emily Werner interpreted the Kauai study: "the most salient turning points for troubled individuals occurred when they met a caring friend." See Werner and Smith 1992.

39   Interview at Chemawa with Karen Graham. May 2006.

Chapter 5

1   Esther Burnett Horne and Sally McBeth, *Essie's Story: The Life and Legacy of a Shoshone Teacher* (Lincoln: University of Nebraska Press, 1998), 66-67.

2   Adams 1995: 197. Quoted by Cora Folsom in "Memories of Old Hampton," Cora Folsom papers, Hampton Institute: 107.

3   Adams 1995: 201. Quoted in *Talks and Thoughts of the Hampton Indian Students* (February 1898): 3.

4   Sally Hyer, *One House, One Voice, One Heart: Native American Education at Santa Fe Indian School* (Santa Fe: Museum of New Mexico Press, 1990).

5   From a collection of unpublished interviews conducted by Tessie Naranjo and Margaret Archuleta, 1996-1999, Heard Museum Archives. Quoted in *Away from*

Home: American Indian Boarding School Experiences, 1879-2000 (Phoenix, AZ: Heard Museum, 2000), 75.

6   Troutman 2009: 195-96. From Horne and McBeth, *Essie's Story*, 49.

7   Harmon 1998: 156-57.

8   "Christmas," *Chemawa American* 30, no. 10 (Jan. 2, 1929).

9   "Local," *Chemawa American* 31, no. 16 (Dec. 25, 1929).

10   "Local," *Chemawa American* 31, no. 11 (Nov. 20, 1929).

11   *Chemawa American* 34, no. 10 (Jan. 18, 1933).

12   "Patriotic Pageant,"*Chemawa American* 30, no. 17 (Feb. 20, 1929).

13   "Senior Notes," *Chemawa American* 31, no. 23 (Feb. 19, 1930).

14   "Local," *Chemawa American* 29, no. 33 (May 23, 1928).

15   *Chemawa American* 30, no. 19 (Mar. 6, 1929).

16   "Local," *Chemawa American* 30, no. 4 (Nov. 14, 1928).

17   "Local," *Chemawa American* 30, no. 18 (Feb. 27, 1929).

18   Founded in 1923, the American Indian Defense Organization focused its efforts on two related battles: protecting Native landholdings by abandoning individual allotment policies, and the reclaiming of Indian culture that had been destroyed by the assimilationist policies of the Indian Office. For more, see Adams 1995: 330-31.

19   K. Tsianina Lomawaima, *They Called It Prairie Light* (Lincoln: University of Nebraska Press, 1994), 151.

20   Mrs. Turney's retirement notice, interestingly, explains that she had attended Chemawa herself at an early age, studied piano "under one of the best piano teachers in Salem," and later became the "official government Indian pianist" at the 1903 World's Fair in St. Louis, Missouri. See "Beloved Personage, Mrs. Ruthyn Turney, Retires from Indian Service," *Chemawa American* 42, no. 3 (Nov. 28, 1941).

21   "Traditional Christmas Pageant Presented by Choir," *Chemawa American* 42, no. 4 (Dec. 20, 1940).

22   The crowning of a queen or princess was a process that was proliferating within Indian schools and Native communities. While this pageantry took its cue from the white society that had long viewed "nice" Indian girls as princesses (see Green 1975, 1994), it did encourage the young women to make their own costumes and regalia, leading to the acquisition and retention of cultural knowledge.

23   "Pageant, Canoe Prophesies Given Two Nights for Campus and Public," *Chemawa American* 54, no. 5 (Mar. 1, 1954).

24   Shake dance, small boys' Indian dance, hoop dance, eagle dance, Yeechai dance, welcome dance, swan dance, canoe dance, farewell dance, arrow dance, feather dance, and snake dance.

25   All quotations that follow were featured in the "Student Briefs" column of the *Chemawa American* 55, no. 7 (Mar. 15, 1955).

26   "Students Enjoy Holiday," *Chemawa American* 54, no. 5 (Mar. 1, 1954).

27   Untitled article, *Chemawa American* 40, no. 8 (May 4, 1940).

28   "Notice," *Chemawa American* 41, no. 10 (May 2, 1941).

29   "Items of Interest," *Chemawa American* 41, no. 10 (May 2, 1941).

30   This and other quotes from interview with Linda Begay, at the Begay family home in Salem, Oregon. May 2005.

31   Chemawa Annual, 1962 and 1964.

32   Begay interview, May 2005.

33 Interview with Chet Clark, at Bob Tom's home in Keizer, Oregon. Feb. 24, 2005.

34 Begay interview, May 2005.

35 Brent Merrill, "Hatfield Interview: Memories, Truth, and Insight," *Smoke Signals: A Publication of the Grand Ronde Tribe* (Dec. 1, 2001): 1, 3.

36 Chris Mercier, "Hatfield Townhall Meeting in Portland," *Smoke Signals: A Publication of the Grand Ronde Tribe* (Dec. 1, 2001): 2.

37 Margaret Connell Szasz. *Education and the American Indian: The Road to Self-Determination Since 1928.* (Santa Fe: University of New Mexico Press, 1999), 141-46, 156.

Chapter 6

1   Interview with Chet Clark, in Keizer, Oregon. Feb. 2005.

2   "Report of the Commissioner of Indian Affairs," in U.S. House, 48th Congress, 1st Session, *Report of the Secretary of the Interior, 1883*, H.Ex.Doc.1, Pt. 5, Vol.2; Serial Set 2191 (Washington: Government Printing Office, 1883): 9-10.

3   Office of Indian Affairs, *Annual Report of the Commissioner of Indian Affairs for the Year 1902* (Washington, D.C.: U.S. Government Printing Office): 13-14. Cited in Curtis E. Jackson and Marcia J. Galli, *A History of the Bureau of Indian Affairs and Its Activities Among Indians* (San Francisco: E & R Research Press, 1977), 97.

4   Letter from the Commissioner of the Department of the Interior, Office of Indian Affairs, to Superintendent, Grand Ronde School and Agency, January 11, 1902.

5   Potlatching was made illegal in Canada and the United States in the late nineteenth century, largely at the urging of missionaries and government agents, who considered it "a worse than useless custom": wasteful, unproductive, and contrary to the societal work ethic of Canada and the United States. Despite the ban, potlatching continued clandestinely for years.

6   Harrison family papers, in possession of Kathryn Harrison (Harry Jones' eldest surviving daughter). Copies are on file at Grand Ronde's Cultural Resources Department.

7   Cato Sells, "Circular to Superintendents," reprinted in *Indian School Journal* (June 1914): 312.

8   John W. Troutman, *Indian Blues: American Indians and the Politics of Music, 1879-1934* (Norman: University of Oklahoma Press, 2009), 33.

9   Lawrence C. Kelly, *The Assault on Assimilation: John Collier and the Origins of Indian Policy Reform* (Albuquerque: University of New Mexico Press, 1983), 259.

10 Tara Browner, *Heartbeat of the People: Music and Dance of the Northern Pow-Wow* (Urbana,: University of Illinois Press, 2002), 28-29.

11 Charles H. Burke, *Circular 1665: Indian Dancing* (1921).

12 Charles H. Burke, *Supplement to Circular No. 1665: Indian Dancing* (Feb. 14, 1923). Historian John Troutman has noted the degree to which federal dance policy was heavily influenced by missionaries and agency superintendents (Troutman 2009: 26).

13 Troutman 2009: 35.

14 Browner 2002: 29-30. See also Clyde Ellis, *A Dancing People: Powwow Culture on the Southern Plains* (Lawrence: University Press of Kansas, 2003).

15 L. G. Moses. *Wild West Shows and the Images of American Indians, 1883-1933* (Albuquerque: University of New Mexico Press, 1999).

16 Troutman 2009: 87.

17   Benjamin G. Rader. " 'The Greatest Drama in Indian Life': Experiments in Native American Identity and Resistance at the Haskell Institute Homecoming of 1926." *Western Historical Quarterly* 35 (Winter 2004): 429-50.

18   Jethro Gaede. "An Ethnohistory of the American Indian Exposition at Anadarko, Oklahoma, 1932-2003." (Ph.D. diss., University of Oklahoma, 2003).

19   "Indian Karook," *The Chemawa American* 29, no. 30 (May 2, 1928).

20   "The Ghost Dance," *The Chemawa American* 30, no. 9 (Dec. 19, 1928).

21   "Arrows from the Long Bow," *The Chemawa American* 31, no. 4 (Oct. 2, 1929).

22   "Local," *The Chemawa American* 34, no. 4 (Oct. 26, 1932).

23   "Local," *The Chemawa American* 34, no. 7 (Dec. 7, 1932). The Sioux Indian band consisted of Flandreau alumni who traveled the country playing on various vaudeville stages.

24   "Foreign Visitors," *The Chemawa American* 34, no. 6 (Nov. 23, 1932).

25   For a more detailed account, see John Collier's memoir, *From Every Zenith* (Denver, CO: Sage Books, 1963).

26   Troutman 2009: 103.

27   Amelia V. Katanski, *Learning to Write "Indian": The Boarding School Experience and American Indian Literature* (Norman: University of Oklahoma Press, 2005), 7.

28   Interview with Kathryn Harrison. Grand Ronde, OR. Oct. 26, 2006

29   "Artists with Never A Thought of Fame," *The Chemawa American* 35, no. 4 (Nov. 22, 1933).

30   Interview with Floy Childers Pepper by Kathleen J. Cook, April 22, 2002. Oregon Historical Society Archives, call no. SR 1935.

31   "From the Freshman Class," *The Chemawa American* 43, no. 6 (Mar. 26, 1943).

32   "Freshmen Study Diets," *The Chemawa American* 51, no. 1 (Nov. 1950).

33   Katanski 2005 documents this phenomenon with regards to Carlisle's student newspaper, the *Indian Helper*.

34   "Things for a Girl to Remember About Dating," *The Chemawa American* 56, no. 5 (Jan. 15, 1956).

35   "Town Dating Is Scheduled," *The Chemawa American* 54, no. 6 (Apr. 15, 1954).

36   "Boys' Council Helps Develop Citizenship," *The Chemawa American* 55, no. 4 (Dec. 15, 1954).

37   The younger girls at that time lived in McBride Hall.

38   "Home Living—Winona Hall," *The Chemawa American* 52, no. 4 (Feb. 1952).

39   "WARNING," *The Chemawa American* 52, no. 5 (May 1952).

40   Margaret Connell Szasz. *Education and the American Indian: The Road to Self-Determination Since 1928.* 3rd edition, revised and enlarged (Albuquerque: University of New Mexico Press, 1999), 189.

41   "Girls Learn the Answer," *The Chemawa American* 48, no. 3 (Jan. 1948).

42   "Campus News," *The Chemawa American* 38, no. 3 (Dec. 10, 1937).

43   "Jazz," *The Chemawa American* 31, no. 26 (Mar. 12, 1930).

44   "Indian Club," *The Chemawa American* 46, no. 2 (Feb. 1946).

45   *The Chemawa American* 55, no. 4 (Dec. 15, 1954).

46   "Student Briefs," *The Chemawa American* 55, no. 4 (Dec. 15, 1954).

47   Interview with Chet Clark, in Keizer, Oregon. Feb. 2005.

48   Telephone interview with Dee Pigsley. March 2005.

49   Ibid.

50   Commonly known as the Kennedy Report, the formal title of this seven-volume study from the Special Senate Subcommittee on Education is *Indian Education: A National Tragedy, a National Challenge* (Washington, D.C.: U.S. Government Printing Office, 1969). Margaret Connell Szasz (1999) argues that while the late 1960s "was beginning to take on the appearance of another reform period" (186), not until the passage of the Indian Education Act in 1972 was Indian control (i.e., parental and community participation) formally legislated (197-99).

51   "Indians Find Modern Steps Like War Dances," *Salem Statesman* (Sat., Feb. 20, 1965) Section 1: 5.

52   Telephone interview with Max Lestenkof. Aug. 2002.

53   Conversations at Chemawa Reunion in Anchorage, Alaska. Oct. 2002.

54   Caption by Chemawa staff member and photographer Jesse E. Matt, May 1971, in his Album #3, "A Pictorial Portfolio of Chemawa Indian School." It was among albums salvaged by other staff members when the old campus was demolished, and it is now kept by Coach Ed Bartlett of Salem, Oregon.

55   *Parent and Student Handbook*, Vol. 8 (Salem: Chemawa Indian School, July 2009): 9, 27.

56   Ibid., 28.

57   Kennedy Report, 1969. See also Fuchs and Havighurst, *To Live on This Earth: American Indian Education*, which summarizes the results of that study (Albuquerque: University of New Mexico Press, 1972). A more recent assessment of the Kennedy Report is included in Jon Reyhner and Jeanne Eder, *American Indian Education: A History*, (Norman: University of Oklahoma Press, 2004), 251-53.

58   *Parent and Student Handbook*, 2006: 29.

59   Interview with Warner Austin, at Chemawa. May 2006.

60   *Parent and Student Handbook*, 2009: 27.

61   *Parent and Student Handbook,* 2006: 23.

Chapter 7

1   Lester Bangs, "Protopunk: The Garage Bands," *The Rolling Stone Illustrated History of Rock & Roll*, ed. Jim Miller (New York: Rolling Stone Press, 1980), 261-64.

2   David W. Samuels chronicles this special era in the life of the San Carlos Apache community in *Putting a Song on Top of It: Expression and Identity on the San Carlos Apache Reservation* (Tucson: University of Arizona Press, 2004). Both at San Carlos and at Chemawa school bands were founded as part of the government assimilation program, and this training led to students founding their own bands and playing the music they had been exposed to through radio and records. The development of these bands also coincides with the replacement of many Native languages with English.

3   See the account of Paul Revere and the Raiders in Katherine Charlton, *Rock Music Styles: A History*, 3rd edition (New York: McGraw Hill, 2003). Their professional trajectory is also documented online by rock music historians.

4   Bangs 1980: 261.

5   Ibid., 261. For some, this aspiration took the form of everywoman or everyperson an artist, though female garage bands in the mid-1960s did not achieve the same commercial successes as did their male counterparts, and have thus left less evidence (e.g, photos, recordings) of their activities.

6   Max Lestenkof's history is compiled from a telephone interview conducted Aug. 7, 2002, as well as in-person conversations in Anchorage in Oct. 2002 and subsequent electronic correspondence.

7   For more on this little-known episode in American history, see the film *Aleut Story*, a documentary aired on TV in 2005 and available on DVD from http://www.aleutstory. tv/; the brief explanatory article, "WWII internment of Aleuts recounted in documentary" (*USA Today*, 4 Dec. 2005); and Dorothy Jones' book *A Century of Servitude: Pribilof Aleuts Under U.S. Rule* (Lanham, MD: University Press of America, 1982).

8   Telephone interview with Max Lestenkof. Aug. 2002.

9   *Amiq: The Aleut People of the Pribilof Islands, a Culture in Transition, 1981-1983.* Narrated by Larry Merculieff, with original music by Max Lestenkof; produced, directed, and filmed by Susanne Swuibold and Helen Corbett (1985, 58 minutes). Available through the Amiq Institute: <http://www.amiq.org/filmvid.html>

10   *Peter Picked a Seal Stick: The Fur Seal Harvest of the Pribilof Islands.* Narrated by Aleut sealing foremen Mike Zacharof and Timon Lestenkof, with original music of Max Lestenkof; produced, directed, and filmed by Susanne Swuibold and Helen Corbett (1981, 28 minutes). Includes historical photographs from the Bancroft Collection, University of Alaska. Available through the Amiq Institute: <http://www.amiq.org/filmvid.html>

11   Quotes from Ted McGlashan in this and following paragraphs from telephone interview. Jan. 2008.

12   Telephone interview with Rosemary McGlashan, Jan. 2008.

13   Samuels 2004: 15-22.

14   Many Alaska Natives also first knew Max at Chemawa as a Meteors musician, and today they welcome him back to their villages, excited to hear his music.

15   For more on the Akutan gig and on Ted McGlashan's post-Chemawa musical career, see Tim Tapping, "Wild Gentlemen Keeps 'Em Hopping in Dutch," *Fisherman's Journal* (1992). [The *Fisherman's Journal* has since been subsumed by the publication *National Fisherman*.]

16   Katherine Charlton, *Rock Music Styles: A History*, 3rd edition (New York: McGraw Hill, 2003), 112.

17   And at schools and garages across the country. The talent-show craze has dominated evening television programming, and has the most expensive airtime of all, the Super Bowl commercial. Doritos recently invited garage bands to submit their acts online, with the winner debuting during the game on Feb. 3, 2008.

18   Interview with Karen Graham, at Chemawa, May 2006.

19   Interview with Warner Austin, at Chemawa, May 2006.

20   In his essay "Guerrilla Music: Avant-Garde Voice as Oppositional Discourse," Thaddeus Coreno argues that while rock music might present an offense to middle-class sensibility and moral code, there is a paucity of genuinely threatening popular music. Thus, despite youth culture commonly being seen as the site of rapid social change, Coreno maintains that rock music does not offer a viable oppositional discourse for youth. See *Adolescents and Their Music: If It's Too Loud, You're Too Old* (New York: Garland Publishing, Inc., 1994).

21   Interview with Graham, May 2006.

22   The Original Snakeboy's given name is Bill Thompson. Sadly, Thompson took his own life in Portland, Oregon, on Feb. 5, 2008. He is greatly missed by the students he worked with and by blues aficionados throughout the Northwest.

23   Maintained by the Columbia Blues Association at <http://cascadeblues.org/joomla/>
24   Interview with Austin, May 2006.
25   Lawrence Grossberg, "The Political Status of Youth and Youth Culture," in *Adolescents and Their Music:* xxvi.

Chapter 8

1   For some tribes, returning veterans have rejuvenated warrior societies and ceremonial life. Among the Lakota people, for example, new songs are created to honor servicemen, their warrior deeds and victories. In *Indian Blues*, historian John Troutman unpacks the ways dance and powwow gatherings transform the tools of assimilation (e.g., boarding schools, citizenship, and military service) into tools of Indianization, "of Lakota revitalization and celebration." See Troutman 2009: 19-65.

2   Gloria Alese Young, "Powwow Power: Perspectives on Historic and Contemporary Intertribalism" (PhD diss., Indiana University, 1981): 68.

3   Thomas Kavanagh. "Powwows." In *Handbook of North American Indians*, Vol. 2 (Indians in Contemporary Society). Garrick A. Bailey, ed. (Washington, DC: Smithsonian Institution, 2008), 327-37. See also essays in *Powwow*. Clyde Ellis, Luke Eric Lassiter, and Gary H. Dunham, eds. (Lincoln: University of Nebraska Press, 2005).

4   Sonciray Bonnell. *Chemawa Indian Boarding School: The First One Hundred Years, 1880 to 1980* (M.A. thesis, Dartmouth College, 1997): 108-10.

5   Margaret Connell Szasz. *Education and the American Indian: The Road to Self-Determination Since 1928.* (Santa Fe: University of New Mexico Press, 1999), 232. Subsequent administrations have affirmed and strengthened the intentions of this executive order. Most recently, President Barack Obama's "White House Initiative on American Indian and Alaska Native Education," signed on December 2, 2011, pledged the support of his administration to "fulfill our commitment to furthering tribal self-determination and to help ensure that AI/AN students have an opportunity to learn their Native languages and histories and receive complete and competitive educations that prepare them for college, careers, and productive and satisfying lives."

6   "Local," *The Chemawa American* 31, no. 33 (Apr. 30, 1930).

7   "Full Day Pow-Wow Planned by Council," *The Chemawa American* 38, no. 6 (Feb. 25, 1938).

8   "Indian Service News," *The Chemawa American* 34, no. 5 (Nov. 9, 1932).

9   A recording of the Chemiwai Singers is still available on the Canyon Records label: "The Chemiwai Singers—Chemawa Indian School, Oregon," CR-6121-C (1974).

10   See Devon A. Mihesuah, "American Indian Identities: Issues of Individual Choices and Development," *American Indian Culture and Research Journal* 22, no. 2 (1998): 193-226. Mihesuah draws upon the "life stages" paradigm proposed by William E. Cross, Jr., in *Shades of Black: Diversity in African-American Identity* (Philadelphia: Temple University Press, 1991). The same paradigm was also extended by Thomas A. Parham in "Cycles of Psychological Nigrescence"; see *The Counseling Psychologist* 17, no. 2 (1989): 187-226.

11   Derek Lowry, in an interview with Clyde Ellis in Greensboro, North Carolina. June 9, 2001. Published in *Powwow* (Ellis et al., eds., 2005): vii.

12   Interview with Chance May, Nov. 2012.

13   See in particular Mihesuah's 1993 account of women at the Cherokee Female Seminary. *Cultivating the Rosebuds: The Education of Women at the Cherokee Female Seminary, 1851-1909* (reprint, Champaign: University of Illinois Press, 1997).

14   James Howard, "Pan-Indian Culture in Oklahoma," *Scientific Monthly* 81 (Nov. 1955): 215. Howard re-affirmed this position more recently in "Pan-Indianism in Native American Music and Dance," *Ethnomusicology* 71 (1983): 71-82.

15   Barre Toelken, "Ethnic Selection and Intensification in the Native American Powwow," *Creative Ethnicity: Symbols and Strategies of Contemporary Ethnic Life*, eds. Stephen Stern and John Allan Cicala, (Logan: Utah State University Press, 1991), 140.

16   William K. Powers, *War Dance: Plains Indian Musical Performance* (Tucson: University of Arizona Press, 1990), 87, 108.

17   See the essays in Michael E. Harkin's *Reassessing Revitalization Movements: Perspectives from North America and the Pacific Islands* (Lincoln: University of Nebraska Press, 2004).

18   "Termination" refers to a policy that the United States Congress implemented from 1953 through the 1960s in which 109 tribes' sovereign status was no longer recognized by the federal government. Approximately two and a half million acres of trust land were removed from protected status, and twelve thousand Native Americans lost tribal affiliation.

19   See video, *The Oregon Story: The Tribal Economy*. Writer/Producer, Leslie Shearing; Executive Producer, Steven Amen. Oregon Public Broadcasting, 2000.

20   The following recollections are taken from an interview with Chet Clark conducted in Bob Tom's home in Keizer, Oregon, Feb. 24, 2005.

21   Text translated from Navajo to English by Chet Clark.

22   Unless otherwise noted, quotations in this section are taken from a telephone interview with Arlie Neskahi on Jan. 26, 2005.

23   *Intertribal Pow-Wow Songs*. Audio cassette of the Chemawa Singers. Canyon Records, CR-6196 (1987).

24   From an interview on the public radio program "Sound & Spirit." Transcript available at <http://www.wgbh.org/programs/Sound--Spirit-226/episodes/Native-Americans-5038>

25   Ibid.

26   From the "Sound & Spirit" interview.

27   Ibid.

28   Interview with Karen Graham, May 2006.

29   The Performing Arts Club practices are as described in interviews with Warner Austin and others at Chemawa, May 2006 and November 2012.

30   Students pick the name of this drum, and they change it up frequently—sometimes as often as for every powwow. In the fall of November 2012, this drum was called War Party. Chemawa's other drum retains the name Chemawa Nations.

31   Interview with Chance May, Nov. 2012.

32   Electronic communication with Chance May, Dec. 11, 2012.

33   Browner 2002: 40, 38.

34   *Smoke Signals*. A publication of the Grand Ronde Tribe (Mar. 1, 2005): 1.

35   Despite being the smallest segment of the population, Native Americans have the second-largest state prison incarceration rate in the nation, according to a review conducted by the Foundation for National Progress. The review found that 709 per 100,000 American Indians and Alaska Natives were incarcerated in state prisons in 2000. This rate was surpassed only by African Americans, for whom the incarceration rate was 1,815 per 100,000 people.

36   "Chemawa Pow-wow Celebrates The School's 125th Birthday," *Smoke Signals* (Mar. 1, 2005): 6.

37   Inerview with Chet Clark, Feb. 2005.

38   Interview with Bob Tom, Feb. 2005.

39   Interview with Dee Pigsley, Mar. 2005.

40   G'aan also dance prominently at the Apache Girls' Sunrise Ceremony, held each year to mark adolescent girls' passage to adulthood. Because the Natives had been forbidden by the U.S. government to congregate, the ceremonies were held secretly until 1911, when the Apaches were granted permission to assemble on the 4th of July to celebrate the nation's birthday. Choosing this date for one of their most important cultural rituals was a way of insulting their conquerors.

41   Conversation with Bob Tom and Chet Clark, Feb. 2005.

Chapter 9

1   George E. Vaillant, *Aging Well: Surprising Guideposts to a Happier Life from the Landmark Harvard Study of Adult Development* (Boston: Little & Brown, 2002), 95.

2   The Rockefeller Foundation has commissioned a comprehensive review of resiliency studies across disciplines: "Resilience: A Literature Review," by Patrick Martin-Breen and J. Marty Anderies (2011). The psychology studies are particularly relevant for boarding school students. A good overview is Bonnie Benard's *Resiliency: What We Have Learned* (San Francisco: WestEd, 2004). See also Grotberg 1998, Werner 1993, and Neal Conan's 2002 interview with Nan Henderson on National Public Radio's "Talk of the Nation."

3   Child 2000: 92.

4   Johnston 1989: 30.

5   "Former Students Organize in Alaska," *Chemawa American* 34, no. 14 (Mar. 15, 1933).

6   "Local," *Chemawa American* 30, no. 22 (Mar. 27, 1929).

7   "News Notes," *Chemawa American* 35, no. 4 (Nov. 22, 1933).

8   For an extensive exploration of the cultural loss that has occurred among Native American women who attended school in the Northwest, see Debbie Ann LaCroix, "Indian Boarding School Daughters Coming Home: Survival Stories as Oral Histories of Native American Women" (Ph.D. diss., University of Oregon, 1993).

9   Troutman 2009: 217-28.

10   Troutman 2009: 228-33. Joe Morris also self-published his own autobiography in 2001 when he was eighty years old.

Index

Note: Italicized page numbers refer to photographs.